fP

Other books by Robert Kuttner:

Everything for Sale: The Virtues and Limits of Markets

The End of Laissez-Faire: National Purpose and the Global Economy After the Cold War

The Life of the Party: Democratic Prospects in 1988 and Beyond

The Economic Illusion: False Choices Between Prosperity and Social Justice

Revolt of the Haves: Tax Rebellions and Hard Times

Other books by Sharland Trotter:

The Madness Establishment

Delinquent Justice

Family Re-Union

Reconnecting
Parents and Children
in Adulthood

Robert Kuttner
Sharland Trotter

The Free Press

New York   London   Toronto   Sydney   Singapore

THE FREE PRESS
A Division of Simon & Schuster, Inc.
1230 Avenue of the Americas
New York, NY 10020

For information regarding special discounts for bulk purchases,
please contact Simon & Schuster Special Sales at 1-800-456-6798
or business@simonandschuster.com

Designed by Lauren Simonetti

Manufactured in the United States of America

1 3 5 7 9 10 8 6 4 2

Library of Congress Cataloging-in-Publication Data

Kuttner, Robert.
Family re-union : reconnecting parents and children in adulthood /
Robert Kuttner, Sharland Trotter.
p. cm.
Includes bibliographical references and index.
1. Parent and adult child. 2. Adult children--Family relationships.
3. Adult children of aging parents. 4. Sandwich generation--Psychology.
5. Intergenerational relations. I. Trotter, Sharland. II. Title.
HQ755.86.K88 2002
155.6'6--dc21   2001059780

ISBN 0-684-82722-0

We gratefully acknowledge permission to reprint:"When Death Comes,"
from *New and Selected Poems* Copyright © 1992 by Mary Oliver
Reprinted by permission of Beacon Press, Boston

We appreciate permission from Rachel Naomi Remen, fromTom Riderm
and the estate of Suzanne Lipsett, and from Dan Lowenstein to reprint
poems from the collection, *Wounded Healers*, edited by Rachel Naomi Remen.

The lines from *The Fantasticks* are from the song "Never Say No,"
by Tom Jones and Harvey Schmidt, copyright 1960 (renewed) by Tom Jones and
Harvey Schmidt-Chappell & Co., owner of Publication and Allied Rights
throughout the world. All rights reserved. Used by permission.

"Hello in There," Words and music by John Prine © 1972 Walden Music, Inc., and Sour
Grapes Music Inc. All rights administered by WB Music Corp. All rights reserved.

For our parents and our children

Contents

Chapter 1
Regret and Reunion

The *New York Times* Metropolitan Diary quoted a sardonic item sent in by a man with grown children aged twenty-two and twenty-six, proposing a message for his telephone answering machine:

If you require financial assistance, Press One.

If you are in emotional turmoil over an impending breakup with a romantic partner, and require a few hours of sympathetic discussion, Press Two.

If you are being treated unfairly at work or school and wish to displace your anger to a nuclear family member, Press Three.

If your car or household appliances need immediate repair or replacement, Press Four.

If you are telephoning to inquire about our well-being or to pass a few moments of pleasant topical conversation, please check the number you intended to dial.

Underneath the barbed humor is deep regret and longing, tinged with bitterness. Doubtless the twentysomething children could compose a message of their own: "If you are calling to criticize my lifestyle, press one. If you are skeptical of my live-in companion, press two. If you are worried about my career, press three. If you wonder when I am going to produce grandchildren, press four. If you feel that I'm insufficiently appreciative of all that you've done, press five. And if you just want to communicate love and support, well, that would be nice for a change."

We suspect that the conflict of the adult generations is the cause of as much bewilderment, regret, and self-defeating behavior as the battle of the sexes. Nearly everybody struggles with these issues and everybody has a story to tell. Few people discuss them comfortably. Often, all of us find ourselves reenacting family scripts of which we are barely aware.

Having observed innumerable families struggle with this dialectic of evolving closeness and distance, having seen it professionally in a therapeutic context, wrestled with it in our own family from both sides of the generational divide, having watched friends struggle, we discern a common pattern: As kids grow up, parents' expectations and demands often lag behind their children's actual developmental stage. As children become adults, many parents unconsciously deal with the loss of the parental role by continuing to infantilize their long-since-grown children. Many adult children become hypersensitized to what they take to be criticism, and demonize their own parents. Both sides seek relief from pain, conflict, and frustration in the lowest common denominator—distance. Though everyone hoped for something better, patterns ossify. Paradoxically, achieving more authentic family connections is the key to real personal autonomy. Strategies for bridging these family chasms is the subject of our book.

Charles Dickens began *David Copperfield* with the suggestion that all of us want to be the heroes of our own life story. No audience to that drama is more intimate than our own families. No emotions are more charged. No set of hopes and fears is more poignant.

As young children, we want loving parents who will give us patience, support, and protection while we are growing up, and then plenty of room to become ourselves when we are grown. As adult children, we want from our parents a generous appreciation of who we have become.

As new parents, we imagine that we will be the wise and loving mothers and fathers that our own flawed parents never were. We will raise accomplished and appreciative children. And when our children are grown, we hope, they will come to understand what we did for them, and perhaps bless us with grandchildren. They will be grateful for the parents we are.

Children and parents spend a lifetime yearning for each others' affirmation. It hardly bears saying that life often mocks these hopes.

Achieving a satisfying blend of closeness and distance in grown families is a universal human challenge. Most people under the age of fifty have at least one living parent. Nearly three-quarters of adults have children. There is no escaping these relationships, even if one finds them painful and seeks to shunt them aside.

Everybody lives with fantasies of what might be or might have been. Everybody has a vivid mental picture of his or her childhood, and of parents as a mix of positive and negative role models to honor or rebel against. As we were writing this book, we found our casual conversation with friends, colleagues, and acquaintances suddenly enriched. As soon as we mentioned the topic, everyone had a story. And the stories were astonishingly diverse, yet universal.

When we began this book, we had both just turned fifty, with newly separating grown children and one surviving parent in her eighties. So we were engaging these relationships on both flanks, as adult children and as parents. By profession, we were a practicing clinical psychologist and a journalist/editor. As a therapist, one of us was also hearing about these issues from her patients. As we discussed this book project with friends, more than one ruefully said, "I hope I have a better relationship with my grown children than I've had with my parents." This double sense of loss is often the shameful and largely unexplored secret of the middle-aged.

This dialectic of connection, separation, and secure autonomy is not just a drama for two-year-olds, adolescents, and young adults. A rebalancing of distance and closeness recurs throughout the life course, with different particulars at different stages of development, right on into old age.

If there is a single message of this book, it is that more satisfying relationships within adult families are worth the struggle; that change is possible except in the most pathological of families. Indeed, general systems theory tells us that if one part of any system changes, the rest of the system necessarily changes. This is also the fundamental insight of family therapy work with family systems. The irony is that many family relationships are built on patterns that seem hopelessly immutable but that nobody really likes. A family system often mobilizes its resources to resist change, even as each of its members craves something better. Improving these patterns can be immensely rewarding.

In a small minority of families, parents have been so abusive that efforts at reconnection will only bring renewed pain. We address this subject in Chapter 7. In such families, the challenge for grown children is to heal themselves and come to terms with a devastating loss in order to move beyond it. But this does not describe most parents. In most of the human family, relationships are not pathological, yet in some sense unfulfilled. Before concluding that our families are hopelessly toxic, they deserve a thoughtful second look.

ONE FAMILY, ALL FAMILIES

We conceived this project almost eight years ago. It was motivated, in part, by the conversations we found ourselves having with other parents of separating young adults, all of whom hoped that their relationships with their adult children would be rich, close, fulfilling, and mutually appreciative.

In our own case, this universal wish was reinforced by yearnings from our two families of origin and from our experience raising our children. One of us, Bob, had lost a father at age nine and had a mother who was loving, bordering on overprotective. At fifty, Bob still had a great deal of unfinished business involving his father, which influenced his relationship with his children, and, indeed, all his relationships. Sharland was the daughter of a father who was distant emotionally; she had lost both her parents as a relatively young adult, when our children were still very young. Her father, a taciturn man, had withdrawn further into himself as his health failed. Her mother, a gentle woman, had then abruptly become very ill. This history of incomplete connection with her aging parents intensified her desire for authentic, respectful relationships with our kids after they left home.

The general wish for close connections to our adult children was further affected by our experience with the older of our two children, Gabriel, a very independent-minded son. Having a firstborn who tested limits sometimes made us feel like inept parents. There were times when we managed to find just the right blend of firmness and love. Other times, the two of us would have clashing styles or strategies as parents, and we would find ourselves in unproductive and demoralizing three-way conflict. Nor was this good for our daughter, Jessica, whose tacit role in the family system was to stay out of trouble.

As Gabe approached high school, we all hit a wall. We had the sense that this was a boy who could grow up to be an original, successful, and self-aware adult—if he could navigate the shoals of adolescence and learn to play to his ample natural stengths. But often, we found ourselves stuck in a cycle of reactivity, where small conflicts would set off a string of emotional firecrackers that ricocheted around the family system. And in a world where alcohol, AIDS, automobiles, and a variety of pharmaceutical temptations surround teenagers, the risks, the stakes, and our foreboding increased almost daily. Gabe's scrapes were still relatively minor, but his creativity and his schoolwork were not managing to engage with each other, and we wondered what perils lay ahead.

By the end of Gabe's ninth-grade year, we made a painful decision. We enrolled Gabe in a one-of-a-kind, year-round school, the Cascade School in Whitmore, California. We had resisted this course. Initially, it felt like a shameful indictment of us as parents and a confession of failure.

Cascade combined a strong academic program with peer groups, wilderness education, theater, and its own version of toughlove to allow teens stuck in self-defeating personal or family patterns to become authentic and compassionate young adults with the capacity to constructively pursue their dreams. Happily, in his two years at the Cascade School, Gabe was able to connect to his own strengths as a person; to throw himself into creative work with self-discipline—and find real satisfaction; and to cultivate social, emotional, and leadership skills.

When Gabe did come home to finish high school in our community, with the same kids with whom he had started kindergarten, it was as a seventeen-year-old with new adult insights. And, miraculously enough, he was as interested as we were in building a closer family relationship. This, we realized, would have to be a relationship that radically changed the traditional parent-child idiom in which the parent is the source of authority.

After Gabe graduated high school and went on to theater conservatory in London, and as our daughter was entering tenth grade, we began to think more systematically about this challenge of constructing a close but not confining, lifelong relationship with our grown children. Though Gabe was now far away, we finally had the loving and mutually respectful relationship with our son that we had long sought. As he was becoming a more interesting and complex young adult, the relationship was becoming richer. But would it last?

Every parent, though perhaps not with the same poignancy, has some version of this wish. Parents, after all, spend nearly two decades interrupting sleep, juggling work and family, changing diapers, containing crises, stressing their marriages, making financial sacrifices, helping with homework, meeting with teachers, sharing in triumphs and setbacks, and often suffering what seems a brutal lack of appreciation—culminating in the teen years when many children, defining selves, are particularly contemptuous of their parents. The deferred reward, if there is one, is a satisfying, mutually appreciative lifelong relationship with adult children and grandchildren. Yet many parents feel that after all the years of diligence and sacrifice, their grown children have little use for them.

So, as imminent empty-nesters, we began work in earnest on this book. We were fortunate to begin with an emotional vocabulary and a set of professional skills, Sharland as a clinical psychologist, Bob as a writer and editor. We also had a personal story with something of a gratifying happy ending—or beginning—in that our daughter was becoming a young woman of strong connections and good values, and our adult son had traversed childhood and come out not just whole, but emotionally available, self-aware, talented, and very good company. In early 1994, Sharland began researching the literature in several different fields, and conducting her own set of intergenerational interviews.

REUNION AND LOSS

Family Re-Union has turned out to be a different book than the one we set out to write, because our lives took an unexpected and tragic turn. In late 1994, we learned that Sharland had incurable, metastatic cancer. For three years, she remained mostly well and living an active life. The coming together in our own family would be more profound and abbreviated than we imagined.

Sharland continued the work on this book, as a research fellow at the Radcliffe Public Policy Institute. She continued seeing patients as a clinical psychologist. Remarkably, Sharland was able to integrate the reality of impending death into her work as a therapist, her role as a mother, wife, and friend, and as an author. Beyond the devastating tragedy that it was, her impending death became the basis for celebrating and more fully exploring life. She approached the last phase of her life not with dread, but with curiosity and engagement.

A month before her death, Sharland told an audience at Radcliffe, "If one is very lucky, a sense of foreshortened time can deepen relationships immeasurably. Although I did not anticipate an end-of-life stocktaking for another twenty-five or thirty years, I am able to see this process that I've been thinking about, reading about, researching, this process of how one comes to terms with one's children as adults, with new intensity and clarity. Mortality allows one to invite intimacy, if one dares look it in the eye. My own children are growing in the face of my impending death. I can see it, feel it. Most importantly, we can talk about it more openly than I would have thought possible. So there is one final paradox: death, oddly, can be a gift of enriched life."

Sharland's candid, exploratory manner of facing her illness and death also invited a profound family reunion. Her engagement with mortality, far too soon, became a quite unexpected chapter in the lifelong drama of attachment and separation in our family. Strangely enough, it was a realization, too briefly, of the yearnings behind the book. In wrestling with Sharland's impending death, each member of our immediate family got to know and respect and love each other more deeply, not just as parents and children but as people.

Although only one of us is composing the words of this particular paragraph, the book is still, emphatically, a joint endeavor. Major portions of this book are mostly Sharland's work. The narrative voice and wise insights are essence-of-Sharland and this is very much a loving collaboration, written in the first person plural.

At the time we began work on this book, we had experienced the intergenerational drama—as children, as young adults, as new parents, and finally as the mother and father of newly grown children. But we had not experienced old age or the near anticipation of death. We had not personally experienced how people in later life do (or do not) achieve fulfilling connections with grown children and grandchildren. Nor had we personally experienced the stocktaking that comes (or doesn't come) toward the end of life, and the long-deferred repair of connections that sometimes takes place and sometimes doesn't.

The Epilogue of this book deals in greater detail with our own odyssey and with the theme of impending mortality as a final chance, paradoxically, for family reunion. Death, after all, is universal. Some of us leave this earth feeling horribly alone. But we can also approach death feeling connection and affirmation. Death is the ultimate, permanent separation. Whether we engage the fact of our own mortality and that of loved ones influences our capacity for connection while we are alive.

Sharland died in November 1997. Although she died three decades too soon and although our children were just twenty-three and twenty, as a family we went through something of the same process that all families can, in anticipation of the death of an aged parent. Sharland's courage in facing death invited all of us to realize a closer connection. For that to occur, a family has to give itself permission to explore one of life's great taboos—mortality. And if a family can face the ultimate taboo subject unflinchingly, it can address other taboos and break loose from old, hierarchical and mythical roles.

As a distinguished family therapist, James L. Framo, has written, when a patient lacks the courage to even try to repair badly frayed relations with an aging parent, "My heavy artillery consists of having them imagine that their mother or father has just died, and they are standing by the grave. What would they regret never having said to the dead parent?"

Another therapist, Lorraine David, who faced an early death from cancer, wrote in a moving essay entitled. "The Use of Terminal Candor":

> I came from a family in which, as far as I know, death or anything unpleasant had never been discussed for at least three generations on both my mother's and my father's side. . . . I [became] determined to change our family's pattern of avoiding such unpleasant topics, such as death, or expression of strong feelings of anger and sadness, so that we could all become more comfortable and less vulnerable during this period of stress.
>
> During the first year of my illness, with its gradual opening and expanding of feelings, particularly around separation and loss, an interesting phenomenon happened. My father suddenly emerged from his cocoon and started participating in a daily athletic program at the Y; and my mother's depression finally dissipated. It was as if confronting the finiteness of my life enabled each of these family members to accept more responsibility for their own lives and their own time limits.

Our daughter, Jessica, was very moved by Hope Edelman's lovely book written in 1994, *Motherless Daughters*. The book is a series of letters, memoirs, and extracts from conversations with women who had all lost mothers at a relatively young age. The common thread is profound regret, not just for the loss of a mother, but for words that had been unspoken in a well-intentioned effort to shield the daughter from the mother's impending death, and feelings that had been kept under wraps afterwards. One woman wrote: "For a number of years, probably ten, I just couldn't deal with her death. In my family, we never even mentioned her name for years because it upset my dad so much. Because it hurt too much to feel, I just numbed out that part of me."

Like the women interviewed in that book, Jessica suffered an irretrievable loss. But unlike most of them, she didn't "numb out"; little of importance had been left unsaid that she wished had been said. Sharland's candor and courage, and her capacity for emotional connection, live on in our children.

THIS BOOK

Family Re-Union is deliberately eclectic. We draw on the insights of developmental psychology, family systems theory and family therapy, and research on attachment and separation. We also draw on fiction, theater, and mythology, where these universal questions recur, often speaking to our hearts in ways that the drier scientific literature does not. We recount the stories of diverse families, relying on case histories and interviews by clinicians, including interviews that Sharland conducted for this book, sometimes with three generations of the same family. And we draw on our own lives as children and as parents.

Our book is intended mostly for non-specialists who are curious about their families. Though it is not quite a "self-help" book, we hope it gives families practical information. We also expect it to be useful for researchers and therapists.

For truly dysfunctional or violent families, this book is not a substitute for psychotherapy or for support groups. We believe ordinary people in ordinary families can do a lot of constructive repair work without extensive professional help, if one or more family members takes a sincere initiative.

The plan of the book for the most part follows the life course. In Chapter 2, we pick up the story with the drama of newly separating young adults and the echoes of issues from early childhood. In our interviews, and in literature, we find examples of healthy and unhealthy separations. The process is a minefield, but there are paths around the booby traps.

Chapter 3 adds some thoughts about the dynamics of families. It explores the lifelong dance of attachment and separation, a dialectic in which growth requires new comprehension of the other, and new balance. We explore the tendency to get trapped in family roles that nobody likes and to trap others in family myths. This chapter borrows some insights from the work of family therapists, especially the observation that by changing our own behavior we alter the behavior of systems.

Next, in Chapter 4, we take a closer look at parents of young adults. This can be a time of new growth for midlife adults, which has the happy side effect of keeping parents from being overly intrusive in the lives of their young adult children. We also pursue the question: Am I destined to repeat the mistakes of my parents?—and find that life offers a good deal of free will. Connecting with an intimate partner, having children, struggling with a career, are pivotal life events when positive or negative associations with one's parents are vivid and raw, and there is either reinforcement of old identities and myths or new understanding and growth. Adult children, moreover, have much to teach parents.

The middle chapters of the book go more deeply into variations in the human family. In Chapter 5, we look at the new extended family in which adult children may have a more prolonged period of dependency than either they or their parents bargained for. We examine conflicts over money and life choices in families where grown children well into their twenties and even thirties return "home."

Chapter 6 addresses divorce, early death, and stepfamilies. A majority of grown children in the United States will find themselves with a stepparent at some point in their lives. Divorce and remarriage raise loaded issues of loyalty and betrayal, and complicate the process of family reunion.

In Chapter 7, we examine other family complications, including seriously abusive families. And what happens to relationships between grown children and their parents when a child doesn't choose the life parents expected? When a child is gay or lesbian? When a child intermarries or rejects parents' religious faith? How do parents keep their disappointments in check and remain affirming of the people their children have become? What do adult children have to teach their parents?

The final three chapters address the later period of life. In Chapter 8, we examine more closely the project of revisiting our parents, coming to know them better as people, partly as a way of freeing ourselves from often disabling myths. In taking a second look at our families, as adults, we enable all three generations to grow.

Chapter 9 is about grandparents in the family constellation, and the role of grandparent as an opportunity for either renewal and closer connection in relationships between parents and now-adult children—or for greater tension and animosity.

Chapter 10 deals with old age and the developmental challenge of stocktaking and making sense of it all as the end of life approaches. This reflection also offers new opportunities for reintegration of families. In old age, we look back on our life. If we pay attention unflinchingly, we find there are still unresolved questions of relationships with our children and grandchildren, and, mythically, with our own parents.

Finally, the Epilogue tells more of our own story, and examines the paradox of impending death as a renewal, reaffirmation, and reconnection of family life.

As we look at the whole life course, we conclude that in nearly all situations, the effort at reunion is worth the trouble. Throughout a lifetime, there is a striking consistency of patterns and ways of breaking through them—or failing to break through them, as they recur and evolve in different contexts and at different stages of life.

There are many doors into this mansion. In some situations, professional help may be indicated. And in a small number of cases, where most relatives are dead or otherwise lost, or where a parent was truly abusive or a family deeply dysfunctional, the best that can be attained is an exploration and a reframing of the meaning of the childhood experience rather than a literal present-day reconnection. One man, semi-joking, reported after a heroic effort at family therapy, "I still hate my parents but now I hate them on a more mature level." Most of us can expect better than that.

Our book is not meant to be encyclopedic. The more complex variations on the theme, such as divorce, adoption, religious and racial intermarriage, the early death of a parent or parents, alcoholism, abuse, and ethnic and sexual preference differences, each has their own small library of books. We include a brief appendix where we suggest other authors whose work we particularly admire.

The theme of family, as a universal human experience and puzzle, is pervasive in literature, in theater and poetry, in biography and memoir, as well as in diverse schools of human psychology. It is as old as the strained relations between Cain and Abel. It pervades Greek mythology, Shakespeare, and modern literary classics like Eugene O'Neill's *Long Day's Journey into Night* and Arthur Miller's *Death of a Salesman*.

This book is not written for any subgroup of the human family. It is for anyone with parents and with children. We think it will be especially useful for parents of newly adult children, looking forward to close but necessarily different family bonds; for grown children with distant or conflicted relationships with parents, but who have begun to have some compassionate curiosity about who their parents really are; for parents in later midlife who want more authentic connections with their adult offspring. It is also for people revisiting family relationships as part of a final stocktaking of their own life.

This book deals mainly with middle-class American families. But with all of its cultural and class variations, the emotional quest for connected autonomy across the life cycle is close to universal. Today, the broadly "normal" family is a far cry from the stereotypical Ozzie-and-Harriet nuclear family of the 1950s. Well-functioning families include all sorts of unconventional and recombinant ones, and any family where real pathology is not overpowering can hope for constructive change.

Is it really possible to generalize about what makes a healthy, multigenerational family? We think so. In a healthy family, there are clear boundaries. Children are neither pawns in their parents' marriage, nor are they made responsible for rescuing it. As adults, children are accorded their parents' respect, and reciprocate by honoring their parents' experience and wisdom. The family ethic encourages and affirms the autonomous development of each family member. Affection is not demanding or possessive. There is a capacity for honest communication, not conducted in an idiom of blaming. The family does not view itself as "us against the world," but is open to other friendships. Is this ideal too much to ask? Perhaps, but isn't it what all of us want? We may never perfectly attain it, but we can work toward it.

This is emphatically a book for all three generations. In reviewing other books that addressed relationships between parents and grown children, we noticed something curious. There were books for parents on how to deal with separating teens; some rather sad books for young adults with irremediably "toxic" parents; hopeful books for the anxious middle-aged on how to repair relationships with grown children; books for adult children of alcoholics and survivors of abuse; books on grandparenting; and books that deal with aging mainly as a management problem but offer little about emotional reconnection. There was virtually nothing that addressed the common dilemmas of the entire life course. Even in fiction we noticed a disjuncture. There are countless "coming-of-age" novels, where the young hero wrestles with how to break the bonds of confinement with his family, but far fewer literary works in which an older person is struggling with his isolation from young adult offspring.

Yet all of us who live out a normal life span pass through all of these stages: the twenty-five-year-old who finds her parents overbearing and not respectful of her adulthood; the forty-year-old who hopes he has a better relationship with his son than he did with his father; the fifty-five-year-old trying to find some emotional solace and connection amid the practical burdens of caring for an invalid mother; the seventy-year-old looking to repair a painfully distant relationship with a midlife daughter. To underscore what should be obvious: *these are the same people at different stages of life.* We are they. How much richer we would be if we paid attention sooner—if we cultivated these capacities instead of waiting for crisis or regret.

As individuals, all of us flatter ourselves to believe that we acquire more maturity, insight, and wisdom as we get older. And for the most part, we do. Nearly all of us are wiser at fifty than at twenty. But we often find it hard to credit that capacity for growth to others, especially to our aging parents or our adult children. If we do, we may be pleasantly surprised and rewarded.

In a society that prizes and celebrates youth, the natural inclination is to emphasize the young. The old have had their hour on stage. But in fact, even old dogs can learn new tricks. And the young, as much as the old, have a stake in family ties that affirm. People are capable of growth and constructive change at all stages of life. So, if there is a unique contribution here amid a forest of books on parenting and on families, it is to emphasize the commonality of all three generations and the universal human capacity for repair, renewal, and reunion.

Chapter 2
Children as Adults, Parents as People

The successful parent of a teenager has learned to function as a kind of benign despot, setting necessary limits and getting out of the way. Even so, most teens still live at home through high school. Parents are still ultimately responsible for their child's safety and development, establishing expectations for school performance, curfews, dating, use of the car, and so on.

Once teens have left home, however, a very different parental role is in order. The psychologist Anthony Wolf, in his delightful and wise book *Get Out of My Life (But First Could You Drive Me and Cheryl to the Mall?)*, offers advice for frustrated parents of teenagers, most of it in the form of dialogues. He adds one coda for patents of young adults, observing that once children are grown, "They are no longer answerable just to us. They become answerable to their school, to their employers, to the police, even to the government." Wolf imagines this dialogue:

"Ronnie, I just got a call from the IRS. They say you filed fraudulent tax returns for the past three years. Well, mister, you can just forget about going out on weekends for the next month."

"But, Dad, Roselyn and I had planned to take the kids to the circus next weekend."

"Well, mister, you should have thought about that when you filed those fraudulent tax returns."

"Aw, Dad."

Parents can't control grown children. But they can help drive them away—or cultivate a lifelong relationship of equals. Parents don't have the power to tell grown children what to do. But they do have the power to signal either respect and appreciation or anxiety and mistrust. If we can learn to do the former, we are far more likely to find the respect is reciprocated, and that our grown children actually enjoy our company.

STARTING YOUNG

The work of achieving respectful relationships with grown children begins when they are young. New parents often get into difficulty by being inconsistent in their behavior toward young children, allowing their own emotional needs and mood swings to overpower constructive parenting. This sends mixed signals, keeps the child off balance, and produces reactive behavior. The same unhappy patterns impede constructive parenting of teenagers or of children who are grown.

The psychologist, child advocate, and puppeteer Susan Linn has produced a video for parents entitled *Take Another Look*. It is directed particularly at parents at risk of abusing young children, but the video contains sound advice for all parents of all ages. It begins with actual footage of exasperated parents "losing it" and screaming at young children. It then cuts to Dr. Linn's favorite puppet and alter ego, Audrey Duck. "Susan," asks Audrey, wide-eyed, "who are those people?" "Audrey," Dr. Linn replies with worldly-wise compassion. "Those are parents."

Dr. Linn counsels parents to keep in mind one word—"ReThink," which is an abbreviation for "Recognize, Empathize, Think." When a child does something that would otherwise trigger an angry reaction, take a moment to rethink—to consider what is really going on (Recognize); look at the situation from the child's point of view (Empathize); then try for a considered response rather than an instant reaction which is likely to be an overreaction (Think). By doing so, you are more likely to preserve your own authority and dignity, more likely to intervene in a constructive fashion, more likely to communicate empathy, reliability, and safety, more likely to model mature behavior.

Parents who can cultivate these habits when their children are young are likely to have an easier time with separating adolescents, and better lifelong relationships with adult children. The parent who learns to rein in his own reactivity when a child spills her milk, teases a sibling, or fails to clean her room will also have a more temperate response when a teenager breaks her curfew or later on when a thirty-year-old announces he is leaving the family business or marrying out of the faith.

As parents of teens, we learn to listen, to forebear, and to pick our shots, using adult self-restraint to limit screaming matches, knowing that we can no longer directly influence more than a few core issues. We watch, often in despair, as our progeny adopt lifestyles and values antithetical to our own, hoping that when the child grows up, some of what we tried to teach will have sunk in.

Yet even skilled, loving parents who have navigated the teen years tolerably well sometimes find it hard to let go of this benignly paternal or maternal conception of their own role, and to shift to one that is not hierarchical at all. It is hard to accept that Mother or Father no longer knows best. At the same time, life presents second chances. Parents who fail to let go gracefully when their children leave home as late teens can learn new behaviors later in life.

The psychologist and family therapist Donald Williamson has coined the delightful term *former parent.* Obviously, as such family clichés as "I'm still your mother!" remind us, as long as a grown child and mother or father are alive, there is literally no such thing as a former parent. But Williamson's point is that parents of adult children need to give up a certain kind of parental authority if their grown offspring are to flourish as adults. He writes: "If the parent is still the psychological parent then the offspring is psychologically a child as far as that relational system is concerned. By definition, an 'adult' cannot have 'parents' in an emotional sense." According to Williamson, "Older parents spontaneously will relate differently once they recognize and trust the adulthood in the eyes and voice and bearing of their former children."

After letting go of the reciprocal roles of parent and dependent child, the goal is to achieve a new synthesis—a reunion between parents and grown children at a deeper and more symmetrical level of attachment. As the psychoanalyst Ronald Fairbairn put it, many young people experience a desperate desire to "escape from prison" yet a simultaneous urge to "return home." Indeed, teenagers often provoke conflict in order to separate yet stay connected: they keep parents engaged by using them as foils for rebellion. Within limits, this is appropriate for a fifteen-year-old. Yet many grown children get stuck in this pattern all of their lives, and associate intimacy with conflict. Either they hold on to a conflictual style of relating, or go to the opposite extreme and choose emotional distance as a way of asserting selfhood.

Paradoxically, the healthy separation of a child and the establishment of a well-differentiated adult self depends on the maintenance of a healthy emotional connection between parent and child. This paradox is resolved by secure adult autonomy that thrives on nurturing emotional connection.

The whole point of raising children, after all, is to allow them at last to venture forth as competent, self-reliant adults. For some of us, as we contemplate the empty nest, this realization is devastating. Seemingly, the better we have done our work as parents, the less our adult children will need us. What a bitter reward! But this conception is misleading. After the turmoil of the teen years, relationships with adult children can be deeply loving—if children don't get stuck and if parents don't drive them away. For a reintegration and rebalancing to occur, however, the terms of engagement need to change radically.

A friend, the mother of an eight-year-old, laments that her son is already growing up too fast; she is already in mourning—

in less than ten years he will be "gone." But he won't be entirely gone, not if she does her job well. He will just be in a very different state of connectedness, one that for some families is actually more emotionally satisfying than childhood. Some mothers and fathers who often feel incompetent and frustrated as parents of young children take far more joy from new roles as parents of adults.

WORRY IS NOT A FRIENDLY EMOTION

It's normal for parents of newly grown children to have worries. But as parents of young adults, we can no longer control our kids—what they do, whom they marry, how they choose to lead their lives. What we can do is communicate either trust or mistrust. If we manage to communicate trust and to cultivate skills of active listening, respectful equality can become the norm. Emotional engagement can become a pleasure rather than a strain. We can actually remain emotionally connected as constructive parents, and reap the joys that we imagined when we first brought our children into the world. But in order for this to happen, it is often parents who have to grow up.

If the mother and father have a better idea whenever a young adult mentions a selection of courses at college, summer plans, career decisions, dress habits, and the choice of friends and romantic partners, the healthy young person will soon just clam up and not share these ideas at all.

Newly grown children will make mistakes. But adults, even when they seem in trouble, need to be treated like grown-ups. The more a young adult seems to be floundering, the more a successful and competent middle-aged parent is tempted to intervene and rescue. This is a mutually reinforcing pattern. The grown child's difficulties may play to the parent's sense of mastery and desire to still be needed. Daddy will fix it, just as he did when the child was three or thirteen. But for the most part an adult does not need Mommy or Daddy to fix things, and excessive meddling will prolong what psychologists have called the "learned incapacity" of the child who knows that a parent will come to the rescue. The rescue will also create confused feelings of distance and resentment. Even the most intelligent of parents can have astonishing blind spots in this respect.

Two mothers of grown daughters, Susan Jonas and Marilyn Nissenson, collaborated on a book on mother-daughter relationships in adulthood, which they hopefully titled *Friends for Life.* Yet as they painfully acknowledge in their book, these mothers were struggling to keep their own controlling impulses from swamping any kind of relationship.

Susan recounts how she and her daughter, Sarah, then twenty-six, had been together for several days on a cross-country car trip.

> It was basically a wonderful trip. But I couldn't help noticing that Sarah was continually picking and chewing at her cuticles.
>
> Several times when she was driving, against all my better instincts I reached over and guided her hand away from her mouth. . . .
>
> Finally one day, just outside of Memphis, I couldn't stand it any longer. I said, "You're twenty-six. You're too old to have your fingers in your mouth." She turned red and screamed at me. "All you do is criticize. What I do with my hands is my concern."
>
> I yelled back, "But it looks awful. You're a very pretty girl, and I can't stand it when you do something so unattractive."
>
> She said, "Nobody minds but you. My friends don't think there's anything wrong with me."
>
> And I said, "Your friends aren't going to tell you. That's what a mother is for."
>
> We didn't speak for two states.

Susan recalls another fight with her grown daughter. She has given Sarah two chairs for her apartment and then is irritated that the daughter's cats have clawed them "to death."

> I remarked to her that the cats had ruined those pieces, and she said, "Well, you said you didn't want them back." I

said, "Yes, but I didn't realize they'd be ruined." I said, "Well, maybe you want to drape some sheets over them to make them more presentable." She got huffy. "Well, Mom, that's what happens when you have cats." The presumption being that she'll always live with wrecked furniture.

I told her that I would pay for the new stuff that she needed, and that we should try to find sofas and chairs that her cats can't destroy, but that it would help if she would keep their nails clipped. By this time she was quite short with me. . . .

Both of these accounts, of course, raise multiple alarm bells. A twenty-six-year-old may or may not be too old to chew her nails (a number of prominent and successful people are nail-biters), but she is certainly too old to have her mother pull her hand away from her mouth.

A young woman with her own apartment needs less furniture and more autonomy. Moreover, a gift is a gift. Once the mother has given the daughter the chairs, it's up to the daughter to take care of them (or not). Daughter Sarah seems not to mind that the chairs have stuffing coming out. This is a natural consequence that she will have to live with. Eventually, if she wants her apartment to look nice, she'll learn to protect the furniture from the cats. But instead of letting natural consequences teach a logical life lesson, Susan proposes to buy her twenty-six-year-old more furniture, and negotiate over how the daughter will take care of it.

As she acknowledges, this mother was taking too much responsibility for the life of her adult daughter. Not surprisingly, her daughter was behaving like an adolescent. If mothers of adult daughters really want to be Friends for Life, they will back off and allow their daughters to become adults.

This is not to say, of course, that parents of grown children necessarily keep a totally hands-off attitude in all circumstances. In serious crises, parents, even of grown children, need to act. But parents who keep their own needs and reactivity in check, and who offer their grown children clarity and reasonable boundaries, are likely to be rewarded both with higher-functioning adult children and more satisfying lifelong connections.

For both generations, the best outcome is a relationship whose ground rules do not force the son or daughter to choose between autonomy and approval; between sovereignty and love. Parents watch grown children make different choices than they might have made, yet wise parents know when and how to express opinions. Parents particularly need to pay attention to their own issues and keep these from needlessly compromising relations with grown children.

There are lots of ways promote distance in adult children. One can be relentlessly critical, like the mothers in *Friends for Life*—or relentlessly approving. The authors of the book *Ourselves and Our Children* quote a young attorney whose mother embarrasses him by boasting of his accomplishments. "She introduces me to strangers saying, 'This is my son, Freddy. He works in a storefront law office, after graduating at the top of his class in Columbia Law School. I'm so proud of him! Freddy, tell Mr. Davis about the extraordinary man you defended in court last week. What a case! And of course we won.' I feel like a prize pig at a county fair."

It is hardly worth belaboring that such behavior on the parent's part is almost guaranteed either to drive the child away—or into a continuing relationship that is overly enmeshed and unhealthy for both parent and adult child. Sadly, many things that might be shared lovingly by the son may never be known to this mother, because her presence is simply too suffocating and the son runs the other way.

Sons of such mothers may overcompensate not just by keeping their mothers at bay but by having difficulty with intimate relationships in general. Unless he takes steps to alter the pattern, this adult son is at risk of reenacting his issues with his mother in his choice of an intimate partner, either by repeating them or by going to the opposite extreme. He may choose a mate who conforms to his unconscious image of his mother (and then resent the confinement). Or he may choose one who is cool and distant (and sometimes long for greatly intimacy). Either way, he is in thrall to an overly entangled connection to his mother.

Paradoxically, this mother will enjoy a closer lifetime relationship with her son the lawyer if she can back off some. This does not mean, by the way, that the son's putative difficulties with intimacy are the mother's "fault." Once in adulthood, grown children have almost endless opportunities to change relationships for the better. This son can firmly make clear that he finds his mother's descriptions embarrassing and unwelcome.

We should also resist ethnic or gender clichés that lead us to just give up on the prospect of change. Readers from backgrounds in which mothers are stereotyped as overly enmeshed with sons will assume that the brilliant lawyer and his mother just had to be . . . Italian . . . or Jewish . . . or Chinese. There is some truth to these broad patterns—the domineering Jewish mother, the emotionally distant WASP father; the Irish father of *Angela's Ashes* who oscillates unreliably between abusiveness and sentimentality; the all-wise and accepting African American grandmother—but these clichés are also oversimplifications. Patterns of excessive entanglement and excessive distance come in all ethnic flavors and all are subject to revision.

In some families, there is an almost pathological determination to avoid conflict, which translates as a refusal to entertain change that might prove disturbing and conflictual, even if it ultimately led to richer and more authentic connections. Children are tacitly or overtly coerced to conspire in this idealized picture and not to threaten it. However, the result, almost inevitably, is either relationships that are far from authentic, episodic conflicts, or disabling symptoms on the part of some family member who has been denied full adulthood by the pressure to follow the family script.

Joanne, the divorced mother of sixteen-year-old Kelley, was desperate to have Kelley accept her new fiancé. The mother arranged for a family camping trip, browbeating the daughter to join them. On the first day, they hiked for several miles and then pitched tents on a small campsite. After they retired, unmistakable sounds of sexual activity emanated from the tent of Joanne and her boyfriend. Needless to say, this family trip backfired. The last thing this family needed was to have the mother rub the daughter's nose in her own sexuality with a new and resented prospective stepfather. Kelley was embarrassed and resentful. Relations between mother, daughter, and boyfriend remained frosty. What is remarkable here is the mother's blind spot. Why didn't her intellect overrule her impulse? How could she possibly have thought that her display of raw power would be sufficient to win affection and trust? Kelley endured the trip, but seldom confided in the mother. We all have such blind spots, and we pay dearly for them.

FROM REACTIVITY TO ACTIVE LISTENING

Conflicts between parents and separating young adults are inevitable. A young adult's job, developmentally, is to push parents away. A parent's job is to learn how to let go gracefully, without letting go of the love and support that our adult children still need.

In conversations with young adult children, effective parents spend a lot of time just listening. What parents hear from a grown daughter or son is processed, not as an invitation to intervene—but as information, as data. Constructive parents ask friendly questions. The less quick parents are to pounce, the more parents are likely to hear (and the more information will be entrusted in the future). Such parents may be pleasantly surprised at how much adult children actually want to share.

A related goal is to disengage reactivity; to monitor one's own feelings and cultivate the capacity to consider what it feels like to be your grown child. The psychologist Jon Kabat-Zinn, in his work on stress reduction and on parenting, invokes a core teaching of yoga and meditation to encourage people under stress to cultivate a capacity to "respond rather than react." Reactivity is instantaneous, automatic, and usually part of a deeply ingrained pattern. An instant reaction, even if meant constructively, is more likely to reflect your own issues and to provoke a defensive counterreaction. A considered response is more likely to reflect your life wisdom as an older adult and to be taken seriously.

Respectful listening achieves a number of constructive

things. It damps down the urge to give (often half-baked) advice that reflects the parent's own worries and issues (which may not be pertinent). By asking questions, one gets to accurately understand what a daughter or son is really saying, to appreciate the deeper questions or issues behind what is being said, to let the child know you have heard what is being said, and to invite a calm exploration of implications and alternatives. Listening thoughtfully and posing questions rather than proffering instant advice also brakes one's own reactivity.

Family quarrels typically entail familiar roles and deeply scripted patterns. When parents react rather than respond, they are probably reenacting an old script. When children are young, parents are just learning how to proceed. Mother and father may have different approaches or premises. When children are quarreling, or when a child needs limits to be set, parents frequently operate at cross-purposes with each other. Before long, there are angry voices, hurt feelings, and a sense of lack of respect and misunderstanding all around. When parents act in haste, repair can take far longer than the original quarrel. Responding, as opposed to reacting, involves the use of one's intellect to complement and temper one's emotions. What is really going on here? Why is he/she behaving this way? How can I intervene constructively, rather than just popping off? How can I support my partner? Yogi Berra memorably said that "You can observe a lot by watching." By analogy, you can hear a lot by listening.

In the case of a very major life decision by an adult child, such as a career move or the choice of a partner, it's sensible to let a lot of active listening take place over time before weighing in. If two parents have different views on the subject, it's particularly important to hold your fire until you can discuss the matter and either reach a consensus or agree to disagree respectfully. Adult children don't need to be protected from the fact that their parents sometimes disagree. But if letting parents in on a major decision or crisis mainly triggers argument between parents, adult children are less likely to share anything.

A bitter one-liner recently made the rounds in retirement communities: How do you have a good relationship with your grown children? Keep your wallet open and your mouth shut. That advice may yield superficial cordiality (along with a lot of resentment). But it hardly bespeaks a good relationship. There are times when the parent of a young adult needs to express a concern, as a parent. But this should be done sparingly, respectfully, and after a good deal of listening.

Obviously, there are times when parental interventions are required. If a young person is making what seems an ill-considered or disastrous choice, or is in serious legal or psychiatric trouble, parents have an obligation to involve themselves. But how parents insert their views, whether they second-guess relentlessly or carefully choose and time their interventions, determines whether their concerns will be understood as loving or just infantilizing and meddlesome. Some insecure parents of adult children give advice almost continuously—it's their most familiar role, a way of working off nervous energy and of feeling needed—and then wonder why their children don't really want them around. Parents who give advice in a manner that affirms rather than deprecates their grown son or daughter's capacity to be adult will be rewarded.

Sidney Callahan, a psychologist, author, and mother of six adults, proposes what she calls the "good-friend test." What if your twenty-five-year-old engages in behavior that you abhor? The test, she suggests, "is applied by asking yourself: 'How might I approach a good friend in a similar situation?' The answers you come up with in this imaginative exercise help in handling conversations with your adult children." If a good friend's behavior, say table manners, bothered you, perhaps you would just make allowances; "or you might tactfully bring the matter up in private at some propitious moment. You would not, however, *not* automatically and peremptorily correct a fellow adult's manners at the table—not if you wanted to remain friends." This is also good advice for thirty-year-olds who find aspects of their sixty-year-old parents irritating.

Of course, table manners may seem a trivial irritant, but the basic "good-friend" rule holds when far more consequential conserns arise. If an adult seems on the brink of a disastrous decision, about a partner or a career, the parent is still far more likely to play a constructive role if the engagement begins with a lot of active listening.

Edwin Klingelhofer, a psychologist who works with families, recounts the case of Al, a twenty-three-year-old who continues to live at home and shows no inclination to move out. He works twenty hours a week in a music store, and has no other immediate plans. He is not rude or uncooperative, but the parents are unhappy with the status quo. They have several options: to kick him out, to give him a deadline for moving out, to charge him rent, and so on. But as Klingelhofer observes, before making demands, the parents first need information. It may be that Al just likes living at home. Or that he has tried to find other work, and failed. Or that he is afraid of being turned down. Or he is unsure of what he wants to do. The best outcome will likely result from an accurate appraisal of the situation. Often, it is astonishing how little parents know about their children, especially when they create an atmosphere in which it feels unsafe to let them in on much.

Except when genuine disaster seems imminent, it's wise to wait to give advice until it is solicited. One mother thought her thirty-one-year-old daughter's boyfriend was an unsuitable jerk. She left few of her misgivings unspoken. The daughter had her own doubts, but her mother's constant badgering drove her closer into the arms of the unsuitable young man. Had the mother just restrained her verbiage and listened, she might have given her daughter room to express her own doubts. It's hard to improve on the words of the 1960 musical *The Fantasticks:*

> Your daughter brings a young man in,
> Says, "Do you like him, Pa?"
> Just tell her he's a fool and then:
> You've got a son-in-law.

RESPECTFUL PARENTING OF ADULTS

Suzanne and her only daughter, Lisa, twenty-six, were in the car returning from a visit to a cousin who had recently given birth to a baby boy. They were chatting companionably when Lisa took her mother aback by declaring, "I'm pretty clear that I'll never have children."

This was completely out of the blue. Suzanne, approaching sixty, had been imagining grandchildren. Her instant thought was abrupt dejection, followed by irritation at her daughter's glibness. Here's what she might have said:

"Oh, Lisa, how can you possibly be so sure? You're only twenty-six. You'll probably change your mind as you get older."

Or: "A lot of women these days keep putting off having children and then it's too late. Do you want to end up like Aunt Jeanne, dealing with fertility nightmares and adoption agencies?"

Or: "A woman's life isn't complete really until she has children. And just who, young lady, do you think will take care of you in your old age?"

Or: "What, after all I've done for you, now you're going to deny me grandchildren?"

Or: "That's so selfish and so typical, Lisa. You're only thinking about yourself again. Given how you've turned out, sometimes I'm not so sure I should have had children."

What an amazing capacity we have to wound our loved ones. Beyond the immediate issue at hand, think what these comments would have communicated: You're foolish and incapable of adult decisions. You don't have the right to make up your own mind about important things. I am wiser about life than you are. You can't rely on me to appreciate life from your point of view. My needs are more important than yours. As long as you're around me, you'll need to choose between loyalty to me and your own selfhood.

With a choice framed that way, most healthy daughters would opt for their selfhood. We and our children, we and our parents, have the power to push each other's emotional buttons in a way that creates instant distance. If we let reactivity take over, a close moment can be spoiled in an instant, and these defeats tend to cumulate.

Here's what Suzanne actually did. She thought for a few seconds, and invited a less emotionally charged exploration. "Whether to have kids is a deeply personal decision," she said. "A lot of people agonize over it. Your dad and I did. And society certainly doesn't make things easy for mothers these days."

These comments communicated thoughtful interest, not worry or coercion. They invited Lisa to ask her mother questions about her own experience, without making that experience a definitive or necessary model for Lisa's life. They suggested a mother who had done some growing up, who was essentially comfortable with herself—someone who could be trusted. The comments created emotional space for further nonjudgmental conversation.

Lisa had not yet told her mother that she was in the middle of her second painful breakup with a boyfriend in less than a year. Eventually she was able to say that perhaps she really did want children, if she could imagine finding a reliable partner. It was men she was dubious about. By resisting the temptation to pounce, Suzanne allowed Lisa's real concern to emerge from the conversation. Often young adult children really have other issues, with which they are not fully in touch, beyond the one that surfaces in a provocative remark. They are waiting to see whether parents can be trusted with an intimate conversation.

Look at all that would have been lost had the discussion gone in the other direction. Instead of a conversation that allowed Lisa to express her real concerns and seek support and advice from her mother, Lisa would have been reinforced in her wary expectation that her mother's attitude would be judgmental, demeaning, and useless. Suzanne would have lost a priceless moment that brought mother and daughter closer together. From Suzanne's perspective, the actual conversation signaled: I believe you are a good and worthy person. I trust you to make good decisions. I am here to listen, not to dictate. From Lisa's perspective, the conversation meant: I can take some risks with my mother without being shot down. She takes my views seriously. She recognizes me as an adult and loves me as an adult.

Why did the conversation go in the more constructive direction? First, Suzanne responded rather than reacted. She made room for her intuition that something else was behind the slightly provocative opening remark, and took enough time, through respectful listening, to allow Lisa's real concern to emerge. She was honest about her own issues, but in a manner that communicated trust and empathy rather than superiority and condescension. And second, Lisa had enough maturity to recognize trust when she saw it and not to just bait her mother to provoke a further reaction.

Our parents don't always live up to the behavior of the good Suzanne. Some of the time, our parents, as imperfect humans, sound more like the imaginary bad Suzanne. Certainly, those of us who are parents of young adults would much rather sound like the wise and loving Suzanne. The point is, we can. Just as development doesn't stop after age eighteen, it also doesn't stop after age forty-five. Parents of grown children are themselves capable of growth.

Like Lisa, young people occasionally let their parents in on important questions with which they are wrestling. By doing so they are taking an enormous emotional risk, for it remains true that knowledge is power. When they open themselves, their dreams or fears, to parental counsel and scrutiny, they know all too well that they might be ridiculed or thrust back into the role of small child. It is therefore normal for grown children to hide much of their inner lives from their parents, who still represent all-powerful authority figures from childhood. So these moments of emotional availability are rare gifts to parents, and should be treasured as such. Our reward will be more such conversations.

For many parents, who were less competent, reliable, and wise than they hoped to be during the maelstrom of the childhood and adolescence of their offspring, having children leave the nest can be a time to gain perspective on their own lives and their parenting, and to become better parents of adults than they were of children. Some mothers and fathers eventually conclude that they are better grandparents than they were parents (see Chapter 9). This shift, however, reflects not just the fact that the grandparent-grandchild bond is often sweeter and less emotionally overwrought than the parent-child connection. It also certifies that Grandma and Grandpa have spent a lifetime growing up. Certainly, one hopes that we have more life wisdom at sixty than at thirty! Why should the benefits of that emotional growth be saved just for grandchildren? Why not share it with grown children?

Adult children often make choices of which we disapprove. If they involve values very different from our own, it is only human to see these choices as reproaches of our own lives. Yet if our relationship is well grounded and rooted in respectful listening rather than tense reactivity, it is possible to express an opinion or at least to ask thoughtful questions about the choice being made. We may not change our child's mind; but if we are lucky, we may give a son or daughter pause and invite a more considered decision. If nothing else, we will model adult behavior, and keep crucial lines of communication open.

Our dear friend Ann Anderson remarks, a bit ruefully, that maturity as a parent comes when you realize that your children are not going to live the life you had in mind for them—and that it's okay. You can still love and respect them, and expect love and respect in return. Parental disappointment can entail everything from career to political and religious values, to choice of a mate, to domicile and lifestyle (see Chapter 7). But, as hard as it is sometimes for us to acknowledge this fact, each generation gets to make its own choices. And, while they might not be our choices, they can be valid and rewarding ones worthy of our affirmation.

In fact, we have more influence than we often think. One of the most quietly satisfying surprises for the parent of newly launched adult children comes at a moment when some utterance or action betrays the fact that, despite all manner of rebellion, a lot sank in after all. During all those dinners, when they were fooling around or teasing each other or being disrespectful, they were hearing even if they weren't listening. And all that time, we parents were teaching, positively or negatively, by example.

A daughter is living the details of her life rather differently than we hoped, but—mirabile dictu!—she shares some of our values. A son, the one who was addicted to video games, tells us about the terrific novel he's reading. A daughter who took music lessons until sixth grade and then gave them up is mysteriously buying classical CDs, citing the influence of a boyfriend. A son who has followed a very circuitous career route turns out to be pursuing a set of professional and political goals not all that fundamentally different than our own. Or maybe they are quite different. But he has grown into a lovely adult. Hosanna.

TEACH YOUR PARENTS WELL

There are few writings aimed at young adults on how to repair relationships with middle-aged parents. More prevalent are books with titles like *Divorcing a Parent* and *Toxic Parents*, reinforcing the belief of many grown children that their parents are hopelessly destructive and commending declarations of independence followed by wary and self-protective distance. Even in happier families, most children in their early twenties are not yet interested in pursuing closer connections with parents, for they have only recently escaped the confinements of childhood. Developmentally, as Donald Williamson observed, most healthy young adults are too busy separating. And most lack the life experience to think that such an enterprise might be worthwhile.

Children in their twenties with parents who are impossibly judgmental, or meddling, or whose style of manipulation is to lay on guilt, often find themselves coping by distancing. They resist demands for frequent phone calls, or regular dinners, and just happen to go to college or take jobs on the other side of the country. While it's normal and often salutary for young adults to keep difficult parents at a distance, it's a shame to get stuck there or to assume that parents are beyond redemption.

Two psychologists, Barbara Zax and Stephan Poulter, in *Mending the Broken Bough*, a practical book about mother-daughter relationships, suggest that young adults can improve relationships by cultivating the same kind of respectful curiosity that we commend to parents. Children in their twenties can also give themselves permission to set respectful boundaries, communicating love rather than distance. If parents seem overly intrusive, they can plan relatively short visits, but try to make those visits heartfelt rather than just dutiful. Parents, in turn, may be satisfied with less lengthy time commitments.

For parents, one of the real gifts of a lifetime of connection with a grown child is an expansion of horizons. Our kids pursue interests we never would have thought of. Even in their twenties, adult children can teach a lot to their parents. And parents, if they can put aside their role as authority figures, can learn from grown children and take these teachings as a sign of a job well done.

Bob recalls: *When Gabriel, our son, was in his early twenties, he produced and acted in a Sam Shepard play at the Edinburgh Festival. He had some encouragement that it would be picked up by a more established producer for a run in London. Despite some misgivings, I contributed money to the venture, and we would occasionally discuss the play and its finances on the phone. This whole idea, of course, was a calculated risk; Gabriel had just become (barely) autonomous financially; this venture put him back into an emotionally loaded economic dependence on me.*

I realized that I was at risk of using financial help as a misguided currency of love and connection. Still, I thought the play reflected real enterprise on Gabriel's part and that we had a close enough relationship that a modest investment was a constructive support and the risk an acceptable one.

In one phone conversation, however, Gabe's financial projections sounded optimistic. I started asking more pointed ques-

tions, communicating skepticism bordering on distrust. Though I could feel my anxiety level rising, I ignored my usual advice to slow down and pay attention. Finally, Gabriel, acting more adult than I, said evenly and lovingly, "Dad, you're really winding me up here."

In an instant, we both grasped the emotional stakes. Gabe was saying: You've given me this money. You need to trust that I want this venture to succeed as much as you do; that I am behaving conscientiously as an adult. Otherwise you had no business giving me the money. As Gabe later told me, my anxiety made it harder for him to own his very real achievement. The play's financial success was turning into a test of my respect. At the time, I was mostly oblivious to that.

Without realizing it, I was thinking of his dubious schemes as a fourteen-year-old, and I was treating him like one. In that moment of mutual stress, Gabe was exercising more mature reflection and self-control than I was. He was modeling how to be an adult. Instead of taking offense, I gratefully backed off.

In the end, the play lost money, though not for lack of diligence on Gabe's part. Nonetheless, it was well reviewed and turned out to be an important boost both to his theater career and his self-reliance. It was money well spent. More important for our family, in the course of these conversations our emotional vocabulary as father and son deepened—not because I was supporting or advising him, but because I was learning to respect his insistence that I let go.

Chapter 3
The Psychology of Families

Each of us is born attached to a mother. From birth, we begin to separate. The process is charged with ambivalence. A mother, and by extension both parents, is a source of comfort, nourishment, security, affirmation. But to become an autonomous person, the child must find his or her own way. Yet as adults, we still want the love and appreciation of our parents—if we can have it without too much backseat driving. And as parents of grown children, we want to feel that all our labors as parents will be rewarded by a satisfying lifelong relationship. Thus the paradox of attachment and separation.

In his classic coming-of-age novel, *Portrait of the Artist as a Young Man*, James Joyce recounts a playground dialogue in which an older boy, Wells, teases young Stephen Dedalus by asking if he kisses his mother every night before he goes to bed. Dedalus answers: "I do." Wells then announces, to general laughter, "O, I say, here's a fellow says he kisses his mother every night before he goes to bed." Dedalus then says, "I do not." And Wells sings out, "O, I say, here's a fellow says he doesn't kiss his mother before he goes to bed."

Joyce writes, "They all laughed again. Stephen tried to laugh with them. He felt his whole body hot and confused in a moment. What was the right answer to the question?"

From the terrible twos to the tumultuous teens and into later life, the question lingers: Are we supposed to cherish our parents, or reject our parents? Love our mothers, or not love our mothers? We find it difficult to imagine that we can have it both ways. It is hard to appreciate that respectful separation is rooted in respectful attachment, throughout the life span.

The combination of continuing dependence mixed with a fierce desire for autonomy produces a cacophony of mixed signals, to self and others. The complex relationship between secure autonomy and connection with others is a lifetime challenge. It is developmentally normal for newly grown adults to put some distance between themselves and their parents. But many young adults remain stuck in the developmental task of separating, a decade or two after they have reached chronological adulthood. Their own selfhood comes to be defined as emotional distance from their parents. Unresolved family issues of distance and closeness become a template for other relationships and an obstacle to comfortable intimacy. New financial pressures on the young often defer genuine autonomy and add to these strains. Both generations settle into familiar patterns that are somehow the wrong blend of distance and connection—when what they need is a different brand of each.

At thirty-three, Philip Roth, as "Portnoy," wrote that "a Jewish man with parents alive is fifteen years old, and will remain a fifteen-year-old boy till *they die!*" But this sense of awkwardly reverting to the child role when parents are around is not limited by ethnic group, gender, or social class. It is close to universal. In Turgenev's mid-nineteenth-century classic, *Fathers and Sons*, Arkady, the son, returns to his parents' home after graduating from university. "[H]e was conscious of a faint feeling of embarrassment—the embarrassment which generally overcomes a [grown child who] returns to a place where everyone is accustomed to regard him and treat him like a child." King Lear's daughters could not manage their tyrannical father.

The dilemma is woven right into our language. The very word *child* means a young person who is not yet an adult as well as a fully grown person in relation to parents. Our language has no distinct word for an adult child.

As midlife adults, frustrated at our inability to connect with grown children in mutually satisfying ways, we often have similar frustrations with aging parents. Despite forebodings that our own parents will soon die, leaving painful, unfinished emotional business, many of us seem unable to make emotional headway. It is too easy to settle for the strain of cordially distant relationships, with awkward telephone calls and polite, ritualized, clenched-teeth visits. Fortunate is the family that transcends these traps of role and repetition, and achieves ongoing growth, respect, and a satisfying blend of connection and autonomy.

TRANSCENDING FAMILY MYTHS

In nearly all families, there are family stories or myths that both convey family values and sometimes become straitjackets. These myths define one's identity within the context of family and shape one's conception of oneself. They amount to an intergenerational transmission belt of strengths and weaknesses, traits and values. We tell ourselves stories in order to make sense of our lives and selves. Sometimes these narratives are empowering, but often they are partly disabling of self and of other. My mother was always the victim. I was the good child. My brother never was any good at being responsible. My father thought none of us ever was good enough. People feel the need to escape the confines of family in part to outgrow the constraints of these myths.

Sometimes these family myths are congruent—that is, we have roughly the same conception of others in the family that they have of themselves. Other times, family members wouldn't recognize, much less accept, the image we have of them. Often, we only have the most fragmented and incomplete picture of our parents' or grown children's actual lives. We may be afraid of letting our parents/children know us deeply for fear of ridicule, shame, or weakness. We imagine what the response will be, and decide the gamble is not worth the risk. So both parent and grown child stick to the myth, which is at least predictable if not comfortable. Invariably, these illusions get in the way of rich, empathic, and nurturing connection based on real knowledge of self and other.

As the family therapist Ivan Nagy observed, every family weaves a complex tapestry of legacies and stories that are a mix of explicit and unspoken values, handed down from one generation to the next. These family narratives are renegotiated, implicitly or explicitly, in marriages and by every parent and every child. They can be nurturing or toxic, and sometimes are both. Through compassionate revisiting of family myths, anger and aggression within families can become transformed into a capacity for reparation and reunion. With self-reflection, we can cultivate a capacity to integrate both good and bad aspects of earlier experience and come to a more or less balanced understanding of why our parents behaved as they did, and what their family legacies are all about.

A family narrative helps shape individual identities. Our first and probably most profound sense of identity is formed in the context of "who I am in this family." We may have a dim or a strong sense of our parents' narrative. Certain things about the family past, mythic or real, we know because they tell us. Other things we know without consciously knowing. Still other things we observe (children are incredibly astute observers of their parents). And the narrative of our parents has a profound influence on the personal mythology that each of us constructs for ourselves, the story that becomes known to our own children.

In many families, there is a collusion among family members not to speak openly of certain things, because to acknowledge the dark side of family life, the hostility that sits beside tenderness, is also to acknowledge vulnerability, fear, shame, and sadness. Often family secrets turn out not to be real secrets at all, but common family knowledge, surrounded by a conspiracy of silence. To break the family code of silence is really to risk breaking down barriers to emotional communication. Such a risk contains both hope and fear: the hope for a more enduring honesty and openness; the fear of inviting potentially overwhelming conflict and dissolution.

Some families have a poignant need to present an attractive picture to the outside world, often to the detriment of actual family relations. One family sent to relatives and friends an annual Christmas letter that some recipients knew to be painfully at odds with the parents' true feelings. The parents proudly trumpeted a son's career choice and new job—which the father had bitterly tried to dissuade. They affectionately announced a daughter's marriage that the mother had opposed. The letter needed footnotes, disclosing what the parents really felt (and maybe giving the children's side of the story). Such letters express a desperate wish for a storybook family; but the parent who thinks the children is ignorant of those mixed messages is making a grave mistake.

Children see parents as both all-powerful—and vulnerable. Even at a relatively young age, children sense their parents' vulnerability and seek to protect them. These patterns, motivated by love and compassion as well as fear, can become barriers. Dr. Rachel Naomi Remen, medical director of the Commonweal Cancer Help Program in Northern California and author of *Kitchen Table Wisdom*, tells the story of a patient of hers named Gloria who was fifteen and dying of leukemia. The girl's parents had put a large sign at the nursing station instructing doctors, nurses, and other medical personnel not to discuss with the patient anything about her diagnosis or her condition. One night, setting up an IV for the girl's 2:00 a.m. chemotherapy dose, Dr. Remen's eyes met Gloria's. The girl was awake, waiting. "Dr. Remen," she asked, "am I dying?" In a split second, Dr. Remen, in her first year as a medical resident, had to make a decision about whether to honor the parents' wishes or to be honest with her patient. She told Gloria that the disease was growing despite the best medical efforts, and yes, she could die. "She closed her eyes for a moment and then told me she had known. She asked me not to tell her parents. She didn't think they could bear it."

If mutually protective distance is the style of (non) communication in some families, others press toward "togetherness" and an intolerance for individual differences. Indeed, such families define the differences among family members as a problem and anxiously go about trying to "correct" those differences, rather than accepting or even celebrating them. Families who are in constant conflict simulate emotional closeness, but have trouble expressing such human needs as love, gratitude, and affirmation, or respectfully accepting differences. Bickering and argument are the modus operandi.

In such families, there is often over-entanglement without real intimacy. Loving moments abruptly turn into bitterly conflictual ones; genuine intimacy is too threatening. Conflict becomes a proxy for connection. Real intimacy has to begin with an effort to come to terms with what we truly think and feel—as opposed to what we "should" think or "ought" to feel—and real curiosity about the other person.

HEALTHY CHANGE

People, as creatures capable of reflection, learning, and growth, can change patterns, even when the patterns seem hopelessly locked in place. One family we talked with had experienced a terrible loss. A beloved son had committed suicide in his mid-thirties. The son had been a brilliant scientist, and the pride of the family. The suicide had been triggered by a minor but humiliating career reversal which set off an abrupt bout of depression that caught his friends, family, and doctor entirely off guard. Terrible guilt and shame ensued. The parents were inconsolable, and buried their grief. Out of respect for the parents, the other children stopped mentioning the deceased brother. He had died just before Christmas. Each succeeding year, the holiday became a time of tension and private unacknowledged pain instead of connection, mutual support, and remembrance.

This pattern, in turn, affected the entire emotional style of the family. The family members, thinking they were protecting both each other and their own feelings of grief and loss, got into the habit of tiptoeing around emotion. They avoided discussing not just the son's death but emotionally sensitive subjects in general. Distance became the lowest common denominator, a basis on which the family members could at least simulate relationships. It affected not just the immediate family but relations with aunts, uncles, nephews, nieces, cousins, and grandchildren—and relationships in general.

Eventually, a younger brother, after both psychotherapy and an experience with a group forum, resolved that he did not want his aging parents to die without having come to terms both with his brother's death and with the family's pattern of reciprocal silence. He began mentioning the unmentionable, insisting that family members start talking about it. He got in touch with his extended family and initiated difficult conversations. He explained this odyssey to his college-age children, who had been told little. After some very painful moments, not only were family members able to speak of the deceased son. His memory became a source of solace as well as grief. Together, they learned to celebrate his memory, and even to find comfort in it. The entire family loosened up emotionally and found life more joyous.

This change occurred because one family member took the initiative. Once he began breaking the tacit family convention, speaking (kindly and compassionately) of what had been deemed taboo and unspeakable, the old pattern was no longer viable. This brother, of course, took a risk. He was exposing himself to his own raw, unresolved grief, as well as to the possibility that his parents and other family members might have responded with hurt or anger or deeper silence. But they did not. Indeed, they responded, eventually, with relief and appreciation.

A great many people in families are imprisoned behind walls of mutual distance, because it is the least painful alternative they can imagine and nobody has offered anything better. Perhaps they have taken emotional risks in the past, only to have been rebuffed and humiliated. Perhaps they are absolutely certain—psychologist Edward Shapiro calls this "pathological certainty"—that my mother is never going to change, or my father is always going to belittle me, or my brother will forever play the big shot at my expense, just as he did when he was eight and I was four. As the family mourning the lost son found, even patterns that conceal (and offer false protection from) horrible pain can be changed.

There are many possible patterns and strategies of change. A desire and initiative for change on the part of one family member can be triggered by a crisis or a life change, by psychotherapy, by a group experience, by deliberate strategies of family reconnection, by religious or spiritual engagement. It doesn't require anything as dark and dire as a suicide.

The experience of marrying, or having a child, can throw a constructive monkey wrench into old patterns. To acquire a mate is to bring into the family someone whose own family patterns are usually quite different. The newcomer will likely notice things that have been invisible to the family. These can be sources of irritation and silent endurance—or constructive pattern change. A new daughter-in-law can decide that her mother-in-law is just impossible to be around, and can cope by trying to minimize contact. Or she and her new husband can accept the insights that the newcomer brings to the situation, and experiment with constructively altering the family dynamics.

Having a child triggers powerful feelings about one's own childhood. If grandparents are at hand, young adults who experienced a few years of autonomy may suddenly find themselves thrust back into a more intimate tie with their own parents; this may be a closer bond than they entirely welcome. They may feel whipsawed—with simultaneously new adult responsibilities as parents, and a reversion to the role of child in the company of anxious grandparents.

One new mother experienced her mother-in-law as a terrible backseat driver. Her infant was premature and colicky. Whatever she did, the mother-in-law had a better way. When she tried, sometimes with difficulty, to breast-feed, mother-in-law worried about baby's nutrition and kept recommending bottles. When the baby paraded in a diaper, Grandma worried about a cold. When mother dressed the baby warmly in winter, mother-in-law preached the benefits of bracing fresh air. This new mother began crying two days before the mother-in-law arrived for a visit, and stopped crying a day after she left. A sense of utter defeat, and conflict with her husband, invariably ensued. The young father felt a divided loyalty and found himself irritated at both the women in his life. For the wife, the simplest solution was to keep mother-in-law at bay.

Yet as more children came, the younger woman gradually

became a more self-confident mother; she got better at firmly but politely standing her ground; and the older woman backed off and turned into a loving grandma. The two made their peace. The mother gradually realized that at least some of her short fuse around her mother-in-law had to do with unresolved issues involving her own mother. And as the young father matured and learned more about the process of parenting, he was better able to help navigate the shoals of his wife's relationship with his mother.

Some families talk more than others. In this family, differences between the young mother and her mother-in-law were never openly thrashed out. Yet maturation and mutual acceptance ensued anyway. In other, more verbal families, constructive change is negotiated. In all such situations, one can cope by choosing to flee or to grow. Flight is a false solution, because distances invariably mask unresolved issues that haunt not only the immediate relationships but patterns in other ones.

THE FAMILY AS A SYSTEM

Until well into the last century, psychotherapy was heavily reliant on the work of Sigmund Freud. The enterprise took place between a therapist—usually a psychiatrist—and a patient. In Freud's understanding, adult individuals carried around misconceptions or complexes from childhood which in turn led to neurotic symptoms that were disabling in adult life. Through the analysis, these could be understood at both an intellectual and emotional level, and disarmed.

The individual's family of origin was of interest mainly to the extent that it had been the source of injury or neurosis. In Freudian psychotherapy, the individual is treated in isolation; the therapist functions as the stand-in for mother, father, and other significant sources of buried feeling, through the process known as transference. Tacit feelings for mother or father can be elicited by the process of guided free association; they are "transferred" onto the therapist, "worked through," and exorcised. The patient, thus freed of neurotic thought patterns from childhood, is able to live a richer life.

By contrast, family therapy, which evolved in the 1960s and 1970s out of marital counseling, developmental psychology, general systems theory, and dissatisfaction with traditional psychoanalysis, looks at the family as a system. Family therapy, in its several variations, deals with the dynamics of the whole family and the actual family, not the family of the patient's distant memory.

As family therapy has evolved in the past four decades, it has increasingly emphasized not just marital or parent-child issues and conflicts, but the lifelong project of understanding and improving relationships between adults and their own parents and grown children. Family therapists did not pursue this approach out of a sentimental belief that adult children and their parents needed more togetherness. Rather, their research and observation suggested that an overly entangled or overly distant relationship between adult children and parents usually reflected profound, long-entrenched patterns of relating that spilled over and often proved disabling or emotionally impoverishing in other contexts, including relations with lovers or spouses, children, colleagues, bosses, and friends.

Some family therapists, rejecting Freud, build on a different school of psychological thought known as object relations theory, which holds that adults carry around with them internalized images from childhood about how key emotional objects in their lives (mothers, fathers, partners, children) are "supposed" to behave (see Chapter 4). Therapists encouraged families to examine myths and revise roles. By the 1980s, clinicians treating individuals had integrated many of the insights of family therapists. Very useful work continued to be done in individual psychotherapy, but it was no longer dominated by Freud.

In our view, ordinary families can learn a great deal from the insights and techniques that family therapists have used to work with troubled families. This doesn't mean "playing therapist." It just means learning how to disengage our own preconceptions and reactions, to become more dispassionately curious about our parents and children, as people, and to practice active listening. What follow are some key concepts.

As the pioneering family therapist and theorist Murray Bowen observed, an overly entangled or overly distant relationship with parents in adulthood is suggestive of a "poorly differentiated" self. Attaining a more realistic, mature, and balanced connection between parents and grown children, therefore, could be enormously enriching generally.

The psychiatrist Harold H. Bloomfield, reflecting on his own politely distant relationship with his parents, writes, "No matter how we try to rationalize our distance and our resentments, or think that we have the relationship 'handled,' there are emotional wounds and even health problems that we suffer from the unfinished business with our parents." He adds, speaking of his patients, "Many of the here-and-now conflicts people have with their spouses, lovers, ex-lovers, bosses, partners, or children are in part emotional reenactments of unresolved conflicts with parents." Dr. Bloomfield urges his patients to make peace with their parents, "not primarily for your parents, but for you."

In traditional Freudian therapy, the parents of adults undergoing treatment were of interest to the therapist mainly as distant sources of underlying pathology, but were otherwise passive bystanders. The parents of young adult patients were very deliberately, often painfully, kept out of the therapy loop, in order to let the alchemy of the transference operate and to avoid compromising confidentiality. James Framo, another pioneer family therapist, writes that the traditional psychotherapist would tell the concerned parent, " 'No, I can't tell you how Suzie feels about you' (but with the private, unexpressed thought, 'She'd be okay, you smothering bitch, if you'd stop driving her crazy.' ")

Framo observes that in traditional therapy, "The therapist, having never seen the parents, has relied on the patient's description of what they are like—that they are 'cold, rejecting, overwhelming, exploitive, double-binding, disappointing, too loving and possessive, undependable, irresponsible,' and so on. Instead [of coming to terms with parents] the patient is led to the conclusion that the real satisfactions of life are available from other relationships, from one's mate and children, from friends, or from work. In short, most [traditional] therapists write off the family of origin as a therapeutic resource." Ironically, of course, the same people who are counseled to look to their children rather than their parents as a source of satisfaction may well find, twenty years later, that their children in fact have the same disdain for them that they had for their own parents.

In treating couples in marital distress and children with psychological problems, family therapists addressed the entire family system. Often, a child or young adult with perceived problems was merely the *identified* patient—the bearer of symptoms or self-defeating behaviors on behalf of a dysfunctional family. The underlying pathology was neither in the patent nor in parents or siblings, but in the system. "The symptomatic person provides a focus for the family's emotional energy and distracts them from their own anxiety," according to the family therapist and author Monica McGoldrick. When one family member is the bearer of family distress, others can feel superior and have someone to care for. Systemic therapy produced a way to "reframe" the definition of the family problem, and an idiom less of blame than of systemic dysfunction.

One of the founders of what is termed *structural family therapy,* Salvador Minuchin, wrote that "A therapist oriented to individual therapy . . . tends to see the individual as the site of pathology and to gather only the data that can be obtained from or about the individual." By contrast, a family therapist "sees [the individual] as a member of different social contexts, acting and reacting within them."

Out of these diverse strands of work came a whole set of concepts, which can enlighten a relatively normal family that desires greater harmony, mutual acceptance, and respect. Most schools of family therapy agree that the family needs to be understood as an emotional unit which operates as a system. In systems, behavior is reciprocal and reactive. When a family system is stressed, some members will "overfunction" while others "underfunction"; each is compensating for the behavior of the other. An overfunctioning spouse may be successful at work, dominant in the relationship, and "concerned" about the passivity of the other. The partner may be passive, given to bouts of depression or physical illness. The more that the overfunctioning spouse does for the partner, the more the underfunctioning one retreats and is typically perceived by both as the "sick" one. But it is really the system that is dysfunctional. For the overfunctioning partner, instead of redoubling efforts to "help" the "sick" member, the task becomes to change one's own behavior so that the passive one is enabled to take more responsibility for his or her own behavior. A key idea of family systems work is that by changing your own behavior, you begin to change the behavior of the system.

Murray Bowen observed that families, as "living systems," responded to stress in ways that temporarily reduce anxiety but that create other problems. A key concept is "triangling" (also called triangulating). The fundamental triangle in relationships is mother, father, and child. Triangles get recapitulated in other relationships. Often, people in families with high levels of anxiety unconsciously try to reduce the anxiety level by displacing it onto others. A married couple will try to deal with conflicts in their own relationship by making the child the problem. The child will absorb the anxiety and find ways to act it out. Two siblings will make a third, or a parent, the odd one out. Monica McGoldrick, a student of Bowen, observed: "By validating each other's view of how 'obnoxious' or 'incompetent' the third person is, the first two shore up their own perceptions, gain a sense of moral righteousness, and probably lower the anxiety each had in dealing with the third person." But somebody in the system, and the system as a whole, pays.

Triangulating, even in ordinarily perceptive people, can be entirely unconscious until we cultivate the capacity to recognize it. Family therapist Harriet Lerner, author of *The Dance of Anger*, tells this story on herself: Following a visit to her aging parents in Arizona after her father's heart attack, she became annoyed that one of her young children, Ben, was behaving more rambunctiously and concerned that the other, Matt, was having trouble sleeping. After a discussion with a colleague, she realized that she had been displacing her own apprehension about her parents onto uncharacteristic short-temperedness with her children.

> At the dinner table the following night, I apologized to the whole family for being such a grouch and a grump and I explained to Matt and Ben that I was really feeling sad . . . because Grandma and Grandpa were getting old and Grandpa's heart attack was a reminder to me that they would not be around forever and that one of them might die soon. "That," I explained, "is why I've been so angry." I also wrote a letter to my folks telling them how much I had enjoyed my visit and how, after my return home, I'd come in touch with my concerns about their aging and my sadness about my eventual future without them.
>
> What followed was quite dramatic: Both boys relaxed considerably and the fighting diminished. Each asked questions about death and dying and inquired for the first time about the specifics of their grandfather's heart attack and grandmother's cancer. I stopped feeling angry and things returned to normal.

Lerner adds that her father not only responded to her letter but wrote letters to his grandchildren, explaining what happens when someone has a heart attack and describing his own case. "He concluded his letter to Matthew by directly addressing the subject of his own death. These letters, which were factual and warm, began the first correspondence between the generations."

Unspoken fears are generally more terrifying and disabling than spoken ones. By stepping out of role and noticing what was really going on, Harriet Lerner modeled how to constructively face a huge life drama, an impending death, for both her children and her parents. The unspeakable could be spoken. The older and younger generation could engage, based on compassionate curiosity rather than unvoiced misassumptions and terrors. They could be mutual sources of support. She observes, speaking of triangles generally, "It is not simply that we displace a *feeling* from one person to another; rather, *we displace anxiety in one relationship by focusing on a third party, who we unconsciously pull into the situation to lower the emotional intensity in the original pair.* For example, if I had continued to direct my anger toward my misbehaving boys (who, in response, would have misbehaved more), I would have felt less directly anxious about the life-cycle issues with my aging parents. In all likelihood, I would not have identified and spoken to the real emotional issue at all."

Recognizing such triangular patterns, and working instead to build more authentic one-on-one connections, can reduce the anxiety level in the entire system and can allow each family member a fuller selfhood—a secure base from which to have satisfying relationships. While family relations are often the prime source of such behavior patterns, these patterns carry over into other relations. Thus, improved family relationships can lead to greater emotional and relational maturity generally.

A person with a weak sense of self tends to look to the approval of others for his well-being. Not surprisingly, his feelings and behaviors are "a mixture of compliance with and rebellion against the relationship system." Daily life becomes a constant source of anxiety because even minor tasks or decisions will be overly influenced by a desire to please. When "poorly differentiated" people tend to gravitate to people with similar styles, relationships are usually circular and painfully full of conflict, because each excessively looks to the other for validation.

By contrast, well-differentiated people have a mature sense of self. They are better able to experience authentic emotion because they are less enslaved to the expectations of others and to their own patterned reactions; paradoxically, they are freer to behave with altruism and compassion, because cooperation with others is experienced as a principled and autonomous choice rather than the result of a sense of guilt, rote obligation, or anxiety.

Poorly differentiated families can be described as excessively "enmeshed." The well-being and self-regard of one member is overly dependent on the views and words of others. Even when no such demands are forthcoming, people may act in order to seek approval and then resent the imagined demand. At the opposite end of the spectrum, other families or subunits of families are emotionally disengaged, sometimes to the point of total cutoff. Disconnection seems the only way that disaffected members can get on with their lives. Rarely, however, is this remedy emotionally healthy. Typically, the distance simply paves over hurt feelings and deep longings, and engraves a somewhat crippled emotional style onto other relationships.

FREEING OURSELVES TO RECONNECT

A great many people do not entirely like the family role assigned to them. The sister who was always the troublemaker may have the beginnings of a more mature conception of herself, but family stereotypes and expectations squash her back into her earlier role. The oldest of four who found himself in the role of caretaker may be weary of it, and ready to be taken care of for a change. But family expectations, which he may feel obligated to sustain, keep him stuck. He may alternate between being dutiful and resentful. Many people distance themselves from their families because they are sick of their family roles. Yet, in the absence of resolution of family issues, they often find that their family roles follow them around. In spite of ourselves, we recapitulate familiar family patterns in relationships with others. Emotional distancing invariably suggests unfinished business. Extended cutoffs may seem indicated when family relationships are tense, but efforts at reconnection or at least a common understanding of what has occurred are almost always worth the effort.

All systems theory, whether of the natural universe or of social organisms, offers one central insight. Systems are interdependent—so if the behavior of one part of the system changes, other behavior necessarily changes. This is the hopeful message from family systems theory, for it suggests that constructive change is almost always a possibility. One of Murray Bowen's core precepts is "the only person you can change is yourself." Changing yourself avoids blaming others. However, changing yourself improves the likelihood that other members of the system will change, too. Some families are powerfully resistent to change. But even if they don't change as much as you might like, their behavior will become less disabling of you.

Thinking in systems terms can alter the usual family idiom of fault, blame, and immutable stereotyped roles; it can liberate people to thrive as individuals, and alter the obsessive need to please. By learning to become less reactive and automatic, you can become a calming influence on the entire system. Another student of Bowen, Roberta Gilbert, observes that once families are understood as systems, "Parents were not causes, but rather receptors and conduits of, as well as contributors to, a much larger intergenerational process."

SECOND CHANCES: BEYOND HIERARCHY IN FAMILIES

It takes a radical renegotiation of power between the generations to make possible a rediscovery of the "otherness" of each generation. A parent who is no longer functioning as a "parent" in Donald Williamson's sense can be fully humanized and known as a person. This opens the door to a process of genuine curiosity about this other human being; a desire to explore and learn, rather than to criticize what one assumes one already knows. When family members cannot be genuinely open and curious— and hence empathic—about one another's experience, the result, for each individual, is often a subjective sense of isolation, emptiness, and futility. In such families, ambivalence—a conflicting and fluctuating desire for both closeness and distance— is something to be denied and feared, rather than accepted as an inevitable part of family life.

The psychologist and author Robert Karen observes that "we are dealing with two different sets of parents—the parent we grew up with, whom we struggle with internally, and the living parent of today. The internal parents have mythic dimensions. They are the ones who adored us and wounded us, whom we idealize and demonize, and from whom we separate in order to be more whole. The parents of today, by contrast, are other people like us. . . . They may be difficult and hard to take. But they are not in charge now. The control they have is only what our psyches grant them." By letting go of the mythic parent, we can see our mothers and fathers as actual people.

In families that successfully reintegrate, much of the substance and symbol of hierarchy gives way to equality; parents are accorded the authority associated with life experience and wisdom, but not the authority associated with command. Parents and children see themselves as peers in the experience of being human. Parents acknowledge the adulthood of grown children, and the adult children develop the capacity to see their parents as people and not as powerful, mythic figures.

In learning more about the mythic other, we disarm hot spots. History becomes mere history, emotionally as well as chronologically. The most important thing about the past is that it is past. And the past must sometimes be grieved—and sometimes laughed about. Of course, even in families that have achieved a degree of success in renegotiating old roles and finding a new synthesis based on equality, there are delicate subjects and sometimes family skeletons. Thomas Wolfe asked: "Which of us has looked into his father's heart?" Some experiences of our parents are ultimately unknowable, and in this life no family achieves perfect communication. These family aspirations are ideals that we pursue knowing we sometimes fall short. Even if our overtures are not entirely reciprocated, they will be rewarding to us.

Many of us can take these initiatives ourselves. Some can benefit from psychotherapy, often relatively brief. Some family therapists view themselves as "coaches." They instruct their patients on techniques for interviewing families-of-origin, including extended family networks. By establishing more authentic and less charged one-on-one relationships with members of one's extended family, it is possible to gain a more realistic picture of them, as people, and to gradually break out of old, stale patterns. This, in turn, frees them to break out of disabling, patterned roles. Murray Bowen often said that the family in which one grew up is the best place to learn more about one's self.

Family therapists who coach clients on repairing relationships with parents report several benefits. In the process of interviewing parents respectfully and dispassionately, with genuine intellectual curiosity, people tend to become more empathic. We begin to see our parents as ordinary people who struggled just as we struggled, rather than the mythic and often fearsome figures of childhood. "Divested of their magical power, the parents need no longer be unrealistically idealized or denigrated."

Other family therapists, such as James Framo, began inviting their clients to bring parents and siblings right into the consulting room, as a dramatic way of reframing misconceptions and allowing adult children and their parents to rebuild relationships. Framo, in a review of his life's work, reported that most of his patients initially had an "enormous opposition and intense fear" of the idea of involving their actual parents in their therapy. Typically, patients protested that their parents wouldn't come, that they were too old to change, "I don't think they could take it; it would destroy them." People fear that dark family secrets will be revealed; that the therapist will side with parents, who will gain new power over them; that they will be sucked back into an overly entangling set of connections and be smothered. Patients object that things are at least tolerable, and why take the risk of making them worse.

This resistance is itself revealing. However unsatisfying the relations in the family system, people are deeply invested in them. It is easier to suffer than to risk change. Like all systems, it is the nature of a family system to seek equilibrium or "homeostasis." The system's dynamics remain essentially stable as long as everyone sticks to his or her familiar role, and all members of the family unit are part of a tacit bargain to keep patterns the same—until something disturbs them. Constructive change is resisted, yet once it occurs, it is often welcomed.

Framo reports that when asked, parents in fact are usually willing to participate—and his patients are surprised to learn the depths of their own misconceptions. He quotes a patient: "You know, she's just a little, old, unhappy woman; what in the hell have I been afraid of all these years?" Even parents in their seventies and eighties are receptive to the invitation to improve relationships. Indeed, older parents have often been suffering in silence, despairing that their grown children could ever understand, much less appreciate them, or that negative patterns could be improved.

The psychologist Samuel Osherson quotes a colleague recounting how adult men sometimes have preposterously mythic conceptions of their fathers. "'Big Al? Do you want Big Al to come in?' a man might ask me after going over the struggles he's had with his father. There's often fear and awe in his voice. Then Big Al arrives for our appointment and turns out to be a tiny, eighty-five-year-old man, short and gentle. But the father of childhood lives on in these men's minds."

Dr. Susan Forward, author of *Toxic Parents*, tells of a middle-aged man who had a highly controlling mother, and who hesitated to pursue a more authentic relationship with her throughout his adult life. Now that she was eighty-two and recovering from a heart attack, his excuse was that she simply couldn't take it. But with the encouragement of both his therapist and his mother's physician, he managed to begin the first real conversation in years. He reported,

> I got the ball rolling by asking her if she had any idea about how I felt about our relationship. She said she wondered why I always seemed so irritable around her. That opened the door for me to quietly talk about how her need to control me had affected my life. We talked for hours. I said things I never thought I'd be able to say. . . . A couple of times her eyes filled with tears. The relief was unbelievable. I used to dread seeing her, but she's just a frail little old lady. I can't believe how many years I was afraid of expressing myself to her.

The villains of Dr. Forward's book are the "Toxic Parents" of the older generation. However, most of us do not have parents who warrant the label toxic. And it is possible much earlier in life for either generation to take the initiative to change old, unsatisfying patterns. By the time a parent is in her seventies or eighties, it is usually the adult child who needs to take the initiative if change is to occur at all. But how much more constructive the outcome would be if either parent or adult child did not wait so long, and if initiatives were taken out of compassion and not just anger.

By stepping out of role as "child," we can start behaving more as adult peers, and we can let go of a lot of anger. Learning for the first time some biographical facts of which our parents have been reticent or ashamed, we can become adult enough to treat our parents with compassion. Framo recalls, "One father, who had been abusive to his children when he was drunk, disclosed [in family-of-origin therapy] how he had lost his parents when he was six years old and how he had been shifted from one foster home to another, in some of which he had been severely beaten, not given food, and had been sexually molested. Following this disclosure his children, astonished at hearing this for the first time, clustered around the weeping father and hugged him." Another of Framo's patients commented, after a session with her parents, "I cannot reconcile my hatred all these years of my father with that poor pathetic person I saw in the session." The patient, Framo observes, was struggling "to integrate the internalized representation of the father with the real person who was her father."

Sometimes, one parent has to die before authentic connections can be established with the other. One of our interviews for this book was a joint conversation with a father in his eighties and a daughter in her fifties. The daughter had long had a bitterly conflictual relationship with her mother, who was rigid and judgmental. The daughter felt that nothing she did was good enough to win her mother's approval. The father, a gentler person, did not interfere, for fear of provoking the wrath of the mother. The daughter worked with a Bowen-oriented family therapist to improve the relationship with both parents, but made only modest headway. She was able to become more self-confident as an adult, but her relationship with her mother remained strained. In the daughter's fifty-first year, her mother died. Subsequently, she reached out to her father, and their relationship became markedly enriched. She could mourn the relationship with her mother that she was never able to achieve. Her father, at eighty-two, was capable of dramatic personal growth and reconnection.

Most Americans cannot afford intensive private psychotherapy, much less therapy with entire families. And in an era of managed care it is necessary to be on the verge of suicide or homicide before most insurance plans will pay extended psychiatric benefits. Yet a great many adults, probably a majority, often find relations with their extended family a source of disappointment rather than comfort. Here, the insights and techniques of family systems work, while stopping short of formal "therapy," can be of immense benefit.

It's clear that most young adults need to experience a good deal of growth and maturation before they are motivated to give their discarded families of origin a second look. Often, they need to endure the struggles and joys of raising their own children, or to navigate other life passages. We believe this enterprise of reconciliation can be deeply rewarding, even if not storybook. We return to the challenge of reconnecting with our families in Chapter 8.

Chapter 4
Parents Growing Up

Late midlife can be a time of integration, greater emotional coherence, and in Erik Erikson's wonderful word, generativity. It is normal, developmentally, for people in the latter half of their lives to want to give something back. This helps explain why many people who had bumpy experiences as parents are sweet and generous grandparents. It is also easier logistically, once children have left home, to be more thoughtful parents. We can back off some, to the role of interested and appreciative observer.

As parents of young children, our daily life is just plain exhausting. So much of what we do involves split-second timing—getting home in time to relieve each other or a baby-sitter, dashing to day care and just making it to work, worrying about mishaps, exacting discipline that is neither too indulgent not too harsh, resenting having to be policemen of wily and unappreciative adolescents. It takes real work to hold one's own anxiety and volatility in check ("You did *what?*"), to simultaneously negotiate with a teen and with a partner whose premises about what makes for good parenting may be quite different. Parenting a teenager often coincides with the years when one's professional life is going at full tilt; or, if one is less fortunate, it may be a period of career reverses and stresses to a marriage.

Haste and fatigue are the enemies of thoughtful parenting, but they seem to be the environment of the modern nuclear family. Split-second timing is the enemy of calm wisdom. As parents of young children, few of us have the time to be our best.

Yet this hectic, pressure-cooker environment changes dramatically when children are grown—and there is every reason to take full advantage of this change. By definition, when children are no longer living in the house, there is a dramatic qualitative change. Our connections with our kids now come in relatively short moments: phone calls, or visits, or occasional excursions. If we can appreciate it, this logistical shift offers a surprising gift: though these encounters are relatively brief, they no longer have to be rushed. If we are no longer juggling our other commitments with caring for young children whose safety depends on our vigilance, we can slow down some and invite more responsive and thoughtful conversations. In the course of doing so, we can signal our grown children and ourselves that things have changed. We are no longer treating our children like kids, our children are no longer rebelling as a natural developmental step toward adulthood—and maybe we can start being the parents we always hoped to be.

For parents open to constructive change, this letting go of old roles and responsibilities can be a time of their own emotional growth. The wise parent whose child has recently left the nest will view the relative calm and solitude as an opportunity for renewal—repair of the marriage, attention to the self, opportunity to pursue new challenges in work and recreation. The late forties and fifties, the typical parental age when children leave home, are an appropriate time for stocktaking and course correction.

THE LIBERATED NEST

There is a wonderful paradox here, if we notice it. The more the parent is attending to his or her own unfinished business, the less he or she will be overcrowding the newly adult child by imposing anxieties that are often more about us than about our children. Giving ourselves permission to truly let go and tend to our own needs for a change, paradoxically, sends the grown child a signal of trust and invites lifelong connection. Conversely, a parent worried about "the empty next"—what comes next for me now that my children are gone?—is at greater risk of foisting his or her own anxieties on separating young adults, and making the whole process more difficult.

In the 1980s, there was a TV commercial for a breakfast cereal that supposedly promoted youthful health. In the commercial a teenager wonders where her parents are, and sees a note on the kitchen table that they are off playing tennis. "Tennis?" says the teenager in baffled wonderment. "They don't play tennis." The camera then cuts to the product. Beyond the purported virtues of the cereal and the plain good sense of prudent diet and physical exercise, there is a larger unintended point here. How much healthier for the family unit that Mom and Dad are working off their own stresses and establishing a pleasant reconnection on the tennis court rather than hovering over their seventeen-year-old's every movement. The note communicates that the parents have a life; even more important, it communicates trust that the daughter will not invite a motorcycle gang over to trash the house while mother and father are out whacking around a tennis ball. The Special K is the least of it.

For some parents, whose identity has been so powerfully defined by their parental role, letting go can be excruciating. Middle-aged parents may feel conflicted about whether they should honor and deepen existing commitments—personal and professional—or whether this time of life invites new beginnings. To some extent, the adolescent identity crisis is mirrored in the midlife identity crisis. At a time when young adults need their parents to be steady and stable (so that they can safely separate), conflicts can intensify, career crises can occur, marriages can unravel, parental unhappiness can become more glaringly obvious. In such situations, anxieties about one's own life, one's eventual rendezvous with mortality, one's connections with one's partner, and so on, can too easily be displaced onto separating children. This is, of course, unwise. It distracts us from taking care of our own business, and signals our young adults to keep their distance. It produces exactly the opposite of what both generations so poignantly want.

Looked at from the parent's point of view, a child leaving home is both a kind of liberation and a loss. The empty nest produces feelings of profound parental ambivalence. On the one hand, there are new opportunities, to pursue travel, hobbies, and to repair and revive a marriage, or perhaps to find a new partner. On the other hand, there is the loss of what is often the central emotional role of early midlife—the parent of young children. There is also worry, often legitimate, about how these fledglings will fare in a cruel world. All of this produces understandable anxiety, which the wise parent learns to manage.

One woman we interviewed, in her seventies, recalled her younger self as a confused mother of four, who had focused her energy and her considerable intelligence on being a good wife and mother. Although she had always wanted to paint, that desire had taken a back seat to the raising of young children. When her youngest son left for college, however, she packed up her art supplies and went to another country for several months, to paint, "to figure out who I was, other than a wife and a mother." This created something of a crisis in the family, as everyone, including her husband, wondered whether she would come back. But it also gave her grown children room to define themselves as adults. Instead of hovering over their decisions and worrying about their young adult lives, she was tending to the task of her own renewal. When she did return home, it was with a stronger sense of herself that allowed a new, more secure set of family connections, adult to adult.

Interactions between separating parents and young adult offspring are full of discontinuous, inharmonious episodes, pulls and pushes between conflicting forces—loyalty issues, secrecy issues, protective impulses on both sides. In family system terms, the separation of a young adult is a charged situation because it radically alters the family dynamics. As the family therapist Jay Haley observes, the greatest stress to a system occurs when someone is entering the system or leaving it. The acknowledgment and acceptance of such transitions achieves personal and systemic growth. Failure to accept that the family is in a new stage yields frustration or conflict. Ivan Nagy writes that "every move toward emotional maturation represents an implicit threat of disloyalty to the system." The rest of the system necessarily has to adapt, but sometimes does so in maladaptive ways. Often, it is the young adult who acts out "problems." Sometimes, it is one or both parents.

In many unhappy families, children have long served as distractions or as props, or as scapegoats for marital conflicts. As Haley observes, "In two-parent families, the parents are faced with only each other, after many years of functioning in a many-person organization. Sometimes parents communicated with each other primarily through a child. . . . When the child leaves home, the parents become unable to function as a viable organization." A child, subconsciously perceiving an obligation to stabilize the system, may fail—at graduating college, at a new job, at a love relationship—as a way of restoring stability, albeit pathological, to the family. Parents, often relatively late in life, can do a lot of growing up. Grown children need to keep their own minds open to that possibility, and welcome it. Judith Wallerstein's research on failed marriages suggests that a divorce often reflects one or the other partner's failure to adequately separate from his or her family of origin.

CONNECTED AUTONOMY

We spend our entire lives in a dialectic of connection and distance with other people, especially with our families of origin. A common misconception is to view attachment and autonomy as opposites. On the contrary, it is secure attachment and a realistic view of our parents as people that allows us to be fully autonomous adults. To be an adult is to be capable of both intimacy and self-sufficiency, on terms that we freely choose, rather than on the basis of being trapped in old roles or neurotic feelings of guilt, obligation, unworthiness, or a search for approval.

Attachment is not the opposite of independence; it is the opposite of *detachment,* or emotional indifference. Healthy attachment fosters autonomous exploration and growth, in which young people are free both to assert their differences from their parents and to acknowledge their continuing reliance on them. Parents, ideally, are able to acknowledge and accept their children's differentness yet continue to support them emotionally—and also to let their children know something about their own needs, desires, and dependencies.

The parent-child bond is the archetypal attachment with another. It begins in infancy. A young child is dependent on its parents, initially the mother, for virtually everything. The British psychoanalyst and pediatrician Donald Winnicott was fond of observing, "There's no such thing as an infant"—meaning that one can't imagine a baby apart from its mother; to be a baby is to require adult care and nurturing. Yet to be born is to be separated from the physical body of one's mother. And throughout childhood, from infancy to adolescence, parent and child perform a dance of intimacy and necessary separation, one that foreshadows the same oscillations throughout life.

The great British psychoanalyst John Bowlby was the pioneer of research on attachment and separation. His ideas spanned the fields of psychoanalysis, systems theory, cognitive science, and ethology (the study of relationships in animal species). As Bowlby observed, "All of us find security in being with people we know well and are apt to feel anxious and insecure in a crowd of strangers. Particularly in times of crisis or distress do we seek out our closest friends and relatives. The need for companionship and the comfort it brings is a very deep need in human nature—and one we share with many of the higher animals. . . ." Bowlby studied institutionalized children as well as those separated from parents due to other disruptions. He concluded that severed attachments, whether through early death of a parent, divorce, institutionalization, or abuse, can cause deep emotional loss in young children and can impair their own capacity for emotional attachment as adults.

Bowlby emphasized that what mattered most in early child rearing was the emotional quality of the home, and the sensitivity and responsiveness with which the mother handled ordinary interactions with her baby such as feeding, weaning, play, discipline, and so on. He believed that a baby's smiling, cooing, and clinging are part of an instinctual repertoire of behaviors aimed at keeping the mother close at hand. He repudiated the Freudian notion of the autonomous individual driven mainly by unconscious drives like sexuality and aggression and insisted that all human beings instinctually crave relatedness.

For parents, Bowlby did not propose perfection. He believed, in the wonderful phrase of Donald Winnicott, that if the mothering is "good enough," the child derives comfort, joy, and a secure base from which to explore the environment. Bowlby proposed that children build up mental representations or internal working models of their parents and themselves over the course of the earliest months and years of the relationship. These internal images of self and other—emotional "objects"—form the basis for future relationships. They are not graven in stone, but refined and modified by our experience throughout life.

For example, a child whose parents are psychologically available, supportive, and consistent builds up a model of the self as able to cope *and* as worthy of help. There is no false choice between autonomy and dependence, but an appropriate synthesis. Conversely, a child whose parents are unavailable, lacking in responsiveness, or outright rejecting, forms an internal model of other people as unreliable and of the self as unworthy or unlovable.

Parents are both positive and negative role models. Many of us grow up determined not to repeat our parents' mistakes. Yet, if we are children of parents who had harsh lives, we often fear we are condemned to be just like them. A child of divorce fears being unable to sustain a loving relationship with an intimate partner. Children of alcoholics fear succumbing to drink. Children exposed to abuse when they were young worry about being abusive parents. But most of us have a fair amount of capacity to influence our own destinies. Though there may be some genetic "hard-wiring," as well as lingering aftereffects of a difficult childhood, the very act of looking hard at our families and disarming myths can give us greater control over our own destinies. Some adults remain hopelessly stuck. But most of us, over a lifetime, are capable of attaining a measure of emotional and relational wisdom.

While fiction, theater, and mythology have long appreciated the lifelong capacity for emotional growth, the idea came as something of a revelation for modern academic psychology. Early in the twentieth century, there was no such field as "developmental psychology" or "adult development." There was only child psychology. Psychologists were curious about how children developed, but just assumed that in broadly normal people little of interest occurred developmentally in adulthood. Even in people with serious emotional problems, Freud actually believed that people over the age of about fifty were hopeless candidates for psychotherapy, because they were incapable of much change. Today, developmental psychology covers the full life span, and recognizes that constructive change and growth can occur throughout the life course, right into the eighties and even nineties.

Although a child's capacity for intimate relationships is influenced by the quality of parenting, most of us can transcend difficult childhoods. This has been demonstrated by four decades of evolving research of patterns of attachment and separation. In the late 1950s, a younger American colleague of John Bowlby, Mary Ainsworth, tested Bowlby's theories with a famous and ingenious experiment, one that has now been repeated and refined many hundreds of times by other researchers. Ainsworth was interested in how patterns of mothering affect the child's security in relationships. In her experiment, a team of observers made home visits to babies and mothers over the course of the baby's first year. They observed each mother's style of relating to her baby in situations such as crying, feeding, cuddling, playing, and smiling. Ainsworth devised rating scales to measure the mother's responsiveness to her infant's needs.

She then observed in a psychology lab the same mothers and babies, now about one year old. She first observed the babies in the room with their mothers present; then with a stranger; and briefly, alone.

Ainsworth was able to clearly demonstrate that mothering patterns directly influenced how securely babies connected with mothers—and others. She differentiated three distinct patterns. "Securely attached" babies cried protestingly when the mother left the room, greeted her joyously when she returned, and were easily consoled. Two other groups were observed to be "insecurely" or "anxiously" attached. Some of the anxiously attached babies were ambivalent—excessively clingy, hesitant to explore the toys on their own, and quite agitated when their mothers departed. These babies were eager for contact when the mothers returned, but often continued crying, pulled away instead of pleasurably cuddling, and were difficult to soothe. Another subgroup, labeled "avoidant," seemed almost too self-reliant. They actively explored the room, seemingly oblivious to their mother's presence or absence. When she left, an avoidant infant didn't appear to notice, and when she returned, the baby ignored or avoided her.

At home, the mothers of securely attached children were markedly more responsive to their babies' signals of hunger or pain or readiness to play, while the mothers of anxiously attached children had been rated as inconsistent, overly intrusive, slow to respond, or overtly rejecting. Succeeding waves of researchers statistically confirmed that the attachment patterns formed in infancy influence behaviors that persist well into the school years and beyond.

Other research about parents and children suggests that the causality runs in both directions. Secure attachment is not simply a case of a competent and loving parent passing on that security to her children. As every parent since Adam has suspected, children are born with different temperaments; they are not simply blank slates. Behavioral science confirms that some aspects of children's temperaments are "hard-wired." And a child's behavior can influence a parent's, just as vice versa.

Indeed, an easy, adorable, and winning child is likely to evoke loving and confident behaviors in a parent. Those parental behaviors, in turn, reinforce the child's confidence that she is worthy of love and competent to navigate the world. In this virtuous circle, parent and child both gain self-esteem. In contrast, a colicky, restless, whiny, demanding child is likely to engender fewer delighted smiles from the parent, and more frustration and eventually anger and lost parental self-confidence. These negative messages reinforce the child's insecurity and self-defeating behavior patterns. This cycle of negative reinforcement, however, can be revised and repaired by careful parenting during childhood and self-conscious change on the part of the grown child later in life.

A good illustration of the tricky nature of causality is the history of research and treatment of schizophrenia. In the 1940s and 1950s, psychiatrists were convinced that schizophrenia in children was largely caused by destructive parental behaviors. Mothers were the prime suspects. Psychiatrists used the term "schizophrenogenic mother," and described a constellation of patterns seemingly based on close observation of families with a schizophrenic child. Such children, not surprisingly, had anxious, insecure, and seemingly inept parents—for good reason: nothing that the parent did seemed to make much difference! Psychiatrists of that era, however, made the elementary mistake of presuming that the cause and effect ran from parent to child. The parent "must have" been responsible for the child's schizophrenia. Today, brain science suggests that the causality runs from child to parent. Children, of course, don't give parents schizophrenia, but schizophrenic children do produce (appropriately) anxious parents. Schizophrenia is a disease of demonstrable brain lesions that may be chemical, genetic, or even viral in origin. But it has little to do with parental behaviors.

More garden-variety variations in children's behavior reflect parent-child patterns of interaction whose cause and effect often runs in both directions. While the work of Ainsworth may seem to imply that we are blessed or cursed by what our parents did to us, subsequent research in the Bowlby-Ainsworth tradition suggests that adults can transcend poor attachment patterns in childhood and that constructive change in the parent-child system remains possible throughout the life cycle.

ARE WE DOOMED TO BECOME OUR PARENTS?

In the 1980s a student of Ainsworth named Mary Main, now a professor at the University of California at Berkeley, explored how patterns of attachment in our childhood affected the kinds of parents we grow up to be. In an "Adult Attachment Interview," Main asked adults to reflect on their early interactions with their own parents, memories of separation or loss, and descriptions of the current relationship with each parent. These interviews also provide a window on how one's internal model of relationships works, and whether one feels able to revisit and transcend painful memories.

Main's category of "secure/autonomous" subjects were self-reflective individuals who seemed to have integrated both good and bad aspects of their early experience. Either they had had secure parental attachments as children, or had somehow (with an adult partner or a therapist or a spiritual or other transformative process) worked through painful early experience to come to a balanced understanding of why their parents behaved as they had. The children of these parents, assessed via the Ainsworth experiment, tended to demonstrate secure attachment patterns.

A second group of subjects seemed self-reliant, indifferent to, or skeptical of, intimate relationships, and had trouble remembering very much about their childhood bonds. And the majority of their own children were classified as avoidant of attachment.

The third group, which Main called "preoccupied with early attachments," often became flooded with emotion during the interviews, particularly with intensely negative memories which they had not been able to integrate. Their own children, for the most part, displayed the ambivalent style of attachment that Ainsworth first described.

But lest this research seem hopelessly deterministic, Main and colleagues also demonstrated that the relationship styles learned in early childhood merely establish predispositions; they do not doom us to inevitable patterns. Human beings, unlike the goslings studied by animal psychologists, are capable of emotional learning throughout the life cycle.

More recent research, observing the parenting styles of mothers and fathers of young children, confirms that patterns of poor attachment in early childhood do not doom one to be an ineffective or anxious parent. Attachment researchers now differentiate those who have enjoyed "continuous security" from those whose secure attachment patterns are "earned." This is a charming choice of terminology in a body of research that is otherwise fairly dry and quantitative. It connotes effort, hard work, reward, and just desert. By taking the trouble to learn something about who our parents were, why their own efforts sometimes fell short, and by working hard on other relationships, we can become more compassionate people—and better parents. Even for those who suffered from weak or ambivalent attachments as children, empathy can be cultivated.

One study found that parents whose warm and competent parenting style was "earned" (as opposed to patterned from their own childhoods) could be just as effective mothers and fathers as those whose parenting was rooted in a secure "early working model" of what it meant to be a parent, carried over from childhood. "[I]t may be that attachment to a spouse whose own model of attachment is secure may be helping to enhance the parenting behavior of the at-risk parents." The authors further speculate that parents whom the study rated as "earned-secure" may have become "more involved with their [own] parents at this time and may have been attempting to come to terms with their earlier relationships with their parents." Though there is little professional engagement between this line of research and the family systems approach described in Chapter 3, these two very different schools of human psychology have arrived at the same insight via entirely different routes: By compassionately engaging our families of origin, we can promote healthy change in ourselves.

Nearly all of us are capable, through insight and effort, of improving relationships both with our parents and our children. No matter how toxic our childhoods, we are creatures who can influence our destiny. Some of us may have to work harder than others to earn such relationships. For parents of children who are still at home, the important lesson to glean from the body of work on attachment and separation is not that adult patterns of relating to others are indelibly set in early childhood. It is, rather, that the process of having a good relationship with your adult children begins when your children are young; and that autonomy is not the opposite of attachment—rather, it is the lifelong capacity for connection with others that makes us whole and vividly alive individuals.

GROWTH AND RECONCILIATION

This enterprise, of building authenticity into adult family relationships, is a lifelong process. It is often hard work, but it is deeply rewarding and very much worth the trouble. Mark Twain (Samuel Clemens) famously remarked that when he was fourteen, he was amazed at how ignorant his father was, and when he was twenty-one, he was amazed at how much the old man had learned in seven years. This ironic, self-deprecating remark is usually taken to mean that the young Clemens himself grew up during those seven years, acquired more mature insights about his father, and stopped rebelling for the sake of proving his own manhood. But there is a deeper, unintended, meaning to the remark. If we, as parents, wish close and mutually respectful relationships with our grown children, we too need to change our own acts. A parental stance of authority and firmness that is appropriate when dealing a with a fourteen-year-old will surely backfire if applied to a young adult of twenty-one—or twenty-five, or forty. Perhaps Clemens's father did learn a few things in those seven years, after all. Otherwise, Clemens might have gone on thinking him an ignoramus.

It is the developmental task of young adults to break away. But the behavior of their parents during these crucial years has great bearing on whether, and on what terms, they will come back. In great works of literature, a common theme is the idea that the young adult (usually a young man) must make some dramatic break with his family (usually his father) in order to become his own person—an authentic adult. There is a whole literary genre known as the *Bildungsroman*—the coming-of-age novel, which usually includes a break with parents. The Oedipus myth and its many variants entails the symbolic or literal killing off of the father, so that the son can assume his place as an adult. The poet Robert Bly, in his 1990 book *Iron John*, observes that countless myths have at their center the odyssey of the young man who must leave home and attach himself to some mentor other than his own father, before he can return home as an adult. In Thomas Mann's epic saga, *Buddenbrooks*, each generation of a merchant family needs to define its own course and radically differentiate itself from the one that came before.

There are far fewer literary works about family reconciliations. One, interestingly, is Homer's *Odyssey*. After more than a decade, Odysseus finally returns home. His son, Telemachus, doesn't recognize him. Odysseus says, "I am the father whom your boyhood lacked." Homer writes "Salt tears burst forth from the wells of longing in both men, and cries burst from both as keen and fluttering as those of great birds." Telemachus, out of loyalty to his father, had been resorting to endless tricks to keep a band of suitors from marrying his mother and usurping the kingdom. He has just about run out of tricks, but the miraculous return of Odysseus vindicates his efforts. As the psychologist Samuel Osherson comments, reflecting on the significance of this reunion scene, "The message is that for a man to grow up he must find the good and the strong in his own father—he must find the heroic in the figure he hardly knew."

Too few sons, we suspect, achieve this. In Arthur Miller's play, *Death of a Salesman*, father and son desperately crave each other's affirmation but tragically never get it. The father, Willy, is crushed that the son Biff, now in his thirties, has never lived up to Willy's dream for him. Willy alternates between harshly condemning Biff and trying to manage Biff's life in the wild hope that his actions can yet make a success out of his son. Biff, not surprisingly, is both ashamed and resentful. He rubs his father's nose in the old man's own failures and hypocrisies. Each attempt at reconciliation ends with Willy furious and Biff leaving. Willy, now also failing in his business, can think of no way out other than to commit suicide and leave Biff the proceeds of a life insurance policy in a last, pathetic effort to give his son a paternal legacy. Just before the suicide, son and father, rage spent, both break down. Biff hugs Willy through sobs. Willy says—in Miller's stage directions Willy is astonished and elevated—"Isn't that—isn't that remarkable? Biff—he likes me!" But this only redoubles his determination to proceed with the suicide.

Throughout it all, Willy's wife, Linda, tries to interpret son to father and father to son. But the two men never manage an emotional connection that is other than mutually annihilating. The play could be used as a family therapy text. In many families, fathers do not know how to give love to adult children in ways that respects their adulthood, and mothers as the traditional carriers of emotion, cannot make up for this gap.

One adult daughter told us how her father, in town for a visit, grandly proposed gathering the entire family together to celebrate an upcoming wedding anniversary. But the proposed weekend was not convenient for several key family members and the father was adamant about not changing the date. Feeling rebuffed, he agrily declared that, instead of underwriting an unwanted gathering, he would donate the money to charity.

Later, his older daughter found herself alone with her father in the kitchen and tried to reopen the conversation. Her father glared at her, picked up his newspaper, and went into the other room. It felt uncannily familiar, this suddenly stalled communication, and her father's retreat into hurt and angry silence. "My father grew up in poverty," says the daughter. He is bitter that he wasn't given to as a child, as a young person. . . . It should say on my father's tombstone: 'Nobody ever gave me anything.'"

This awkwardness with strong feeling is characteristic of fathers who came of age early in the twentieth century. Is this man replaying some family script he himself learned in childhood? Did he feel so cheated of his own father's (or mother's) caring that he now makes excessive demands—under the guise of generosity—of his own children? What he reaps is a bitter, locked-in, self-punishing silence that dares others even to try to understand the sad secrets of his heart.

The father, apparently, is equally uncomfortable with giving—and with taking. He resents giving, and has difficulty taking the emotional risk of asking for what he needs. His attitude is, "At my age, you shouldn't have to ask. . . ." The people who really love you should know without having to be told, what you want what you need. They should, in effect, be able to read your mind. As observed by the psychoanalyst Donald Winnicott, it's the fantasy of early infancy: The baby, feeling hungry, fantasizes the breast and, lo and behold, the breast appears, giving the baby the illusion that the breast is his or her creation, that mother and baby are one. The gradual disillusionment, meted out by the mother in small enough doses so that the baby can cope, is a critical aspect of healthy separation and autonomy—and to the existential pain of being human and therefore alone in our own bodies.

In too many families, impasses like the reunion fiasco are not unusual. Hurt feelings are not voiced; anger, though keenly felt, is buried and never resolved. The risk of breaking down barriers to emotional communication runs deep. Such a risk contains both hope and fear: the hope for a more enduring honesty and openness, the fear of inviting potentially overwhelming conflict, dissolution, humiliation, and ultimate abandonment.

Often, it is grown children who need to take constructive initiative if patterns are ever to change. They will require more than one effort, and are less likely to bear fruit in the heat of argument And such initiatives are more likely if they begin before parents are into advanced age.

Vivian Greenberg, a clinical social worker who runs groups for midlife people who have strained connections with parents, recounts an episode from one session in which a forty-nine-year-old nurse, obviously intelligent and sensitive, described her relationship with her mother as hopelessly distant, "like polite strangers." Before Greenberg could respond, a youthful seventy-year-old woman in the next chair said, "Better talk to your mother—and *now*—because you don't know how much time is left. Just tell her that you feel strange with her; that you know she's trying to protect you, but that's not what you want. Tell it how you feel it—straight from the heart, that's all! Your mother sounds as if she's afraid of something, probably of getting close. Maybe she was hurt by her parents when she was little, I don't know. But don't you be scared. She'll thank you for opening the floodgates."

Not that it's always so easy. Such breakthroughs are rarely instantaneous. They require real effort and persistence. If a forty-nine-year-old, with a mother around eighty, has waited so long to initiate a more authentic relationship, she will have her work cut out. But these initiatives are worth taking.

MOTHERS AND DAUGHTERS, FATHERS AND SONS

The project of staying connected as autonomous individuals is experienced somewhat differently by men and women. In the 1970s, feminist scholars of human development began drastically revising the views of Freud and his disciples. The psychoanalyst Nancy Chodorow, in a very influential series of books and articles, proposed that girls and boys had a radically different experience of early development, stemming in large part from the fact that the mother was the dominant figure for children of both sexes. Sons naturally identified with fathers, daughters with mothers. As sons grew older, they needed to break away. But because of the closer and more natural mother-daughter bond, Chodorow argued, "feminine personality comes to define itself in relation and connection to other people more than masculine personality does. (In psychoanalytic terms, women are less individuated than men; they have more flexible ego-boundaries.) Moreover, issues of dependency are handled and experienced differently by men and women."

As the British psychoanalyst Melanie Klein had observed a generation before, in the act of mothering a woman produces a double identification. By identifying with her child, a woman also identifies with her own mother, and thus experiences and reexperiences herself as a cared for, and by extension, a caring person. This, of course, assumes that she enjoyed a satisfactory daughter-mother bond as a girl.

At the risk of oversimplifying a rich, complex, and still evolving literature, this "relational" view of women, as further elaborated by psychiatrist Jean Baker Miller and social psychologist Carol Gilligan, suggested that relational continuity between mothers and daughters contoured women's emotional styles. It was normal for girls to be initiated into the company of womanhood without a dramatic disjuncture, as part of the process of coming of age. By extension, women were therefore socialized to be more comfortable than men with emotional connections generally. Other theorists, citing both human cultural history and the behavior of other primates, contended that it was nature's way for the father to be "instrumental" and the mother to be "expressive."

Unlike a girl, a boy coming of age must make a dramatic break with both his mother and his father to prove his manhood. He is also likely to be the son of a father who himself has been socialized to be tougher and less emotionally available. This father-to-son modeling provides yet another source of emotionally distant manhood. Therefore, if the challenge for men is to rediscover their fathers once they are secure in their own manhood, the task for women is a more gradual evolution of the mother-daughter relationship. Both paths lead, ideally, to secure autonomy with a capacity for mature attachment.

Father-daughter connections, by contrast, are often the most remote of the four parent-child gender variations. Mothers are intensely involved in the rearing of children of both sexes. While fathers may pursue manly connections with sons, often outside the company of women, fathers and daughters often tend to dwell in different worlds. At the same time, there is an echo of the Oedipal myth in father-daughter relationships. This has been called the Electra complex, in which the daughter seeks, metaphorically or literally, to seduce the father (or the father seeks to sexually abuse the daughter).

Just as both parents sometimes have difficulty letting go of sons, a father may experience a daughter's normal separation as a kind of symbolic betrayal. Quite legitimate concerns about a daughter's emergent sexuality may get all mixed up with a father's unconscious fantasies. A father may see a boyfriend or husband as a rival. The father may also indulge a daughter excessively. His wife then is at risk of seeing her daughter as a rival for her husband's affections, and feeling like the odd one out.

These themes are also ancient. Three of Shakespeare's best known works, *King Lear, Othello,* and *The Merchant of Venice,* all dealt with fathers' obsessions with supposedly faithless daughters. Lear, the father of grown daughters, is hypersensitive to what he perceives as filial ingratitude. Yet he is unable (in an all too characteristically male way) to clearly express what he expects and needs from his daughters, especially his youngest and favorite daughter, Cordelia. That this theme is both ancient and contemporary is reflected in Jane Smiley's novel *A Thousand Acres,* which explicitly borrows the Lear theme relocated to a late twentieth-century farm in Iowa, where a father who had been abusive when his children were young imagines himself betrayed by adult daughters and goes slowly mad.

Adult daughters often find themselves in the position of caregivers with aging fathers. This can be a time of awkward distance, in which the father recedes into what seems to be geriatric passivity. Or it can be one of sweet reconciliation, repair, and renewal.

The historian Doris Kearns Goodwin, in a lovely memoir, recalls how she and her father bonded around their love of baseball. Whenever they played, he would come home from work and quiz her about how the Brooklyn Dogers had done that afternoon. Her assignment was to fill out a scorecard of each game, even though he could have just as easily read the box score in the newspaper. This ritual led to a lifelong shared love of baseball, and a close emotional lifelong connection with her father that deepened after her mother died while Doris was still in high school. She took the trouble to learn more about her father's story, which led to a continuing bond with her father in his advancing age. Her research for the book, long after his death, led her into a more profound appreciation of her family's odyssey.

Emphatically, this conception of gender, attachment, and separation is only a broad generalization. It is cultural, not genetic. It doesn't describe all societies, or even all American families. But in theory at least, the pattern supposedly predisposes women to a greater level of comfort with intimate talk and emotional connection.

A mother and a grown daughter who compare notes about courtship and sexuality, or about tending to a new baby, or who just have an easier time falling into conversations about feelings rather than computers, football, or the stock market, are more likely to have an easy and intimate relationship as both mother and daughter age. In many of our families, the women are typically the transmitters of emotional business. How many of us live in extended families where a weekly phone call begins with a perfunctory "Hi, how are you?" from Dad, who, after an awkward sentence or two, says, "Just a minute, I'll put your mother on." Grown sons certainly have mixed feelings about how close they want to be to their mothers. And while fathers and sons often yearn for connection, they may either see each other as irrevocable rivals, or just lack an emotional vocabulary. (One of our out-of-town relatives, when he gets Bob on the phone, immediately starts talking about the Red Sox. It is his way of emotionally connecting.)

On the other hand, as we have seen, some mother-daughter relationships carry an intense emotional change that is negative. And taken to an extreme, the new "relational" view of gender runs the risk of setting up an ideal of emotionally engaged womanhood that is hard to attain in the real world—a feminist counterpart to the traditional idealization of motherhood. In our interviews, many mothers complained that the child-rearing books don't prepare them for the deeply ambivalent feelings, the anger, the mood swings, that even the most normal and loving parents invariably experience.

In her book *Mother Love, Mother Hate*, Rozsika Parker, a British psychoanalytic psychotherapist, challenges the cultural idealization of motherhood which would have us believe that mothers are primarily loving, kind, and infinitely patient. She argues that love and hate can alternate with dizzying rapidity in the course of a day or an hour. A mother with two children might experience acute conflict and rage in relation to one, while having much more manageable feelings for the other. "The social conditions of mothering," says Parker, "can work to render maternal ambivalence manageable or unmanageable." She observes that today's conditions of parenting intensify maternal mood swings.

WHAT DO WOMEN (AND MEN) WANT?

Just as actual mothers often give the lie to the idealized picture of motherhood, not all grown daughters enjoy easy relationships with their mothers. Precisely because of the close emotional connection, conflictual relations between mothers and daughters can be excruciating to both. Many mothers carry around emotional wounds from their own childhoods that carry over into their mothering. In cases where women and their mothers are overly attached, relentless conflict is a perverse form of intimacy. Vivian Gornick, in her memoir *Fierce Attachments*, recounts a walk with her seventy-five-year-old mother. "She is capable of stopping a stranger in the street when we're out walking and saying, 'This is my daughter. She hates me.' Then she'll turn to me and plead, 'What did I do to me, you should hate me so?' I never answer. I know she's burning and I'm glad to let her burn. Why not? I'm burning, too."

In Penelope Lively's poignant novel *Moon Tiger*, an old woman, lying in a hospital bed, is reviewing her life. Her great passion was a wartime romance with a pilot who was killed in battle; she has not shared this with her family. One of her disappointments is her politely cordial relationship with her daughter, Lisa. "She was a disappointment to me. And I, presumably, to her . . . I took her to museums and galleries; I tried to encourage opinion and curiosity. Lisa, growing older, became ordinary. She began to bore me. And I sensed her disapproval. I have attracted disapproval all my life. Usually, it leaves me indifferent, occasionally it delights me. But the disapproval of a child is oddly unsettling."

Lisa comes to visit in the hospital. They make small talk. Lisa tells her mother about a rugby match, and a theater excursion. And Lisa thinks, but does not say, "And on Monday afternoon I visited the man who has been my lover for four years now and of whom you know nothing nor ever will. Not because you would disapprove but because you would not. And because since I was a small child I have hidden things from you: a silver button found on a path, a lipstick pilfered from your handbag, thoughts, feelings, opinions, intentions, my lover. You are not, as you think, omniscient. You do not know everything; you certainly do not know me. You judge and pronounce; you are never wrong. I do not argue with you; I simply watch you, knowing what I know. Knowing what you do not know."

The scene is chilling for its total absence of compassion. It is a far cry from the idealized "relational" mother-daughter connection. Knowledge is power. And in families with tacit power struggles, one resists the power of the other by denying her knowledge of one's true self. What a dreadful prospect, nearing the end of life, to have only this mutual distance.

Sociologist Lillian Rubin, who has written a compelling analysis of how families are coping with the new economic realities, has also written poignantly about her own experience as the daughter of "illiterate immigrant" parents who cannot fathom exactly what she does for a living. Rubin's professional gain her mother experiences as loss. "In all these years," Rubin writes, "she has never spoken a word of pride or praise for any of my accomplishments, at least not to me. She may brag to friends and neighbors about 'her daughter the doctor' and round them up to watch TV when she knows I'm doing a guest appearance on some national show. But when, in hurt and exasperation, I once asked why she'd never told me she was proud of what I'd achieved, she answered angrily: 'Proud? What do I get out of it? It's like I don't have a daughter. I see my friends' daughters taking care of them; they go to lunch, they take them shopping. What do I have? You live 3,000 miles away, and even if you didn't, what would I have? You're too busy.'"

In families like Rubin's, and in many others, unfinished business stretches even toward the end of life. Fully acknowledging the impending death of an aging parent is often difficult, particularly if child and parent have tiptoed around painful emotional issues. Death closes the book and forecloses the prospect of a richer relationship, except in memory. In facing the death of a parent, children face the fact that mother or father will die without being able to go back and have a life in any way different from, or happier than, the actual life lived.

Most people are only remotely aware of their emotional roots in previous generations—and of the impact on ourselves of earlier psychological events. We know scattered facts—the chronology of births, marriages, deaths; we know a few well-worn family stories but little about the emotional undertones and the richer inner lives of our forebears. To plumb these depths takes effort and initiative, empathy and humor.

Writer Victoria Secunda offers a whole typology of unfortunate patterns in mothering—the Doormat, the Critic, the Smotherer, the Avenger, and the Deserter. The Doormat mother doesn't know how to separate, and uses her vulnerability to keep her daughter tethered. The Critic always has a better way ("My mother will not get off my back about being single. She even ran an ad in the personals listing all the qualifications *she* has in mind for a suitable mate for me"). The Smotherer (or in Harriet Lerner's term, the Pursuer) tends to do the feeling work for the child, makes sacrifices for her, and insists that she be happy. Avenger mothers are narcissists—bullies. Except for Deserters, who have difficulty emotionally connecting at all, all of these mothers are excessively involved in their daughters' lives, but without real compassion.

Each of these types, Secunda contends, tends to beget daughters with characteristic problems. Doormat mothers often produce rescuer daughters; Smotherers produce overachievers; and so on. And daughters are at risk of repeating the patterns with their own children. Daughters learn both explicit and tacit lessons from mothers—whether they experience themselves as loving and lovable people; how they are supposed to behave around men, and around women; how work fits into their lives whether they experience the world as a trustworthy place.

As with any other relationship between parent and child, a mother-daughter connection begins improving when one party or the other takes the trouble to depart from the script and seeks compassionately to know the other. The therapists Barbara Zax and Stephan Poulter write, "The more you understand and have insight into the parts of your mother that you possess, the easier it will be to separate your life from hers." And, we would add, the more autonomous you are, the easier it will be to reconnect in a healthier way.

The issue of gender and parental attachment has taken something of a new twist with the "men's movement." While many feminist psychologists and social critics were positing that the entire pattern of women's early development and socialization and greater comfort with intimacy was culturally constructed rather than genetic (and hence potentially available to men as well as women), an emergent men's movement was taking these insights in two opposite directions. Some, such as Robert Bly and Sam Kean, wanted a return to a more rough-and-tumble, earthy version of father-son bonding. Others, mainly psychologists of men's behavior such as Zick Rubin, Samuel Osherson, William Betcher, and William Pollack, were observing that men's emotional detachment was partly rooted in the affective distance they had with their own fathers. To become more emotionally whole, men needed to have more intimate relationships with fathers (and sons); this, in turn, would make them more emotionally available to wives and lovers, and ultimately to themselves. These seemingly opposite visions partly overlapped. One evoked hunting trips and bonding around a common trade; the other evoked Dad tenderly playing in the nursery and learning an emotional vocabulary. Both involved hugs and even tears.

Prodded by more egalitarian values and by their new roles as more engaged parents, many men today feel empowered to seek closer father-son connections throughout the life course. We have encountered dozens of novels and memoirs in which sons recount a longing for a closer connection with fathers. This genre, though not totally unprecedented, is in many ways the product of the gender revolution of the 1960s and 1970s. Before that tumultuous era, men may have tacitly felt such longings, but there was little cultural permission to express them or act on them.

The novelist and social critic James Carroll (who is also a dear friend) won the National Book Award for his memoir about his father, *An American Requiem.* The father, Joseph Carroll, a lawyer and career military officer, served as head of the Defense Intelligence Agency during the Vietnam War. In his youth, he had also thought about becoming a priest. James Carroll, the son, did become a priest, albeit a radical, antiwar priest. Eventually, he would leave the priesthood, marry, and have children. The unbridgeable political differences between the Carrolls blended in a complex way with the son's need both to be his own man and yet to love his father.

James Carroll recounts one especially poignant story concerning his younger brother, Dennis, also an opponent of the war, who was seeking conscientious objector status. Dennis, who had not spoken to his father for two years at that point, tells James that he is planning to ask his father—now a recently retired three-star general—to act as his lawyer at his CO hearing. "You can't do that," James says. "Dad would never help you, and it would only be cruel of you to ask. . . . He's ashamed of you. He hates what you've done."

But Dennis does ask his father, and to James's astonishment, General Carroll does represent Dennis at the hearing, and in full uniform. "I am here today," he tells the draft board, "not because I agree with what my son just said—obviously, wearing this uniform, I don't—but because I know with absolute certitude that his position is sincerely held, prudently arrived at, and an act, if I might add, of heroic integrity."

Dennis gets his conscientious objector status—and also his father's blessing. James is crushed. "It wasn't only that I envied Dennis, confronting as I had to, yet again, how little I knew of my father's true capacity. It was also that I saw Dad, for the first time, as a 'child-changed father,' in the phrase Cordelia used of Lear. Dennis had touched him in that dark corner of the self. . . ."—in a way, apparently, that James had not.

The story also reminds us how different family realities can be for different siblings. It evokes the biblical story of Esau and Jacob, in which the one brother makes off with the father's blessing that the other brother so desperately craved. No wonder these family transactions are so highly charged.

Only in rare moments, such as the day when James was ordained as a priest, did much expressed emotion flow between father and son. On that day, young Carroll, in the vestments of a priest, places his hands on the head of his father, who is kneeling at the altar rail. "As I do, it is as if an electric current flows through me, because instantly his body convulses. The movement in his shoulders explodes into quaking. . . . My father is racked with sobbing. . . . Oh, what gratitude for the raw physical sensation it is to touch the man with whom I can no longer speak. I want to fill the abyss inside him, and I do not care if what I fill it with is myself."

Nearly a decade later, when James decides to cease being a priest, he breaks the news to his father, in words he has carefully rehearsed. "I'm leaving the priesthood, Dad, because I want to have a life like yours, with a loving wife and children."

"'Children?' Now his eyes flashed. I glimpsed the full force of his feeling. Yes. Hatred, sure enough. 'Why would you want children?' he said. 'They would only grow up and break your heart.'"

Despite his own efforts to effect a rapprochement, by the time James had the maturity to seek true reconciliation with his father, too much damage had been done; the father seemed rigid and the breach irreparable. And by the time the father reached the age when he might have softened, he had early Alzheimer's disease. James Carroll ends the book with an account of his father's funeral, and he concludes: "My father was dead. A fallible man. A noble man. I loved him. And because I was so much like him, though appearing not to be, I had broken his heart. And the final truth is—oh, how the skill of ending with uplift yet eludes me—he had broken mine."

James Carroll had to write his father's story twice, first as a novel (*Memorial Bridge*), then as autobiography, before he felt he had fully integrated its meaning. Philip Roth likewise treated his father both in fiction and in memoir.

Samuel Osherson, reviewing a long-term study of 370 men

who came of age in the 1960s and conducting his own interviews, found that most American men have profound unfinished business with their own fathers. Other studies have rooted male depression in poor emotional connection between fathers and sons. Survey after survey has confirmed that most sons growing up in postwar America reported little time and little emotional connection with their fathers.

In all eras, men have looked to their fathers as role models for how to behave as husbands, professionals, friends, and as the parents of their own sons and daughters. But for the most part, Osherson wrote of the postwar generation, actual fathers were traditionally distant and somewhat baffling figures. "What [stands out] in men's talk of their fathers is a mysterious, remote quality. Whether describing heroes, villains, or somewhere in between, most know little of their fathers' inner lives, what they thought and felt as men. The first man in our life was a puzzling, forbidding creature." Osherson's own father, he writes, "felt like a heavy weight to me, an immoveable force I could neither approach nor avoid, pressing on me with his remote sadness and distant judgmental quality."

To be adult, young men indeed need to separate from both parents. But because in most families the nurturing tends to come almost exclusively from mothers, "For many boys the only way to let go of what seems feminine is to devalue or ridicule it," Osherson suggests. Conversely, "We do not learn to be cared for, to get nurturance and intimacy from, men—beginning with the first men in our lives, our fathers, and ending with ourselves."

The gender revolution did not cause this rupture between fathers and sons; the shift from agrarian to industrial society did. But the revolution in sex roles has both exacerbated the consequences and created new opportunities for growth and reconnection. Men are now expected to accept and support wives with professional aspirations, as well as taking more of a nurturing role in their families. Many men lack an inner mental vision of this new role as appropriately manly. However, at least some men are adjusting to new roles, and vowing to have closer and more authentic connections to their sons than they had with their fathers.

FREEDOM TO ENGAGE

In the past four decades, American society has experienced radical and hopeful changes in traditional gender roles that our society has not yet fully integrated. In the 1960s, women broke out of their assigned domestic place and asserted equal rights in the workplace, the polity, and the family. Sexuality became more open for both genders, and traditional hierarchical marriage was no longer taken for granted. New possibilities for women, combined with economic pressures and new stresses on child rearing, caused divorce rates to soar. For many of us, the yearning for family reunion is compounded by the wound of parents separating via divorces at some point in our childhoods, before we were developmentally ready to separate from them.

As values changed, some men welcomed the invitation to pursue better balance between their striving and nurturing sides. Others felt displaced from traditional gender roles with clear boundaries. For a time, some women, exhilarated by new possibilities, tried to have it all—supermom, career woman, superlover. A great many found the effort exhausting. And some women felt emotionally displaced by the increased male role in the home. All of these social changes in a fairly brief time span reinforced new questions about how men and women were "supposed" to behave—with parents, partners, and children.

There were also very long lags in how society assimilated these profound changes. As the sociologist Arlie Hochschild has observed in two extremely perceptive books, the "stalled revolution" in the workplace—where women still encounter glass ceilings and bear the brunt of excruciating work/family dilemmas—is a mirror image of the stalled revolution at home, where mothers still do the lion's share of housework and child rearing. Supposedly liberated fathers still boast of "baby-sitting" (when did a mother ever describe herself as baby-sitting?) and books with titles like *The Mommy Track* and *The Price of Motherhood* still resonate as a description of the huge career sacrifice women make when they become mothers. Nobody speaks of the sacrifices of a Daddy Track; it is just taken for granted that Dad goes off to the office or factory.

The Harvard social psychologist Richard Weissbourd, an advocate of active fathering, reports that schools, hospitals, day care centers, and other institutions that interact with mothers and fathers continue to signal parents, in gross ways and subtle ones, that they still consider mothers the primary parent. Weissbourd recounts his own experience in parent-teacher conferences and in hospital emergency rooms. "Would you tell your wife to pack your son an extra pair of shoes tomorrow?" the third-grade teacher tells Weissbourd, one of the few fathers meeting with the teacher. At the hospital, where both parents are present while their three-year-old is getting stitched up after a backyard mishap, the nurse explains how to deal with the bandage and when the boy needs to come back in, addressing and making eye contact with the mother, as if Dad were a potted plant. Weissbourd writes that he took comfort in seeing infant changing tables in airport men's restrooms—until he noticed one enterprising business traveler using the table to work on his laptop computer.

While roles and possibilities for women and men have become newly open, archetypal images of struggles between fathers and sons, mothers and sons, fathers and daughters, and mothers and daughters linger. They recur in literature going back to antiquity. Conflict between fathers and sons pervades classical mythology and the texts of all the great religions. It is no accident that Freud drew on Oedipus to try to explain the rivalry between fathers and sons and the deeply ambivalent bond between sons and mothers. Each dyad—mother/daughter, father/son, mother/son, father/daughter—presents patterns that suggest broad generalizations about gender. But there are probably more variations within these categories than between them.

Although there are dramatic differences in the way different theorists and critics have addressed the subject of gender in parent-child attachment and separation, one common inference is important for our purposes here. Virtually all these scholars conclude that these differences in family relationship patterns are less biological than a function of the way boys and girls are raised and socialized, and of the different gender roles habitually prescribed in the family and society. They are more cultural than genetic, and Chodorow and others point to cultures where men play a very different role in the family and child-rearing patterns.

It therefore follows that society is capable of changing its patterns, as it has in the gender revolution that has placed more women in workplaces and given men greater responsibilities at home. And individuals—male and female—are capable of breaking out of stereotyped gender roles, with respect to intimate partners, aging parents, and children. Chodorow's recent work suggests that men and women are capable of widely varying patterns of attachment, intimacy, and coming of age. It is a mistake, she suggests, "to think that all little boys are physically aggressive and all little girls are not, that all men are uncomfortable with dependence, and that all women need relationality."

One can read these diverse currents as signaling hopeless confusion—just the latest variant in the eternal battle of the sexes. But we read these trends far more hopefully. Despite their seemingly contradictory messages, most of these currents of thinking express poignantly common yearnings: that both sexes be free to explore the full range of human possibility; that women and men alike be able to become compassionate adults who enjoy both relational connection and professional accomplishment; that men be allowed to take pride in their manhood and women in their womanhood, but without narrow constraints based on stereotyped traditional roles.

As the enormous changes of the past two generations suggest, women are not doomed to be the subordinate and often privately unfulfilled helpmeets that Jean Baker Miller described writing in the late 1970s. Nor are men doomed to be economically and politically privileged strivers but emotionally stunted clods. This new sense of possibility has to be good for the project of reconnection and reunion between parent and adult child.

In the course of researching this book, we sought out people in midlife who had loving, lifelong connections with parents. We were curious, among other things, about what those relations had been like when the young adult was, say, twenty-one. One memorable story came from Richard Parker, a longtime political activist, scholar, and writer who now teaches at Harvard's Kennedy School of Government.

As a student at Dartmouth in the late 1960s, Richard had been a political radical. His father was a moderately liberal Episcopal priest, in a politically conservative corner of Southern California. Father and son, like so many of that generation, argued about the Vietnam War. The father didn't really like the war, but considered himself a patriot. He had organized discussion groups and even got a group of ministers to sign a letter opposing the war's escalation. The son, on the other hand, was on the front lines of militant protest and draft resistance.

His father and mother both expressed concern for his physical safety. Richard, in turn, felt passionately that his father, despite his agreement that the war was wrong if not immoral, was playing it safe. Richard remembers pushing his father very hard, accusing him point-blank of hypocrisy. At the end of one long and heated conversation, the father said thoughtfully: "I guess our difference is that I am called to be a priest and you are called to be a prophet."

This father knew how to communicate deep love and respect in the face of personalized political disagreement and rebellious provocation. Despite the taunting, he could acknowledge his son's idealism, and manhood. The two men maintained a close lifelong relationship as loving adult father and grown son. What more could we want?

Chapter 5
The New Extended Family

The challenge of grown children is to hold on while letting go; to become autonomous adults whose self-reliance is strengthened rather than weakened by mutually affirming connections with family. This enterprise is hard enough psychologically and developmentally. It is further complicated by the conditions of modern life—families that are strewn across the country, or many countries; families in which working parents barely have time for children, let alone their own parents; divorced and recombinant families with multiple sets of stepgrandparents and his-and-hers offspring; and families caught off balance by the downward mobility of the young.

Today, increasing numbers of grown children live for extended periods in their parents' homes, usually for financial reasons. Despite general prosperity, this is the first generation of American young adults who expect, in large numbers, to be less affluent than their parents. Both realities tend to prolong a psychological dependence that neither generation really wants.

A century ago, most young men and women stayed at home until they married and could afford their own place. But in the affluent era after World War II, it became the norm for adults to move away and start their own homes, as young singles as well as newlyweds. However, in the 1980s and 1990s, as housing costs surpassed salaries, millions of young adults deferred leaving home. Millions of others attempt to set up housekeeping on their own, but return to their parents' homes for prolonged periods. According to the U.S. Census Bureau, more than half of all young adults between age eighteen and thirty are living with their parents. That number increased by almost 50 percent between 1970 and 1986, and increased again between 1986 and 1999.

The high cost of housing defers getting started. One indicator: in 1973, 43.6 percentage of Americans age twenty-five to twenty-nine owned their own homes, as did 60.2 percent of those age thirty to thirty-four. By 1990, those statistics had fallen to 35.9 percent and 51.5 percent, respectively. Rents, as well as the cost of buying, are outstripping incomes. Those of us who were young adults in the 1960s and 1970s can fondly remember following the norm of spending a week's pay on a month's rent and living nicely, even in our twenties. While broad economic prosperity returned in the 1990s, wages and salaries for millions of young adults failed to keep up with rising rents. Today, young adults are doubling and tripling up, often paying a third or even half of their salaries for a share of a crowded rental in a dubious neighborhood.

In the 1960s, four years of private college cost $10,000 to $12,000. Today, it may cost more than $120,000, and state universities cost more than private college cost a generation ago. In many occupations, salaries have not kept up with living costs. One middle-class grandmother matter-of-factly commented, "You have to start putting money away for your grandchildren's college education as soon as they're born. There's no way their parents are going to afford it."

Adults now in retirement, who grew up relatively poor during the Great Depression, had the happy experience of starting careers and raising families during the great postwar economic boom and catching a national tailwind. Even those born in the 1940s who came of age in the 1960s experienced substantial upward mobility. But children born from about 1965 onward often face a very different financial experience.

Often, grown children kids will return "home" after a career reversal, a psychological trauma, or an early divorce, sometimes bringing along a young child of their own. The adult "child" who moves back home can be a thirty-five-year-old.

In these situations, conflicts reflect more than the ghosts of childhood—more than parents and children having difficulty letting go of old roles. They reflect present setbacks and practical needs. While some conflicts are inevitable in these circumstances, they can become supercharged because parent and adult child fail to disentangle the practical questions from the emotional and symbolic ones. These young adults have suffered serious setbacks and need their parents' emotional or financial help at precisely the developmental moment when they most want to stand on their own feet and be respected as adults. Such moments often lead both generations to send mixed messages—of both support and resentment.

All of this, needless to say, is emotional dynamite. Ordinarily, an adult child doesn't want to be "home," except as a last resort. It is shameful to have to confess failure to the parents whose very sphere of authority you want to escape. For the parents, no matter how much they love their children, the empty-nest years are a time to relax, downsize, and plan retirement after long years of having offspring at home, not a time to tend adult children.

BOOMERANG CHILDREN

Psychotherapists Jean Davies Okimoto and Phyllis Jackson Stegall describe a couple, Tom and Ann, in their early fifties, who were quite enjoying the privacy of their empty nest. They had turned one of the kids' rooms into a guestroom and the other into a den for Tom. They enjoyed cooking together in their newly remodeled kitchen. "Their sexual relationship had never been better; when [their youngest] Susan first moved out, Tom said, 'You know, Annie, we can make love in any room in the house.'"

"It all changed abruptly one evening when Tom and Ann got a phone call from their daughter. At first, Ann did not recognize Susan's voice because she was crying so hard."

Susan, twenty-four, had been jilted by her live-in boyfriend, Bob, who was also her co-worker. She couldn't stand seeing him every day at work, and she could no longer afford the apartment alone. "Mom, I just want to come home," she said. And so she did. Susan moved into the guestroom. She was depressed and withdrawn, staying in her room, playing the stereo loudly, leaving dirty dishes around. After a month, she still was not seriously looking for a job.

The parents, trying not to push her too hard, began quarreling with each other. "One evening, after Ann wondered what they might have done wrong, Tom exploded in fury. 'Enough! She's twenty-four years old—not some, lovesick teenager. I want my house back! I want my wife back!'"

As Akimoto and Stegall observe, these parents have suffered four losses: the loss of their image of their daughter as a competent young adult; the loss of their self-image as successful parents; the loss of a newly intimate marital relationship; and the plain loss of territory. The authors note that in their urge to express support and sympathy, they never discussed at the outset what it would mean for Susan to be living in the house again, as another adult. So in their desire to be supportive, they actually contributed to her infantilization and prolonged dependency. The authors cite several other stories, but their sage advice is consistent: there need to be ground rules and an explicit set of understandings. How long do you think you need to stay? What are fair expectations about your contribution to the household? How will we respect each other's privacy?

As parents, we may feel guilty that some past parenting failure of ours may have contributed to the present crisis, angry that our adult offspring has thrown in the towel too easily and reverted to the dependence of childhood, and resentful at the invasion of our space. We may feel ashamed that we have so much while our adult child has so little. None of this helps us to see what is needed in the present—which is to help our grown child get through this crisis and regain mastery and autonomy. Paradoxically, to be helpful to the adult child, we need to take care of our own needs, and to be very alert to the danger of triangling and scapegoating.

Such dilemmas grow even more slippery when a grown child

returns home with small children, often after a divorce; or when there are more than transient emotional problems. It is still more complex when the parents are themselves in a second marriage and the returning child is a stepchild to one of the spouses. In such cases, it may make sense to consult a professional therapist. But short of extreme situations, parents of boomerang kids can accomplish a lot by being clear about their own needs and emotional issues, and by negotiating a firm and fair contract. In such situations, guilt, anger, and resentment are three emotions that can blind us to what is really required.

Okimoto and Stegall write: "If you are a stepparent [of adult children] who has held the expectation that your partner's children would never be much of a factor in your life, you will need to rethink this. If you have married someone who cares about his or her children and those children have a crisis, are in need, and turn to your partner, they will be in your life. . . . Sometimes it helps to accept this fact by asking, 'Would I really love and respect my spouse if he or she were the sort of person who wouldn't come through for an adult child in crisis?'"

Of course, coming through in a crisis doesn't mean accepting permanent dependence. As a parent who feels the need to deliver for a troubled adult child, you may be caught between your own complex feelings, those of the child, and the needs of your spouse (who may well have different needs, different emotional hot buttons based on a different family-of-origin history, and may just size up the situation differently). If there is unfinished emotional business between parent and child—if they are too enmeshed or overly distant—such situations will almost invariably provoke crises. Typically, the families that get into the most difficulty in these cases are those that are still battling ghosts of the past rather than coming to terms with what the present situation requires.

The situation is also emotionally loaded for the child. An adult child who has returned home may be acting out feelings of deep resentment, without quite realizing it. The child may be engaging in provocative behaviors—refusing to contribute to the household, being noisy and slovenly, bringing disruptive friends around—as a way of acting out resentment. But these are the behaviors of a rebellious teenager, not a mature adult. Both child and parents, whatever their differences, should have one goal in common: to get the child back to adult responsibilities in a reasonable time, with their friendship intact.

Parents, in spite of their best judgments, may cling to a rescuer role. One woman, whose forty-four-year-old son is on his third marriage, told an interviewer: "I thought it would be over by now. I never know what to expect next. He has five children, needs my financial help, and still behaves like the child he was and I suppose always will be. I would like not to have to worry about him any more and finally have a clear head. I'm seventy-six and I deserve a break. . . . Constant heartache, that's what it is. Therapists have told me to let go already and not make myself so miserable, as there's nothing I can do about it. But believe me, it's not that easy. I keep asking myself what I did wrong."

Parents who keep making allowances for adult children will only defer their children's adulthood. In the Steve Martin film *Parenthood*, we cheer when the aging grandfather, played by Jason Robards, finally asserts authority and makes it clear to his dissolute, manipulative, ne'er-do-well grown son that it's time to get on with his life. The father, at long last, has insisted that the son get a real job or move out of the house. Eventually, the son packs up. It's not clear that father and son will ever see each other again. We can imagine that if the father had asserted some toughlove earlier on, his son might have grown up sooner and the two would still enjoy a relationship.

The multigenerational family is again becoming less of an oddity. In the nineteenth century, when most Americans were farmers, three generations often shared the same farm. During the Great Depression, grandparents, parents, and children often lived under the same roof as a matter of economic survival. Among African American families, where single parenthood is prevalent and poverty widespread, grandmothers often become primary parental figures and as many as four generations share a home. And in immigrant families, long-term multigenerational families are more common, both for economic reasons and because such families are more normal in many cultures of origin. Even more than in the case of short-term boomerang kids of middle-class families, where both parent and child are eager to reclaim separate domiciles, permanent multigenerational households require generosity and compassion.

PARENTAL PURSESTRINGS

Only in the past couple of decades has the issue of financial support of grown children been a problem except for the wealthy. For centuries, the rich have worried about how not to spoil their children. Many tycoons, like John D. Rockefeller, went to great lengths to impose spartan routines on their offspring, so that growing up amid wealth would not turn them into coddled and ineffectual adults. Nelson Aldrich, a fourth-generation rich kid, writes in his memoir *Old Money*: "For many beneficiaries [of family bailouts], a life spent without having to take the risk of paying the cost of consequences is, quite simply, an inconsequential life."

But for most of our history, most Americans of both generations struggled financially and expected their grown children eventually to enjoy a higher material living standard than the parents. According to the urban anthropologist Katherine Newman, the new downward mobility of the young creates a variety of emotional strains. Parents may feel guilty if they don't provide support, and resentful if they do. Adult children may feel deprived if they don't get help, but tethered if they do.

Grown children may think parents have more money than they do, and resent the fact that it isn't being shared. "I'll never have what my parents had," a young woman named Lauren in a suburb of New York tells Newman. "I can't even dream of that." Many young adults, seeing the nice suburban house their parents still live in, or their pleasant retirement to Florida or Arizona, may think their parents are more affluent than they really are. Yet with skyrocketing medical costs and lengthening life spans, upper-middle-class parents who have a pension plan and clear a few hundred thousand dollars on the sale of the family home may have enough for a secure but hardly a lavish retirement. Only about 2 percent of Americans leave net estates worth more than $675,000, the exemption on the federal estate tax in 2001. As Newman observes, even if aging parents are inclined to pursue rescue missions and "to ignore the cultural prescription that calls for every generation to stand on its own two feet," the financial reality is that most lack the means to go on supporting their adult offspring indefinitely.

Nonetheless, many moderately affluent and somewhat guilty older parents are often tempted to subsidize their grown children well into adulthood. Although some circumstances warrant financial support, the risk is far greater that parents, like the well-meaning authors of *Friends for Life* quoted in Chapter 2, will err on the side of excessive financial help, thus depriving their children of the need to come to terms with their own financial reality. Some help is welcome; too much can be disabling.

There are no hard and fast rules here. But parents are wise to be alert to several questions: To what extent is the grown child contributing to living expenses to the best of his or her capacity? Is he/she living beyond reasonable needs or means? To what extent will financial aid trigger a reversion to dependency and resentment? How much is too much? In the past, has financial help from parents led the child to redouble his or her own efforts, or to slack off?

What about the parents' issues? Is the financial help part of a carefully thought out and mutually discussed plan—or is it impulsive on the part of the parents? Does it reflect misplaced guilt, desire for appreciation, or concerns about appearances and status? Are parents unconsciously using continued financial help to control grown children, as opposed to helping them become independent? Parents who indulge small children and teenagers will reap dependent adults. And parents who keep subsidizing grown children may find they grow up ineffectual, guilty, and resentful rather than appreciative.

THE MONEY TRAP

Affluent parents may just slide unthinkingly from paying full freight for college to still subsidizing children who are thirty.

They may feel that their children deserve to have all their college costs covered so they can devote their full attention to schoolwork. They may feel, given the high cost of getting started nowadays, that it is unfair to saddle children with repayment of college loans as long as parents can afford to pay. But it is wise to insist that college students contribute something to college costs, even when parents can afford them. Whether it's summer jobs, part-time jobs during the school year, or a share in loans, some financial effort on the child's part is likely to make college less of a four-year vacation. It is also wise to make the child ready to assume financial responsibility for his or her life sooner rather than later.

Some kinds of financial help may make sense, but all forms of financial assistance for grown children are tricky. Assistance to help an offspring become a first-time homeowner, for example, is probably the most defensible form of help that is not likely to infantilize grown children. Help with a down payment is a one-shot gift, not a continuing dependence. Because it puts young adults into a position of adult responsibility, part of a down payment is less likely than ongoing subsidy to infantilize grown children or lead to prolonged argument about how the money is spent. The cost of a starter home in most communities is far more expensive relative to the income of the average thirty-year-old than it was a generation ago. In the professional classes, it has become close to normal for even moderately affluent parents to help with a down payment.

However, this is very much an individual family decision. These forms of assistance, when given at all, should be carefully thought through, discussed—and then given freely. It is not sensible to offer down payment help until a child's financial situation is sufficiently stable to suggest reasonable assurance that the monthly payments can be met. Otherwise, the result may be a distress sale (in both senses of the word) or an implied obligation for parents to help with mortgage payments as well—and prolonged dependence and conflict over money. But once given, the money should not be the subject of endless discussion. An adult's financial affairs are largely his or her own business. Even if we are appalled at financial choices our grown offspring make with our gifts, it's better not to meddle.

It's also important not to make promises casually or prematurely. One well-meaning father grandiosely promised his twenty-two-year-old son, Sam, on the day of his college graduation that he was no longer subsidizing living expenses but that he would "help out" with a down payment on a house "when the time comes." He imagined that Sam would go to graduate school, presumably get married, and then, when Sam's career and income stabilized and he could afford a mortgage, Dad envisaged himself generously bestowing a check as part of a down payment, just as his parents had helped him. How surprised he was when Sam sought to take him up on the offer—only a few months later.

Sam had two part-time jobs, did not know his long-term plans, and could not really afford a house or even a condo unless his father paid at least half the cost. Nor, even though he was working hard, had he symbolically earned the additional parental help by demonstrating an adult work history. Writing Sam a large check at such a tender age would have signaled continuing dependence and childhood rather than adulthood and autonomy.

Sam's request led to a painful conversation about whether the father trusted him. Why, if Dad was prepared to donate this money, did he rather than Sam get to decide when the time was ripe? In the end, the father held his ground—it was not yet financially time for the son to take on the responsibilities of owning a house, and it was, after all, Dad's money. But this whole conflict might have been avoided if the father, trying to seem generous and hanging on to the image of a provident father with a still-dependent son, had not impulsively made an offer that was premature by several years.

It makes even less sense for parents to put their young adult children on an allowance, to pay for expensive cars, vacations, and other frills. It may be awkward, painful, and guilt-inducing to see our young adults who have been raised in relative comfort struggling to keep a roof over their heads and to put bread on the table. But these struggles promote self-discipline and help children grow into sturdy, self-reliant adults. They build character.

Even in families where parents feel they have struck a good balance between not wanting grown children to live in abject poverty and not coddling them, financial aid to adults is subject to emotional tripwires. Susan is an economist. Her husband, Michael, is a doctor. They are not independently wealthy, but live very nicely on their two professional incomes. They have carefully considered, and endlessly discussed, how to help their grown children, both of whom have pursued careers less remunerative than those of their parents. Their son, Jeff, thirty-one, is a social worker. Their daughter, Lynn, twenty-nine, is an associate TV producer.

Though the children are well past the age of separation, this family still pays the cost of car insurance, health insurance, tax preparation, dental bills, trips home, and gives each child a no-questions-asked four-figure stipend every Christmas as an all-purpose subsidy for the coming year. For the most part, this support doesn't seem to cause the kids to be financial slackers. Jeff works hard for a public agency with very difficult clients, and lives cheaply in Boston where rents are very high. Without the financial help, he'd live in an even shabbier apartment, and perhaps have to give up his idealistic social commitment as well.

Lynn also puts in long hours and is good at her job. But she's in a very competitive field where lots of aspiring people work for relatively modest salaries. Her work is in San Francisco, where rents are even higher than Boston. Unlike her brother, she likes to live well. Lynn eats in nice restaurants, wears good clothes—just as she was brought up to do. She earns nearly $50,000, but her rent is over $1,800 a month and her preferred lifestyle requires parental subsidy. She feels she needs to look her best for work (and for the husband she hopes to meet). Her parents are torn between a sense of guilt that their daughter will probably never afford the living standard she grew up with, and a sense of irritation that some of their subsidy goes for frills.

On a recent visit home, Lynn let it drop that she had just

chipped in with two other co-workers to buy a very expensive engagement gift for a mutual friend. "Nice, if you can afford it," her father said dryly. This led to a furious fight, which ruined the weekend for all of them.

Lynn feels she is working hard and living no more lavishly than most of her co-workers live—and far more modestly than her parents. She also feels somewhat guilty about taking her parents' money, and extremely sensitive to any criticism of her lifestyle. Her father expects Lynn to economize, the way he did when he was her age. Her mother thinks perhaps they are giving her too much money.

These parents are sending mixed messages. Whatever they contribute, they can't reasonably criticize how Lynn chooses to spend it—not if they want appreciation, let alone friendship and trust. If they conclude that they are subsidizing indefensible luxuries, it's time simply to pull back. And it makes sense for a twenty-nine-year-old to pay her own bills, even if parents send a generous Christmas supplement at the end of the year.

The psychologist Lee Hausner tells the story of Phyllis, a young woman from an affluent family, who graduated "from a prestigious university without any career goals," and then "returned to her beautifully decorated bedroom in the family home to consider her options. For the next two years, she enjoyed a luxurious life, paying little attention to her parents' suggestion that she begin looking for a job and moving out on her own."

After two years, and a few halfhearted forays into the job market, Phyllis became overweight, insomniac, and clinically depressed. The parents turned to a therapist, who soon recommended immediate termination of all financial support. The mother and father reluctantly agreed. Before long, Phyllis moved into a shared apartment and got a job. According to Dr. Hausner, Phyllis now describes her two years living with her parents after college as her period of "adult infancy. She acknowledges that she had no real concept of the value of money. She assumed that it would always be there and that she was entitled to whatever she wanted or needed. Fortunately, Phyllis also recognizes that beneath this feeling of entitlement was an unjustified fear that she lacked the competency skills to support herself. She is grateful now that she can independently meet her own needs."

Dr. Larry Stockman, a family therapist, recounts the story of Tom, a young adult with a long history of needing money for routine bills. He made more than enough money to cover his basic living expenses but spent money capriciously, and invariably came to his parents for unforeseen expenses. With some coaching from the therapist, his parents decided to change the pattern.

The next time Tom needed money to repair his sports car, he asked his father, as usual. This time, his father declined to pay. Tom, at first disbelieving, responded indignantly. "But if you don't fix my car, I won't be able to get to work. I'll lose my job. And it will be your fault."

At this point, it's critical for parents not to take the bait. Despite the adolescent effort to induce guilt and the attempt to make the child's problem (the car) into the parent's problem, this father managed to acknowledge both the seriousness of the situation (Tom really does need to get to work), as well as Tom's upset feelings. But the parent needs to model adult behavior, calmly stick to his guns, offer to help strategize about other solutions, and resist the temptation either to bail Tom out yet another time or to snap back with snide, judgmental retorts ("You never could manage to save a dime, could you?" "If you didn't have such an expensive sports car that you can't really afford, you'd have plenty of money to keep it running").

Reproachful comments have obviously not succeeded in changing Tom's behavior. And actions speak a lot louder than words. The fact is, changing the ground rules on an adult adolescent is empowering to the parent. And empowerment can be very calming. A parent who has resolved not to back down is more likely to stay relaxed, and project love and concern, not just refusal of help. These conversations should never be rushed. A grown child needs to know that, even if he isn't getting exactly what he wants, his problems are being heard and respected. Genuine efforts deserve respect, not ridicule. And, though the grown child may not yet realize it at the time, this change in the rules is also empowering to him. It is an acknowledgment, however delayed, of his adulthood.

Parents in this situation are very vulnerable to being split. In the family constellation, some parents play polar opposite roles—the authoritarian father, the weak and submissive mother; or conversely, the hands-on practical mom who doesn't miss a trick, and the frequently absent and hence guilt-ridden father who is an easy touch for young adults. Almost from infancy, children are adept at maximizing any splits in the parental united front, and at playing off Daddy against Mommy, This pattern often carries over into young adulthood.

Parents who resolve to change the rules on young adults who have stayed in a condition of extended adolescence need, above all, unity, or at least a common strategy. Before changing their own behavior and expectations for their grown children, parents are wise to work out disagreements among themselves and agree, at least provisionally, on a game plan. Otherwise, splitting will invariably occur, followed by acrimony and defeat. If parents have been habitually locked into polar roles or have inconsistent ideas of how to proceed, a major shift in expectations for a grown child—you have to pay rent or get your own place; we are no longer subsidizing your car—can be one of those moments when a short-term therapy can help to get parents onto the same page.

One couple, in Denver, was torn between the feeling that their son, a talented but impoverished pianist in New York, really deserved financial support and the feeling that it was high time to cut the cord. The son was thirty. He was reluctant to take much of a steady job, because he needed to remain free for gigs that only occasionally materialized. His mother thought this was both a plausible story and a handy excuse. His father felt the family could afford the several hundred dollars a month help he needed with rent—they had been subsidizing him since graduate school—because he really took his music seriously and housing costs where he lived in Manhattan were extreme.

As the chronic, ritualized argument between the parents continued, the checks kept flowing and the son's dependence persisted. The mother contended it was time for him to face financial reality: "We're not doing him a favor anymore." But the father had always wanted to be an artist; he strongly identified with the son, and felt vaguely guilty about how much money he made as a bond trader. The parents were living comfortably, while the son lived in a slum, for his art. There was family money to go around; it didn't seem fair.

At length, after repeated wrangling and three sessions with a counselor, mother and father concluded that this financial help was nonetheless becoming a crutch; it was keeping the son tethered to them in a way that, paradoxically, created emotional distance. The financial dependence was a vague embarrassment to all concerned. The parents finally agreed on a plan to wean him from the monthly subsidy. They phoned the son and suggested that it was time to taper off the financial help. To their surprise, the son agreed that this was a good idea. Together, they worked out a plan to gradually reduce the monthly checks to zero over the next six months.

Four months passed. Although the deadline was now just two months away, the son apparently wasn't doing much to increase his earnings as long as the checks from Dad kept coming in. After a couple of misguided interrogations, the parents resisted the temptation to question the son regularly about what he was doing to bank some reserves. After the last month of subsidy they waited for the inevitable distress call. But it didn't come.

A few months later, delighted with the son's new responsibility, the father invited him and his girlfriend to spend a week at the family summer vacation home, all expenses paid. The son explored the cost of air tickets, which turned out to be at their peak summer fares. "Dad, I just can't let you spend sixteen hundred dollars," the son said. "It's too much money." The father thought a moment, realized that he was both disappointed and pleased, grasped that something very important was happening, and suppressed the urge to insist.

Both father and son noticed a change in their subsequent phone calls. Conversations about money ceased. The son casually let it drop that he was giving music lessons, working part time for a catering company, and that he had a regular weekly gig at a local piano bar. This was not exactly the big time, but it was reality. He had also moved to Brooklyn. There was a subtle change for the better in his self-confidence, and a lowering of the mutual anxiety level. The son became less guarded in discussing his career plans with his father, and the father realized he was listening more and giving advice less. Though they were two thousand miles apart, they had never felt closer. The frequency of phone calls actually increased. They missed each other. The father felt he had done something really important as a parent. The mother, with heroic self-control, resisted the temptation to tell the father, I told you so. The son had taken responsibility for his life.

What is significant about this story is the symmetrical process of development: the father backing off and the grown son stepping up to the plate. The son brought at least as much to the encounter as the parents did. A year earlier, he might not have been ready to take charge. As a less mature adult, he might have just resented the withdrawal of money and taken it as a withdrawal of love. This time, he understood the gesture, correctly, as an acceptance of his own manhood. Conversely, less mindful parents might have missed the shift, and continued to infantilize him. But this time, both the parents and the son caught the wave. The son was ready to declare: I am a financial adult, despite some inconvenience. And the parents were paying attention.

This sort of progress is almost never a straight line. It's unlikely that these parents will never send their son another check. But they have ceased being his main financial support. Even had this initiative turned out to be premature, it might still have been timely a year or two later. Adults continue to evolve, and so do parent-child relationships. It's a mistake to assume, just because grown children are adults and out of the family home, that change doesn't keep occurring. The parent (and adult child) who is mindful of opportunities to build more mutually respectful connections will be richly rewarded. The enterprise is very different from that of being mother or father of a small child, but no less of a challenge.

Very accomplished parents sometimes are disappointed that their children seem less motivated in life than they were in their own early adulthood. Successful parents are a hard act to follow. Children may look at the stresses of their parents' fast-track life and reject the trade-offs and sacrifices. They may decide subconsciously not to compete and risk falling short. Or they may decide that their parents' materialism is not for them. The pattern of a son following his father's footsteps—lawyers begetting lawyers, doctors begetting doctors, children going into the family business—was more common earlier in the last century. Part of the project of separating from parents and defining one's own course is to choose a different occupation or profession.

Naturally, children who choose less demanding careers will likely find they earn less money, particularly in an era when starting out is harder generally than a generation ago. Even though they have deliberately rejected the economic stratum of their parents, they may still resent, consciously or subconsciously, the fall in their material living standards. Parents may feel an obligation to provide financial support, but this only prolongs dependency. Our experience is that affluent parents do well to err on the side of giving less, rather than more, money to grown children.

Successful parents, of course, do not necessarily produce underfunctioning young adults. Sometimes the high expectations translate, just as the parents hope, into grown children who have very high standards for themselves and who even exceed the achievements of parents. Even so, the strong presence of a parent in the life of a grown child may complicate other aspects of life, such as marital patterns and parent-child relationships in the next generation.

Franklin Roosevelt was the only child of a very powerful mother, Anna Delano Roosevelt. Her doting certainly did not prevent him from becoming a strong, successful, adult man. But it may have had other effects. Even after Franklin was governor of New York and then president of the United States, his mother continued to preside as the mistress of Hyde Park. She was a domineering presence in the life of Franklin and his wife Eleanor, herself a very strong women. Biographers of the Roosevelts have written about the role of an affair that Franklin had, early in their marriage, in creating a union that was a political alliance and a genuine close friendship, but something short of a complete marriage. Eleanor Roosevelt eventually moved to her own home a few miles away from the Roosevelt family compound at Hyde Park. Biographers suggest that it was not only Franklin's affair but also his mother's dominance that drove a wedge in his marriage.

INJURIES OF CLASS

Of course, it is still a fortunate minority of parents in America who have to worry whether they are oversubsidizing grown children. A great many couples in late middle age are just getting by themselves. Children of less affluent families, at least, don't begin adult life with the handicap of being overly coddled. But they may have the opposite handicap—being relied upon to support aging parents or younger siblings. At either extreme, money issues can bind the generations in a way that is emotionally awkward and conducive to undesired obligations, resentments, and conflicts.

The downsizing of the economy that began in the 1970s produced many casualties. Middle-aged workers, mostly men, suddenly found their economic prospects drastically diminished. In some families, children find that they have to grow up very fast, and become economic contributors to the household. Katherine Newman observes, "The older progeny of downwardly mobile families realize that they have to continue draining bank accounts to help pay for the younger brothers and sisters' food, clothing, or college tuition. One has to go back to the immigrant generation to find an analogous situation where young adults were torn between starting their own families and helping to pay for siblings and parents to come over from the Old Country."

By the same token, the explosion in divorce rates produced

tens of millions of economic casualties, usually women. No-fault divorce laws and the eclipse of alimony only compounded the problem. So-called displaced homemakers, divorced women who had stayed home, raised children, and accumulated little in the way of career skills, personal financial assets, or even Social Security entitlements, may find themselves in late midlife awkwardly dependent financially on grown children.

In a sense, this picture is the mirror image of the family in which adult children are yoked to parents by the parents' misplaced generosity. In both situations, parents and children are tied by financial binds. Fathers or mothers who are downwardly mobile may feel humiliated in the eyes of their spouse and children, and in their own eyes. One grown daughter told Newman, "The reason why my father drank and belittled and beat my mother was because he felt he had failed as a man. He wanted to reassert that even though he was being supported by this woman, he could still dominate her completely."

The economic assaults on working-class and poor families leave them more vulnerable to more social problems, on average, than affluent ones. Psychological problems are just as prevalent in affluent families, but affluent families can buy professional help. When poorer families experience alcoholism, child neglect, spousal abuse, physical and mental illness, or low self-esteem, they are less likely to get counseling because social services are available only intermittently and they can't afford private treatment. The poor, by definition, have fewer financial reserves to fall back on in hard times. These are, in the words of the sociologist Richard Sennett, among the "hidden injuries of class." The financial insecurities and social assaults faced by lower-income parents are often turned inward, on themselves, their spouses and children.

Lillian Rubin's classic book *Worlds of Pain* describes domestic life among a sample of working-class families. Often, she reports, there is less ease with verbal communication, more time stress, and more of a tendency to take frustrations out on a spouse and children. There is greater awkwardness about sexuality. Rubin writes that economically insecure working-class men

wonder "what happened to the old familiar world," yet are fear-
ful "that their masculine image will be impaired if they talk
about the things that trouble them." Women, likewise, "tend to
suffer alone. Despite all the publicity generated by the women's
movement about the dissatisfactions women experience in marriage, most working class women continue to believe that their
feelings are uniquely theirs."

Yet people of all social classes and of varying degrees of comfort with verbalizing feelings are capable of improved connections with aging parents and grown children. Not to pursue
more authentic relationships across the generations is to leave
oneself stunted not just in these family relations, but in others.

Midlife adults need to find a good balance of giving support,
financial and otherwise, to adult children and aging parents,
without feeling overwhelmed with family obligations at a
moment when they are seeking a little respite for themselves.
Vivian Greenberg sagely observes that it is a serious mistake to
compare aging parents to dependent children. "Although parents at this stage are usually dependent upon their children,"
she writes, "roles do not reverse so that children become their
parents' parents. Parents remain parents, but now they can trust
their children's dependability."

Even where family life is complicated by financial entangle-
ments and multigenerational living arrangements, all three generations at bottom want the same thing: love, respect, and
connected autonomy. If we can give our parents and our children
that, we will have done a lot.

Chapter 6
Fractured Families, Whole People

In Yasmina Reza's recent hit play, *Art*, there is a climactic monologue in which Yvan, about to be married, reports to his friends on an "insoluble conflict." His tale pours out in one extended, hysterical sentence. The problem is that both stepmothers want their names on the wedding invitation. His fiancée, Catherine, has a close relationship with her stepmother, who raised her. This does not produce conflict in Catherine's family, since her own mother is dead. But Yvan, whose parents are divorced, faces a very different situation. Yvan reports that Catherine "wore me down" and persuaded him that his stepmother's name should also be on the invitation. But Yvan's mother insists that if the stepmother's name goes on the invitation, hers must be taken off.

Trying to broker a compromise, Yvan suggests to Catherine that perhaps none of the parents' or stepparents' names should be on the invitation. ("After all, we're not adolescents, we can announce our wedding ourselves.") This only infuriates Catherine, who points out that her father and stepmother are generously paying for an expensive reception. By the time the monologue ends, everybody is mad at everyone else. Yvan and his mother aren't speaking. Bride and groom are at sword's points. Yvan's mother is angry at her prospective daughter-in-law, and old resentments have been rekindled between Yvan's mother and his father.

The monologue has just about everything—conflicts between the generations, conflict within the young couple, conflict inside and between both sets of in-laws—all interwoven and intensified by mutual interaction. It also offers an almost flawless rendition of the reactivity that family members exhibit when buttons get pushed. As outsiders, we could imagine various solutions, but everyone's pride has been engaged and the conversation is just too charged for reasonable deliberation. Yvan and his mother obviously aren't in the habit of discussing such matters calmly and compassionately, and we suspect that Yvan is at risk of repeating with his wife some of the aspects of his relationship with his mother.

If relationships between parents and grown children are tense, or distant, or frayed, such highly loaded events as weddings or births are almost guaranteed to be emotionally overwrought. Everybody in this tableau wants support and understanding, and nobody gets it. The bride doesn't get it from the groom (or vice versa); the mother doesn't get it from the son (or vice versa); even the bride's kind gesture of wanting her stepmother to be acknowledged blows up in her face. Reza's drama is rendered as hysterical farce, but it is painfully funny because it is so familiar—only a slight caricature of what occurs in our own families all the time.

A family therapist might observe that this family is in some respects overly enmeshed and not adequately "differentiated": that is, each family member is far too invested in the other's actions. But this is partly just for the sake of appearances; the actual relationship between mother and son is rather distant. This paradox represents two sides of the same coin. Parents and children feel compelled to act out intimate scripts that actually feel phony and are deeply resented. Yet at the same time change is threatening; we are more comfortable with familiar scripts, even when they are deeply disappointing or even damaging. Intimacy takes the form of conflict. That helps explain the highly charged blend of simultaneously professing not to care and caring too much.

As the monologue from *Art* suggests, all of these issues of separation and reconnection are even more emotionally charged in stepfamilies. It is difficult enough for parents to agree on values, on matters of discipline and other aspects of child-rearing strategy. A blended family is likely to be more of a challenge on every front. It raises issues of loyalty and rivalry, of who is an insider and who is an outsider, of who has authority and trust.

The challenge of assuming the role of stepmother or stepfather in a blended family with young or teenage children has been the subject of innumerable books and articles. However, little attention has been paid to how divorce and remarriage complicate the challenge of building satisfying connections between parents and children who are grown.

By the time a child reaches the age of eighteen, a majority of families are no longer "intact"—having two living parents who were the child's natural mother and father still living together. More than 65 percent of all Americans will spend part of their lives in families where one generation or the other has experienced a remarriage. With the sole exception of single parents who later remarry, the vast majority of stepfamilies are sequels to a divorce or a death. Divorce raises complex issues for both generations involving loyalty and guilt. So does the death of a parent, though in somewhat different ways.

A child of divorce may carry around lingering feelings of anger or hurt about the divorce but draw comfort from a special relationship with the natural parent. With a parent's remarriage, suddenly there is a stepparent, a foreign adult, in the household. The new adult is the intimate partner of the child's mother or father, but has no special relationship with the young adult child.

On the contrary, the new stepparent is nothing so much as a rival—a rival for the natural parent's affections and a rival to the divorced parent to whom the child still feels loyalty. If there are stepbrothers or sisters in the picture, there is also new sibling rivalry, without the leisure of adjustment that a pregnancy and a prolonged infancy offers with natural brothers and sisters (even in "intact" families, sibling rivalry is often brutal). This sense of rivalry is more intense in young children living at home, but it can be surprisingly vivid in young adult children as well.

Where a remarriage occurs against the background of the death of a parent, the issues may be more muted but no less emotionally charged. To a child or young adult who has lost a parent to death, a remarriage may seem a terrible betrayal.

The child who has lost a mother or father may or may not have adequately grieved the lost parent on a conscious level, but still carries around deeply tender if inchoate feelings of love and loss. The lost parent is often mythologized as one of unique qualities (indeed, there is no substitute for one's own mother or father). Now, abruptly, the living parent is abandoning the one who died and embracing another. Some children can adjust to this new reality more gracefully than others. For many, a remarriage can call forth feelings of abandonment (how easily my mother shifted her affections away from my father; will she also abandon me?) and disillusion (maybe she never really loved my father; maybe she was unfaithful to him all along?) as well as misplaced loyalty and rage (what is this bastard doing in my father's bed!).

If a grieving widow or widower finds comfort in a new partner quickly, all of these feelings are likely to be intensified. A single parent struggling to raise young children after the death of a partner may remarry before grieving is finished, often out of plain loneliness and the need for comfort or the generous sense that the children desperately need a new mother or father. But the children seldom experience it that way. *Hamlet* can be read on many levels, but one of the most powerful is a son's loyalty, grief, and rage at a mother remarrying too soon and thereby usurping the rightful place of both dead father and living son. Whenever the remarriage occurs, even after a lengthy interval, children may well feel that it is "too soon."

A blended family in which one parent has been through a divorce and the other through a death adds further complications. The death of a partner is a profound loss, yet in some ways the aftermath is cleaner and feels more innocent than the aftermath of a divorce. The living parent may feel some survivor

guilt (why did he die and not me?), but for the most part the survivor feels honorable, even heroic. In the case of a partner's prolonged illness, the surviving spouse very likely went through a
profound ordeal as a loving, often selfless caregiver. If the union
was a good one, the surviving partner very likely retains a hopeful view of marriage; the worst fear is likely to be that a new
partner could die, too.

The survivor of a divorce, in contrast, may be experiencing a
whole constellation of feelings involving guilt, shame, and insecurity about intimate relationships. If infidelity or deception
preceded the divorce, there has been a body blow to pride and
self-confidence in the case of the victim. For the perpetrator of
infidelity that led to divorce, there may be shame, or denial, or
both, as well as ambivalence about a new commitment. So,
when the survivor of a death marries the survivor of a divorce,
there can be a kind of moral asymmetry. The survivor of a death
is painted as the innocent victim; the survivor of a divorce can
feel like a dupe, or a cheat, and in any case a failure at marriage.

A further permutation is a blended family in which one partner has children and the other doesn't. This creates yet another
sort of asymmetry. The new partner may feel insecure about his
or her competence to function as a parent—a fifth wheel. Children have an unerring sense of how to rub insecurities raw. A
new partner without kids may be eager to have children, and
this will further complicate the blending.

Parents struggling with all of these crosscurrents are every-
day heroes. Hundreds of times a day, they make split-second
judgments which require prescience and generosity of spirit. If
ordinary parenting requires unimagined patience, love, a capacity for generosity and forgiveness, parenting in blended families
requires us to tap reserves of compassion, energy, and uncommon sense we didn't we know we possessed. And of course, we
don't always get it right. We are constantly blindsided and it all
goes by so fast that thoughtful deliberation is seldom possible.

Although all of these feelings are especially loaded during
childhood, few of the experts on stepparenting and blended families bother to tell us that the feelings also carry over into adult-

hood. At whatever age a divorce and remarriage occurred, step-families complicate the process of redefining a relationship between parent and grown children. Often, the visible relationship between grown children and a stepparent is perfectly comfortable, if a little distant. Because of unresolved issues rooted in a divorce or a death, the more emotionally charged pattern is frequently between child and parent.

Hope Edelman quotes twenty-six-year-old Audrey on her relationship with stepmother and father: At first, Audrey was very resistant to her new stepmother: "I thought, 'Who is this person in my father's life with all her tagalongs, and what makes her think she can become part of my life, too?' I gave her a really hard time until after I left for college. Now, I think of her as my father's wife, and as long as she doesn't try to be my mother, we can get along fine. She's the one who tries to keep the family together, which I kind of appreciate. But my relationship with my father is still a mess. I needed him to help me through those first months after my mother died, and he was off wining and dining all the divorced women in our town. I'm still trying to work through my anger about that. In the meantime, it's hard for me even to have lunch with him."

Two sisters in another family interviewed by Edelman recounted how their father announced he had met another woman just five weeks after their mother's death. "My Dad didn't really deal with the death. He started going out every single night, and then he got together with this woman. She's great today, but he just shoved her down our throats, and we resented it." The sisters displaced the grief and frustration from the loss of their mother onto their father. For weeks, the relationship was bitterly distant. But father and daughters were able to talk, and negotiate. The father, in deference to their wishes, agreed to put off remarriage for a year. Very slowly, the father-daughter relationship began to improve. Edelman observes, "The year gave them time to adjust to their mother's absence, and to the idea of another woman living in their father's house. They also saw that he didn't intend to abandon his daughters."

As observers, we might think that these daughters should

have shown more compassion for their father, or that the father should have had the decency to wait longer before pursuing other relationships. But all of us make mistakes, especially in situations where our judgment is clouded by grief or loss. In time, however, compassion and reparation are usually still possible. Psychologist Robert Karen writes, "The capacity to forgive is an important measure of emotional development." He adds, "[F]orgiveness is not just a by-product of growth . . . the struggle to forgive can *promote* growth."

Parents wresting with old issues of their own need to resolve them before than make real progress with their children. This is especially true when there has been a divorce. Russ and Cindy went through a really nasty divorce. Each was bitterly disappointed by the breakup of the marriage, and each fought over custody of the kids, minute to minute. There were several years when they had each other in court regularly because the terms of the shared custody agreement were not being followed to the letter. They stopped communicating, except through intermediaries. The logistics of drop-offs and pickups became an emotionally charged nightmare. Both knew the children were suffering. Finally, when their daughter was sixteen, their son a freshman in college, custody essentially moot, and both parents were in new relationships, Cindy went to a weekend forum where she had a kind of epiphany. There was no point in holding on to all of this anger at Russ, which was just ruining their relationship with their kids, who were now nearly grown.

Cindy picked up the phone and called Russ. "It finally dawned on me," she said. "I've really been behaving like a complete jerk." When Russ picked himself up off the floor, he agreed that this pretty well described his behavior, too. They met and had a long, constructive talk, the first of several. Once things simmered down, all the negative energy that had gone into continuing the marital fight could become positive energy for their new partners. Both could cultivate better relationships with the children. But this transformation, for which both parents were more than ready, required someone to take a constructive initiative and an emotional risk. Cindy's acknowledging her part in a destructive pattern gave Russ the permission to admit his own role. Had she just gone on berating him for his behavior, both would have remained dug in. Not surprisingly, things improved dramatically with the kids.

In her wonderful book about marriage, *Love, Honor and Negotiate,* the family therapist Betty Carter tells the story of working with a couple, Roger and Cassie, who brought to the therapy the entire litany of stepfamily issues—divided loyalties, different family traditions and styles of child rearing, stress with parents and in-laws, and issues with ex-spouses.

At one session, when Roger had been again complaining bitterly about his ex-wife, the therapist asked: "Why are you still so emotionally involved with her? When are you really going to get divorced?" She added that being "enemies" is a close relationship, "whether it's out-and-out vengeful or just fighting about money." When Roger finally reopened more emotionally neutral lines of communication with his former wife, first by letter, then by phone, his children began to calm down dramatically. They were acting out the conflict that was still engaging their parents, long after the divorce.

STEPFAMILY TRIANGLES

The arrival of grandchildren can rekindle issues that reverberate back through a divorce to the childhood of now-grown children and even one's own childhood. Stella, fifty-nine, is the mother of two young adults, Amy and Peter. They were born when she was in her early twenties. She and her husband, Steve, separated when the children were still in grade school. Steve, a self-confident, gregarious man much like her own father, was a very successful engineer whom she long suspected of cheating on her when he was traveling. As their marriage fell apart, he became more emotionally distant. The more aloof he became, the more insecure and needy she became. Eventually he moved out, leaving her with a deep hurt and a general uneasiness around men.

For several years after the divorce, Stella consumed herself raising the two children on her own and was unable to date men. A round of psychotherapy helped. For the past nine years, she has been married to Charlie, a gentler but somewhat detatched man. Stella's expectations of her marriage to Charlie are more limited, and she displaces a lot of emotion onto her son, Peter, now thirty-six. All the men in her life seem more distant than she would like, and she compensates by filling up the space.

Stella's daughter, Amy, thirty-three, lives on the other side of the country. A lot of Stella's issues with men get reenacted with Peter, who lives nearby. Peter, a developer, is married to Cara, a stay-at-home mom. They have two children, who are five and three. Stella is an adoring grandmother, and very free with her advice. In fact, she advises Peter incessantly where to live, how to decorate the house, how to invest his money, how to treat his wife, and how to raise the children. This relentless involvement reflects her own insecurity and desire to be needed, as well as a subconscious yearning that Peter have the intact, financially secure family as an adult that he was denied as a child. But Stella is trying too hard.

A legacy of divorce can be that a grown child remains in a caretaker role, and eventually begins to resent it. Ever since his father moved out, Peter has been quite protective of his mother. He went to college close to home, and as an adult made sure to live in a nearby community. They have a dutiful family dinner every Sunday. But the mother-son relationship is fraying. Invested emotionally in his own children, Peter is tense around his mother. And the more Stella dispenses advice, the more Peter withdraws emotionally. In fact, Peter, ordinarily an outgoing and confident man, becomes quiet and somewhat formal in her presence. He lets the women do the talking, and just looks glum. This frustrates Stella, who increasingly thinks Peter is becoming emotionally cold and self-centered, "like his father."

Stella pours her feelings into her relationship with her daughter-in-law, Cara. The two talk a lot about everything. In particular, they talk about Peter, and Stella freely vents her frustrations. A family therapist would say they "triangulate," making Peter the odd man out; that Peter is overfunctioning in his work and underfunctioning at home. In fact, Cara considers herself deeply loyal to her husband. Everything his mother tells his wife goes right back to Peter, whom Cara knows to be an affectionate and emotionally available husband. As she recounts her mother-in-law's complaints, Cara rolls her eyes. But all of this only makes Peter more wary of his mother. Cara thinks that by letting Stella freely gripe about Peter, she is managing her mother-in-law. In fact, she is feeding the flames.

This pattern will continue until somebody changes it. Stella is not getting what she professes to want—a closer relationship with her son. Peter is annoyed by what he considers his mother's excessive meddling. Cara thinks she has things under control, but she is actually contributing to the ongoing conflict, perhaps enjoying the feeling of power over both her husband and her mother-in-law. If she is not careful, Peter will begin withdrawing from her, too. The roots of these conflicts are in Stella's divorce, but the damage is being done in the present.

What to do? Stella, if she can manage it, would be wise to give less advice and to complain less about her son to her daughter-in-law. Cara could tell Stella that if she has an issue with her son, she should take it up with him directly. Peter needs to be clearer about his own needs and feelings. He would do well to set some limits with his mother and let his wife know that the conversational daisy chain is unwelcome. Charlie, the stepfather, plays a role in this system, by being emotionally absent. If nobody takes the initiative, however, this dysfunctional system could continue for some time, with Stella feeling vindicated (if frustrated) in her feelings about the emotional distance of her first husband and his son; Peter feeling that the women in his life are ganging up on him; and Cara with a kind of emotional power—for which she pays a price. But, as family systems work suggests, any one person in this system can take the initiative, not by changing the behavior of others but by changing his or her own. This sort of initiative may seem risky and conducive to further conflict. In fact, it is often empowering and calming.

Some difficult situations involving in-laws and grandparents are less subtle. The parents of a man or woman who has gone through a divorce may be bitterly disappointed or disapproving. Despite all the mother-in-law jokes, the mother of a married man often develops a close, loving relationship with his wife, who is after all the mother of her grandchildren. In some divorced couples, the husband's mother actually maintains a closer connection with the former wife than with her own son. This can be a way of staying connected to grandchildren, of identifying with the wife as one who has suffered at the hands of a man, or of punishing the son—or all three. Sometimes this ostracism is seemingly justified by behavior, sometimes not. But painful distance, however "deserved," is rarely fulfilling; more often, both mother and adult son experience the regret of unrealized dreams.

Emily and John Visher, a psychologist and psychiatrist who work with stepfamilies, quote several remarried women and men who experience difficult relationships with current or former in-laws and with parents.

Mary: Since my remarriage, neither one of my parents will have anything to do with me or with their grandchildren. They've disinherited us all completely. John's parents keep some contact with their grandchildren, but only through his ex-wife. . . . John's parents only seem to phone him to complain that he's not doing enough for the kids or for his ex-wife.

Ralph: My mother disowned me when I got divorced. She didn't contact me in any way for three to four years. She told my ex-wife not to let me see my children in the hopes I'd stay married, and when I remarried a woman with children, she wrote my ex-wife that this woman was marrying me to get my money and have someone look after my children. It was a bad beginning to our marriage.

Alice: My new in-laws won't have anything to do with me or my children. They give presents to their own grandchildren, but don't even give a card to their stepgrandchildren. . . . If they come to see us they don't even look at me or talk to me. They just chatter away as though my children and I don't exist. And Dick just basks in their attention and I get so hurt and angry at them, at him, at everybody.

In situations like these, the couple first needs to get back on the same side. The spouse needs to make it clear that parental splitting is unwelcome. Changing one's own behavior can change behavior in the family system. Eventually, grandparents may soften and become more accepting—but not if one partner basks in the favored treatment and reinforces the offending routine.

Alternatively, sometimes it is grandparents who involve themselves constructively and ease transitions, giving grandchildren a needed sense of continuity and supporting grown children through a difficult time. With a divorce comes the shattering of the dream of an idealized family. With a remarriage comes fresh hope and a lot of hard work. Grandparents may see themselves as disappointed, long-suffering elders; they may be mainly concerned about salvaging a connection with grandchildren, especially when the custodial parent is not their child, or when a remarriage makes them feel like a fifth wheel. But in stepfamilies, as in other imperfect families—and there are no perfect ones—reconciliations between parents and grown children are possible and almost always desirable. In chapters 9 and 10, we look more closely at the process of family reconciliations and the role of grandparents.

FAMILY BETRAYALS

Among the most emotionally charged situations are families in which a divorce and remarriage occur after what seems to the children like a betrayal of one parent by the other. During their courtship, Elaine experienced Nathan, a poet, as a dashing and romantic suitor. But the romance collapsed after children were born. Elaine lost interest in sex. From Nathan's perspective, she was pouring all her love into the children. Nathan soon felt confined in what he considered a loveless marriage and harbored a fantasy life that he eventually acted out with other women. As Nathan withdrew emotionally and sexually from the marriage,

Elaine invested even more of her emotional life in being a mother. When the children were late teenagers, Nathan left Elaine for one of his former students, Alissa. A year later, he married her. His two daughters vehemently sided with their mother.

The following winter, Nathan persuaded the girls to join him and Alissa on a ski vacation. Not surprisingly, it was a disaster. The kids were in a state of moralistic, contemptuous rage, wanting nothing to do with Alissa, who is only ten years their senior. Alissa tries hard, but has had no experience with children. Family visits have become mainly a time for the daughters to rake Nathan over the coals for his disloyalty to their mother. If Nathan carries around ample guilt from his first marriage, his children are his ex-wife's instrument of retribution, and with no prompting from her.

Nathan hopes desperately for a closer relationship with his children, but it will require patience and time. The last thing he can do is force it on them. Later in life, they may be ready to understand something of his story, but they do not yet have the emotional maturity or capacity for empathy. They are also at a developmental stage when it is natural and normal for children to push parents away in any case. In their neat and mythic construction of events, their mother is martyred and their father, rather than a flawed human being, is simply treacherous and immoral. In some respects his behavior was deplorable, but there are two sides to every story and he is the only father they have. This family might benefit from therapy, but it will not be pleasant. The children are not ready to cut their father much slack; they might totally resist the idea. The best thing Nathan can do for now is back off, keep lines of communication open, and give up any idea of trying to get them to play intact family or accept Alissa as a stepmother. In time, as the children mature, their own evolving capacity for empathy and curiosity may allow them a more complex and kinder view of their father.

Grown children well into adulthood can have surprisingly strong feelings when a parent remarries. And feelings of loyalty to an absent or lost parent can be combustible, even where the prologue to a remarriage was entirely honorable. It typically takes years before a new family knits together.

Rick and Paula considered themselves extremely lucky to find each other after each one lost a spouse in their early forties. After meeting at a discussion group for single parents, they didn't lose any time. Six months after they met, they were married. Paula, who was just twenty when she first married, has one daughter, Jennifer, who is now twenty-four. Rick's two boys are fourteen and ten.

Paula had been financially stressed, living as a single mother in a nearby community. When they remarried, Paula was grateful to give up her cramped apartment and move into Rick's comfortable suburban house. She assumed that her daughter, Jennifer, in graduate school, would be a big sister to Rick's boys when she was home on vacation. She knows that Rick's two sons miss their mother terribly, and is doing her best to be a mother to them. She has pretty much won over the younger one, Mike. However, Bill, the fourteen-year-old, seems profoundly attached to his own mother and wants little to do with Paula. Bill's grades are falling and he is getting into fights at school.

The real surprise, however, is her own daughter, Jennifer, ordinarily a secure and generous young woman. It feels like she has regressed to a difficult teenager. She is furious with her mother for giving up the familiar apartment. She considers Rick, her new stepfather, an uptight jerk, and Rick's kids spoiled rich brats. Her own father, Brendan, who died two years ago in a car crash, was an actor. Jennifer worshipped him. They were a close-knit threesome, living in a funky flat that was the coolest in the neighborhood. Her stepfather, Rick, teaches business administration. His house is formal and fussy. Jennifer, who idealizes her parents' marriage, can't understand what her mother sees in Rick.

Jennifer, however, is not aware that Paula had been growing weary of being married to an actor who, while charming and larger than life, was financially careless and cavalier about life's mundane details; that, notwithstanding her very genuine grief at his death, she feels as though she is finally married to an adult.

She is a little ashamed of these feelings, which make her feel disloyal to Brendan in death, and she feels she can't possibly share
any of this with Jennifer. Rick is devoted to his own boys, but is
quite at a loss about how to handle an angry twenty-four-year-
old stepdaughter. He is beginning to feel extremely resentful of
Jennifer, who is getting in the way of both his relationship with
Paula and his ability to make his own children feel at ease with
the loss of their mother and the new blended family.

What should this family do? Paula needs to pay more attention to the needs of her own daughter. She needs to do some
active listening. She and Rick should stop pressuring Jennifer to
play big sister. Jennifer has experienced a triple loss—the loss of
her father; the loss of space that had a special meaning for her;
and the loss of a very close mother-daughter connection. The
last thing she will welcome is demands to be attentive to stepbrothers that nobody consulted her about. If Paula gives Jennifer
some respectful attention, Jennifer may start paying more attention to her own feelings, and may gradually stop scapegoating
Rick. Paula is also overdoing the benign stepmother role. Fourteen-year-old boys can be a trial under the best of circumstances.
Paula should back off a little, let Bill grieve his mother, stop displacing the lost mother, and let Rick play a more active role
with his sons.

Rick needs to summon up some superhuman patience with
Jennifer. If he and Jennifer can avoid locking horns, this phase
will probably pass. He needs to let Jennifer feel the range of grief
and rage, and not rise to the bait. They may or may not become
close, but they can become civil. This family could benefit from
short-term counseling or therapy. Unless the parents can exhibit
exceptional insight, skill, and forbearance, the children may
need some venue in which it is safe to give vent to complex feelings which they do not entirely understand, without triggering
equally complex feelings in their parents.

ONE STEP AT A TIME

Harriet Lerner writes that the biggest mistake stepparents make
is to assume, with the best of intentions, that they can just take

over the role of someone's natural father or mother. "Nobody can walk into a family that has a history of its own that did not include her and become an instant mother. The role of mother—any kind of mother—cannot be automatically conferred on a woman when she marries a man with children. Can you recognize the absurdity of such an expectation?"

Blended families often try too hard. Paradoxically, stepfamilies need to resist what seems like the logical imperative to blend until they have had time just to coexist. Most studies suggest that it takes a few years before stepfamilies can stabilize and integrate. James Bray, author of one of the most extensive sets of case studies observing the struggles of stepfamilies over time, writes: "We found that many of our men, usually with a wife's encouragement, assumed an active parenting role too early in the marriage and thus fell into a trap of presuming an intimacy and authority that was still unearned." Bray concludes that the amount of intimacy or authority a child is prepared to accept in the first year or two of a remarriage is comparable to that of a coach or camp counselor, not a father.

At first, it is wise for the natural parent to remain in the primary role, so as to ease fears of abandonment and to minimize crosscurrents that may cause parental authority and constructive discipline to evaporate in a cloud of hurt feelings, recriminations, and guilty short-lived reconciliations. In the case of children who are grown, loyalty issues are no less powerful. A natural parent should spend less effort trying to get grown children to accept as a surrogate mother or father a new partner whom they did not grow up with, and more effort signaling that his or her own love for them is no less secure. If a close relationship with the stepparent evolves in time, what a lovely bonus.

In families experiencing divorce and remarriage, holidays, birthdays, weddings, and the like can trigger old hurts, anger, shame, guilt, and reunion fantasies, as well as competition within and between the generations and ongoing sorrow for the loss of the imagined storybook family. Clifford Sager and colleagues report a wide variety of styles in recombined families.

One of their clients reported a father who insisted on a "once a member of the clan, always a member of the clan" philosophy, and invited his younger brother's present and past wives to family holidays discounting the feelings of others. In another family, a divorced father who had remarried was told by his engaged son that he should come to the son's wedding alone or not come at all. Sager et al. advise, "Between these two extremes there is a range of more flexible behavior that takes into account blood ties, preferences, loyalties, sensibilities, the reality of the loss of the nuclear family, remarriage(s), and sensitivity to the impact of exclusion or inclusion on others."

Stepfamilies are only more intense variations on the issues of loyalty, autonomy, affirmation, and mutual respect that occur in all of our families. Each generation experiences life anew, and we make a terrible mistake if we project our own issues onto our grown children or attempt to use them to compensate for our own losses or disappointments. In most remarriages, especially those that occur when children are old enough to remember a lost mother or father, we can't reasonably expect our children to treat a stepparent as a natural parent. But with some compassion and forbearance, the generations can appreciate each other and share many of the supports of family life. This is also true of other nontraditional families, to which we now turn.

Chapter 7
Family Complications

In general, the message of this book is that family reconnections are almost always worth the effort. Sadly, however, some families have such a terrible history of parental abuse or neglect, either due to alcohol, drugs, or major psychological problems, that grown children who try to reconnect with them will often just be disappointed and more deeply wounded. In such families, the task of the adult child is simply to heal him- or herself.

One challenge for grown children seeking more authentic family connections is to determine whether a parent is in the relatively small category of adults for whom connection, repair, and reconciliation can take place only on a symbolic level. In these families, the actual parent may be so toxic and the history of abuse so appalling that the grown child's challenge is to build a capacity for trusting relationships elsewhere, and not to attempt a futile rapprochement with a parent that will end in deeper disillusion, or worse. This situation is the inverse of the challenge that faces most grown children, who need to let go of mythic images of their parents from childhood in order to form more authentic relations with the people whom their actual parents really are, and by extension to form more authentic relationships generally. In the case of truly abusive parents, the mythic ghosts are all too real.

For parents who have been perpetrators of abuse—to a partner, children, or both—reconciliation is conceivable only if and when they have made profound changes in their own behavior and have come to terms with what they have done. This need for both acknowledgment of one's past actions and making amends is at the heart of twelve-step programs and more conventional forms of therapy. However, seriously abusive parents are often sociopathic, and averse to therapy. They may remain in denial of the past, or continue patterns of abuse, all of their lives.

Even when overt abuse has ended, a spouse who has colluded in past abuse by failing to demand that it cease may feel that the shameful family secret must not be exposed lest it threaten the marriage. The parents, if they are still together, may have arrived at a tacit bargain not to reopen the past. Though the active abuse may have ended (whether it was abuse of a wife, children, or both), an adult survivor of abuse who attempts to alter old family scripts is taking on a much larger challenge with a lower probability of success than the task of renewing emotional connections in families without extreme pathologies.

At the same time, while the physical, sexual, and emotional abuse of children has only recently been acknowledged as a large-scale problem with its own distinctive psychological effects on grown children, most families do not merit the label abusive. Just as it is a mistake for survivors of genuine abuse to think they can manage reconciliations or "change" parents, it is also a mistake to characterize families with common or garden-variety misconnections and frustrations as hopelessly abusive.

CHILDREN OF ABUSE

It is only in the past two decades that Post-Traumatic Stress Disorder (PTSD) as a consequence of abuse has been fully described and well understood by psychotherapists. As psychiatrist Judith Lewis Herman, the pioneering scholar of PTSD and childhood abuse, describes the syndrome, people who have endured repeated and prolonged abuse, especially as children, suffer grave psychological harm that follows predictable patterns. Earlier diagnostic categories typically failed to recognize the connection between the early abuse and subsequent adult behavior, and attributed the victim's psychological problems to other sources.

Characteristically, a child who has been repeatedly abused, whether physically or sexually, experiences herself (and victims usually but not always are female) as powerless, full of shame, and often perceives herself as the one deserving of blame. A common response is what psychologists call dissociation—an emotional shutting down and a subconscious attempt to insulate oneself against all feeling, since feeling is associated with pain and shame. The survivor may also feel profound guilt at having failed to prevent the abuse, and this is true whether the abuse was of one's self or one's mother. Indeed, children who witnessed mothers being abused by fathers often exhibit the same patterns of post-traumatic stress as those who were objects of abuse directly: dissociation and mistrust of intimacy.

Another common response among abuse survivors is "repetition compulsion," a pattern of reenactment of the abuse. Adult children of abuse are often at risk of self-mutilation. Young women prone to degrading, promiscuous behavior were frequently sexually abused as girls. Women who find themselves with abusive husbands often had abusive fathers. A self-loathing combined with a primitive desire for human warmth may drive survivors of abuse to pursue risky and debasing sexual encounters. A father who rapes a daughter will often sidestep his own feelings of guilt by blaming her seductiveness and calling her a "whore." And a child who is repeatedly called a whore may come to behave like a whore. Herman writes, "Almost inevitably, the survivor has great difficulty protecting herself in the context of intimate relationships. Her desperate longing for nurturance and care make it difficult to establish safe and appropriate boundaries with others. . . . Many survivors have such profound deficiencies in self-protection that they can barely imagine themselves in a position of agency or choice. . . . A well-learned dissociative coping style also leads survivors to ignore or minimize social cues that would ordinarily alert them to danger."

What is true of survivors of sexual and physical abuse is often true for children of alcoholics and drug abusers, who may exhibit similar patterns of physical or emotional abuse, even if not sexual abuse. Alcoholism is complicated by the fact that alcoholics may be dry for periods of time, during which they seem to be trustworthy parents, only to fall back into periods of alcoholic rage. Love becomes associated with dangerous unpredictability. The children of such parents may grow up to be mistrustful of relationships generally, or may take on exaggerated caretaker roles.

As Herman observes, "The pathological environment of childhood abuse forces the development of extraordinary capacities, both creative and destructive. It fosters the development of abnormal states of consciousness in which the ordinary relations of body and mind, reality and imagination, knowledge and memory, no longer hold. . . . [T]hese symptoms simultaneously reveal and conceal their origins; they speak in disguised language of secrets too terrible to reveal."

The process of healing from a childhood of abuse can be excruciating, since one's survival has been often based on a suppression or distortion of feelings, one that carries its own disabling consequences. Recovery can come via psychotherapy, support groups, or both. A common and necessary reaction, at least initially, is rage. One incest survivor told Herman: "I have so much anger, not so much about what went on at home, but that nobody would listen. My mother still denies that what went on was serious. . . . At the time nobody could admit it, they let it happen. So I had to go and be crazy."

This is not the place for an extended discussion of physical and sexual abuse. Readers who want a fuller treatment of domestic violence and its adult consequences should consult Judith Herman's fine work and other materials that we cite in the bibliography. There are similarly extensive literatures on alcoholism as a family disease, and on the dilemmas facing adult children of alcoholics. For our purposes here, the issue is when, and how, it makes sense for adult children to attempt reconciliations.

In recovering from the after-effects of childhood abuse, survivors characteristically go through several stages. Survivors first need to keep safe, to protect themselves from repeated bouts of abuse, whether from the original perpetrator or from others, and to regain a sense of personal control. Gradually, they need to name the real problem, to reexperience it in a context of support, to get angry at it and work on rebuilding a shattered inner life. They need to mourn the loss of innocence and trust, to have others (a therapist, a caring support group, or loving intimate partner) bear compassionate witness to their history. Only then is reintegration of a healthy personality possible and likely. And only then is some kind of reconnection with the parent even conceivable.

Therapists who treat survivors of abuse counsel against premature confrontation with families or impulsive attempts at reconciliation. A survivor of abuse in the early stages of recovery may still be exhibiting a variety of self-destructive behaviors, bouts of depression, rage, and volatility. A sudden accusation of, say, sexual abuse that has long been under wraps will more often than not lead to denial by one or both parents. And if the adult daughter seems like a "hysteric" and the father like a normal adult, family and friends may choose to believe the father. This can result in a grave setback for the recovering survivor—a repetition of the abuse in a new form and a feeling that her father's domination of her life will continue endlessly.

At some point later, a survivor of abuse may want to confront her family, as a kind of capstone to her own recovery and as a validation of her own empowerment. Typically, a survivor who at last insists that the truth be told is breaking a family code of silence. As Herman puts it, "In preserving the family secret [survivors] carry the weight of a burden that does not belong to them." When well into recovery, she adds, "survivors may choose to declare to their families that the rule of silence has been irrevocably been broken. In doing so, they renounce the burden of shame, guilt, and responsibility, and place the burden on the perpetrator, where it belongs."

Note, however, that where there has been a history of prolonged abuse, these confrontations are almost part of the survivor's own recovery, not necessarily part of a family reconstruction. If the fantasy is that the abuser will break down, admit past wrong, and change into the loving parent the child always yearned for, that wish is usually disappointed. Herman writes, "A successful disclosure is almost always followed by both exhilaration and disappointment. On the one hand, the survivor feels surprised at her own courage and daring. She no longer feels intimidated by her family or compelled to participate in destructive family relationships. . . . [But] on the other hand, she gains a clearer sense of her family's limitations." Even the bravery of confrontation and truth-telling will not produce the fantasized, intact family.

Some therapists encourage letter writing as a safe way to confront past abuse and rewrite scripts. The letter can honestly tell what occurred, how it affected the one who was abused, and what the goals are now. Dr. Susan Forward, who works with survivors of abuse, quotes one such letter. It begins:

"I want you to apologize for being such a cruel, lousy father. I want you to acknowledge the harm you did."

For those of us who have experienced some bouts of parental anger that bordered on abuse, the question is whether our family is so toxic that reconciliation and reunion are impossible. Although cases of prolonged and sadistic abuse are more widespread than once supposed, they do not describe anything like a majority of families. Rare is the child who grew up without having a parent occasionally break into frustrated rage or administer an occasional spanking. This hardly means we are all "survivors of abuse." In considering the value of reconciliations, the important judgment is whether our family of origin fell into the relatively small category of chronically abusive ones.

This is, of course, something of a spectrum. Parents who are seriously neglectful can do nearly as much damage as those who are willfully abusive. There is also something of a polite disagreement among the experts. Family therapists tend to look more hopefully on the healing potential of reconnections. Specialists on abuse and post-traumatic stress tend to look harder for episodes that merit the label *abuse* and emphasize the risks of expecting too much of truly abusive families of origin. The same is true for adult children of alcoholics, who are often counseled to heal themselves and not to expect too much from an alcoholic parent.

In *Toxic Parents*, Susan Forward puts it this way:

> Fairy tale endings are rare for children of alcoholics. In the best of all possible worlds, your parents would take full responsibility for their drinking, enter a treatment program, and become sober. They would validate and acknowledge the horrors of your childhood, and would make an attempt to become responsible, loving parents.
>
> Unfortunately, the reality usually falls far short of the ideal. The drinking, the denial, and the distortion of reality often continue until one or both parents die. . . . If you are the adult child of an alcoholic, the key to taking control of your life is to remember that *you* can change without changing your parents. . . . You can overcome the traumas of your childhood and their power over your adult life, even if your parents stay exactly the way they have always been.

This advice is sound as far as it goes. At the same time, some recovering alcoholics are truly committed to staying sober and making amends with loved ones whom they have hurt. This process is part of their own healing and central to twelve-step and other programs. If genuinely committed to change—and this is a big if—a parent making sincere amends can be part of repair work that is beneficial to adult children. The personal narratives of adult children of alcoholics seem to fall into two broad categories: genuine reconciliations; and cases of disappointment and then acceptance of the reality that my alcoholic father or mother is just never going to change, and my task is to save myself.

Happily, profoundly abusive families are the exception. The vast majority of parents fall into a vast middle ground, somewhere in between the secure and loving parents that we all want (and want to be) and sadistically abusive ones. America is, famously, a land of second chances. People who were frivolous in their twenties get serious about their lives later on. People start new careers in midlife. C students become millionaires. People who were too immature to have successful marriages when they were young have happy second marriages. In middle age, we may reflect on how little we knew when we were young. Members of our family grow, too.

MIXED BLESSINGS

Children are full of surprises. They choose partners of whom parents disapprove. They pick career paths far from what parents would have chosen for them. They turn out to be Buddhist, or vegetarian, or Republican, or lesbian. They divorce. They move to Montana. When grown children and their parents have major differences over values and life decisions, parents can experience disappointment and even grief.

To children, parental rejection of their own life choices can also seem brutal. Rejection, however, is often temporary and not the same thing as abuse. And reconciliations based on growth and mutual respect remain possible.

Where children choose radically different courses, parents above all need to distinguish clearly between their own issues and dreams—and their concern that an adult child could be in serious trouble. The latter, as we saw in Chapter 5, may warrant constructive intervention. The former simply calls for acceptance that the child is now an adult. Where a grown child pursues a different path, parents need to be respectful and flexible if they hope for a lifelong connection. Children need to accept that some of their choices may have disappointed parents, and communicate respect even as they insist on standing their ground.

Sometimes, it is parents who disappoint their grown children. They sell the family home before children are ready to let go. They remarry someone whom their children find unsuitable. They behave in ways that children consider embarrassing and out of date. Sharland recalls that at fifteen, she did not want to be seen with her parents. Once, on a family excursion to the movies, she asked her parents to walk down the other side of the street. What is developmentally normal for a rebellious fifteen-year-old is not appropriate behavior for an adult. In these cases, it is the young adult children who need to restrain their impulses and to behave like compassionate grown-ups.

The marriage of a child is a moment of great joy and sometimes great conflict. Ideally, it signals that "the family" is continuing; but the parents may not like the direction the family is headed. The partner may be the "wrong" religion, or race, or social class, or gender. He or she may bring along the progeny of a previous marriage. The young adults may choose to be partners but not legally wed spouses. The new union may rekindle old issues and old conflicts in the older couple. For the younger couple, the parents can be a source of support—or of extraneous tension.

In the end, despite many traditions to the contrary, the choice of a partner is the business of children, not parents. Psychologist Sidney Callahan offers her usual sage advice. If I had doubts about my child's choice of a mate, she writes, "I would treat my child with all the delicacy and tact that I would use with a good friend. . . . [T]he questions and doubts a parent has can be voiced in a concerned but rather tentative way. Tentative is important both as a strategy and out of honesty. After all, every parent knows of many successful marriages that were originally opposed by everyone, including the couple's parents and friends." Callahan stresses the importance of speaking "in a delicate, noninfallible mode." If the marriage does go forward, despite parental doubts, "parents should offer support, or at least not work against the relationship. Marriage is hard enough to make a go of without outsiders, especially in-laws, interfering."

If marriage is hard, mixed marriages are often harder, both because of parental and sometimes social disapproval and because of divergent traditions and customs. Each partner brings to a union tacit images from childhood about how a husband, wife, or lover is supposed to behave, and what a mother or father is supposed to do. Often, in a couple, these images diverge. As they settle into the daily routine of marriage, a mixed couple may discover deeply embedded differences in their expectations and styles of communicating that set off unanticipated conflicts.

Mixed Blessings is the title of a modern classic by the late journalist Paul Cowan and his wife, Rachel Cowan. Paul had grown up an assimilated and affluent Jew, Rachel a Unitarian from a WASP family. Their book tells the story of their own marriage and of several other mixed-marriage couples. The Cowans quote a psychiatrist friend, John Pearce, who specializes in what he terms "ethnotherapy." Pearce told the Cowans, "I'll bet when you have a disagreement at night, Paul wants to talk it out and Rachel wants to leave it. When you wake up in the morning, Rachel wants to spring out of bed and begin the day's activity while Paul wants to stay in bed and talk about your relationship."

Paul recognized the pattern. He explained, "I come from a very talkative Jewish family and Rachel comes from a reserved Protestant one, so our negotiating styles are very different. I argue melodramatically, exaggerating to make my point, trying to drag Rachel's feelings out of her. But what I see as a natural, heated conversation threatens her with obliteration. [Later,] I try to heal the wound I've inflicted, hovering over Rachel, asking her how she is. I punish her with words. She punishes me with silences."

Monica McGoldrick describes a new father and mother who came to her for counseling. The father is an ebullient Italian American Catholic, the mother a somewhat withdrawn Protestant. Initially, they were attracted to each other's differences. When they were dating, and then as newlyweds, she liked the fact that he was more emotionally available than most of her family. He was delighted that she was quieter and less prone to mood swings than his mother.

But when children were born, deep-seated cultural differences in the family mode of dealing with conflict created real discord. In the Protestant family, minor annoyances were ignored; the family idiom was reticence. In the Italian family, everything was discussed, often with high emotion. The arrival of children only intensified the intuitive differences about "appropriate" behavior that each spouse brought from his or her family of origin.

Eventually, each learned from the other and the couple was able to come full circle to what attracted them to each other in the first place. The husband, with time, appreciated that every possible irritation or perceived slight did not require endless discussion. The wife came to appreciate the value of exploring and processing important hurts and misunderstandings.

McGoldrick observes that "couples who choose to intermarry are usually seeking a rebalance of the characteristics of their own ethnic background. . . . During courtship, a person may be attracted precisely to the fiancée's differentness, but when entrenched in a marital relationship these same qualities often become the rub. . . ." She adds that spouses from different ethnic groups "may perceive each other's reactions as offensive or insensitive although within each group's ethnic context their reactions make perfect sense. In our experience, much of therapy involves helping family members recognize each other's behavior as a reaction from a different frame of reference."

So far, so good. But note that these two sets of conflicts and negotiations were strictly within the couple. Coming to terms with unanticipated differences in cultural styles becomes all the more loaded when anxious parents or other relatives are intrusive or ostracizing. Eventually, in successful marriages, mindful partners from different backgrounds comprehend and work out differences. But that doesn't mean their parents necessarily bless the union, much less that parents are part of the marital odyssey with its delicately negotiated compromises and hard won compassion.

To parents, a mixed marriage may seem a repudiation of their values and way of life. Parental opposition may reflect simple bigotry on the part of parents, or more complex worry that the marriage and its offspring will be hurt by society's bigotry. Parents may disapprove, or fear disapproval from friends, neighbors, co-workers, and extended family. White families may fear that their child and mixed-race grandchildren will suffer prejudice and loss of status. Among many Asian American societies and among observant American Jews, there is anguish that intermarriage annihilates valued community. For African American relatives all too familiar with society's racism, an intermarriage may seem like sleeping with the enemy or taking risks that could bring disastrous results. Surveys of interracial couples report that women in an African American family sometimes view a black male relative who marries a white woman as betraying black sisterhood. "It feels like you've rejected black femininity in favor of . . . a white standard of beauty," according to one African American man in a mixed marriage that his sister opposed. Parents may also fear that an intermarriage will have a higher likelihood of divorce. Although this was once the case, divorce rates among intermarried couples and couples who marry within a racial, ethnic, or religious community are now converging.

The disapproval of in-laws can leave a spouse wondering whether the marriage partner subconsciously harbors some of his or her parents' beliefs about the outsider. Many of the ostensibly tolerant couples interviewed by the Cowans admitted to a lingering chauvinism about their own ethnic origins. As one man, a Lutheran married to a Jewish woman, put it: "Even though neither of us is very zealous about our beliefs, there's a certain cultural baggage there that we each want, selfishly, to pass on to our kids."

Sometimes, this tacit loyalty to one's own faith is subconscious. It can come out in ways that suggest that even freethinkers have more loyalty to their roots than they imagine. Max Lerner, the son of Orthodox Jews and the veteran of a half-century marriage to a woman of Episcopalian stock, was one of America's great political philosophers and very much a secular universalist. Speaking about his experience in a loving mixed marriage, he referred in passing to his grandson. Grandpa Max said he hoped young Josh would consider himself Jewish. "He's so bright he has to be Jewish," he said.

A family therapist quotes a fourth-generation Jewish American client married to a non-Jewish woman describing a family party. "My mother spent half the evening speaking about Jewish cooking and Jewish holidays, peppering her monologue with frequent Yiddishisms. It took me a long time to realize that this uncharacteristic behavior from my 'assimilated' mother was for the benefit of my non-Jewish wife, whom Mother claims to accept totally."

Unlike earlier waves of one-way immigration to America, many immigrant groups today do not expect to cut ties to their homeland. America is seen as a place to pursue economic opportunity and political liberty, while keeping one's own culture. This is often the case with Asian and Hispanic immigrant groups, who do not want their children to be homogenized into the larger American culture. Julia Alvarez's charming novel, *How the Garcia Girls Lost Their Accents*, recounts: "[A]s soon as we had [migrated], Mami and Papi got all worried they were going to lose their girls to America. Things had calmed down on the Island and Papi had started to make real money in his office up in the Bronx. The next decision was obvious: we four girls would be sent summers to the Island so we wouldn't lose touch with *la familia*. The hidden agenda was marriage to homeland boys, since everyone knew that once a girl married an American, those grandbabies came out jabbering English and thinking of the Island as a place to go get a suntan."

Maria Root, a distinguished clinical psychologist and researcher on mixed marriages, writes that when a child intermarries, parents often go into a kind of mourning for their own lost fantasies of the family's future. "Parents' grief over the race of their child's partner seems to be grief more for what they themselves have lost than for their child. Resolving that grief means that they must reconcile their disappointed hopes with a reality they did not anticipate. They must also honestly face the fact that they grieve not for their child but for themselves and for their assumption that racial sameness would guarantee both a happy marriage and an unbroken family line."

They also may see the marriage as a deliberate attempt to hurt or reject them, or a sign that they failed as parents. A young women told interviewers conducting a study of interracial marriage, "I went home and said I was going to be getting married [to a black man]. . . . [The] whole house just came unglued, and my father went through all, I mean, the drama of throwing me out, disowning me . . . forbade me to come home. His rationales were that this was immoral and that I must be doing it to hurt him. He couldn't figure out what he did, for me to want to hurt him so badly. . . . And then he said horrible things about if we ever had children. . . . So I just left."

Parents who disapprove of a marital partner seldom succeed in blocking the marriage, but they invariably add to its stresses. Maria Root observes, "To be forced to choose between your family and the person you love is a no-win situation. The withdrawal of parental and family love almost always leaves a gaping psychological wound . . . a reminder of the happiness and wholeness that was taken away. As a result, unrealistic pressure may be placed on the marital love to make up for the loss, which is usually a recipe for marital failure."

By disapproving of the union, parents often deny themselves the very connectedness that they fear will be jeopardized by the unconventional choice of a partner. One Michigan woman in an interracial marriage, Christine, told an interviewer, "[Y]ou can't talk very much about problems with your parents because you're trying to make it sound like this is a good marriage and you don't want to . . . give them another reason not to like [your partner]. . . . I think it's almost like your husband has to become a superman . . . he has to be even better, maybe, than a lot of other people, because look at everything I have given up. So I think that puts an edge on the marriage, too."

CROSSING THE COLOR LINE

Society's broader attitudes toward interracial marriage have undergone a revolution in the past half century. In the late 1950s, the Gallup organization found that 96 percent of whites disapproved of racial intermarriage. In 1968, at the peak of the civil rights revolution, 76 percent of whites were still opposed. By 1997, substantial majorities of both blacks (77 percent) and whites (61 percent) said they approved of intermarriage, and the percent approving was significantly higher among younger adults. Though generations of anxious parents and grandparents have worried that the children of intermarriage would "belong" to neither racial group, by the 2000 Census, multiracial was an accepted category, and millions of young Americans, with Tiger Woods, were proudly embracing a mixed heritage.

But this shift is comparatively recent. As late as 1958, when today's midlife adults were children absorbing cultural norms, a Virginia judge jailed Richard and Mildred Loving, an interracial couple who had married in the District of Columbia, for violating Virginia's ban on miscegenation. The judge solemnly declared that God had created separate races. It was not until 1967 that the U.S. Supreme Court, in the aptly named case of *Loving v. Virginia,* definitively threw out all state attempts to ban intermarriage as contrary to the Fourteenth Amendment's guarantee of the constitutional right to pursue happiness, and not until 1984 that the Court ruled that race could not be a factor in custody disputes.

In a generation, attitudes have changed radically among younger people, but parents and grandparents who grew up in the era of segregation can be brutal to children who marry across the color line. One white father told a daughter, a month before her wedding to a black man, that he "didn't want any nigger children coming to his house and calling him grandpa." The black husband-to-be replied, "You don't have to worry about that because we just won't come to your house." Another father told his daughter, "For the first time in my life. . . . I am glad that my own parents are dead so they won't see the shame you've brought on me." Sometimes, these attitudes simply reflect ignorance. A black woman interviewed for a study of interracial marriages recalled, "I think [his parents] didn't envision a middle class in the black community. . . . The feeling was that not only was he marrying someone black, he was marrying out of his class. He was marrying someone beneath him, because I had to be poor." Deciding to go forward with a marriage in the face of such hostility requires an awful choice, knowing that one is likely to incur a permanent emotional cutoff from the family, extending even to one's children.

In one family, a woman in a mixed marriage had been ostracized by her father for twelve years. After he had a stroke, and

was in a nursing home and near death, they attempted to reconcile. She took him for a drive around the old neighborhood,
where she and her husband still lived. Impulsively, the father
asked to see her baby. When he saw the mixed-race baby, he said,
"That is pretty hurtful." Later, after a very emotional day, the
daughter heard him say something that she thought sounded
like "Forgive me." She told an interviewer. "[T]hen he blurted it
out, and it came out loud and clear: 'I forgive you!' . . . And those
were his last words to me. . . . That really rankles with me. I do
have anger for him, and I can't get it out because he's dead, and I
know that for my own well-being I need to forgive him."

One man reported that even when his father was dying of
cancer, he told the son not to bring his interracial grandchildren
to the hospital. "It's like he didn't want the people in the hospital to know he had these black relatives. It would make him not
white or something."

Often, however, time brings reconciliation. The parents get
to know the child's partner, and realize that he or she doesn't fit
the stereotypes. Even so, a lot of damage has been done in the
meantime. One woman reported:

> [My father took] ten years to apologize and say, "I'm
> wrong. It's OK that you married him 'cause he's OK, and I
> like him now. . . . I'm grateful for that. . . . It's probably a
> major step forward for him. But I don't see that as any major
> support. I mean, it's reassuring to me, but . . . if I went ten
> years without his approval, I didn't really give a rip. . . . It's
> like, "So now you're going to bestow your approval on me?
> Like it's yours to give and take?" So I'm grateful for it but I
> have mixed feelings . . . I think he should have loved me
> enough to accept what I did and not have to give or take
> approval."

Another white woman, Julie, recounts how her parents kept
from friends, neighbors, and extended family the fact that she
had married a black man. She and her husband lived some distance away. Mostly, contact was in the form of phone calls and

visits to their home by the parents. Finally, at a cousin's wedding, they could keep the secret no longer. By this time, her children were of college age, and for the first time met aunts, uncles, and cousins—who were far more accepting than the parents had feared. "It just wasted all those years," Julie said sadly.

It takes great bravery to persist with a relationship in the face of parental hostility, and maturity and generosity on the part of the young couple who keep lines of communication open in the hope that the parents may eventually soften. Maria Root writes of a white Seattle woman whose affluent parents opposed her engagement to a black man. "They used expensive and otherwise manipulative ploys, such as the offer of a trip abroad. When she declined, her father stopped speaking to her. She agonized during this six months of manipulation, which she interpreted as a test of the seriousness of her feelings—a generous interpretation that bespeaks both her resilience and her respect for her parents' intentions in spite of her deep disagreements with them. When she and her fiancé refused to budge, the family finally accepted the engagement and now treats them well."

Frequently, it is grandchildren who finally bring acceptance. As one study of multiracial families observes, "It is hard to say whether it was the charm of the child, a realization that the relationship was likely to be a long-term one, a feeling of connection to the child as a blood relative, an unwillingness to be hostile to an innocent child, the importance of a grandchild as a descendant who will live long after one's own death; or something else; but in quite a few couples in which someone in the white partner's family had opposed the relationship and in which the couple had a child, the child seemed to move the hostile family members toward greater acceptance." This study noted that in every white family where there was opposition to the marriage, the opposition lessened over time. But in several cases the healing was incomplete either because there was lingering racism or because of leftover bad feelings of the earlier hostility.

Sidney Callahan writes, "I grew up in a Southern military family of lapsed Calvinists and by the time I was an adult my father and I had ended up disagreeing over a whole range of ideological issues—over race, religion, politics, careers, and money. We disagreed over every life decision I made, from becoming a Christian to the college I chose, to the husband I married, to my decisions to have so many children. Yet we loved each other deeply and learned to get along." Callahan describes her efforts to practice the same goals with her own, now adult children: "My experience in an America full of intrafamily pluralism is that it is possible to live and befriend persons with whom you seriously disagree. Of course, you have to respect those with whom you differ, and want to get along."

How very sad, for both parents and children, that parental rejection of a partner often does nothing but build walls. Occasionally, parents do succeed in blocking a marriage. But for the most part, all they manage to block is the very lifelong emotional connection with the child that they so poignantly sought.

Yet, in a country with a brutal and fairly fresh history of racism, there is often a surprising degree of acceptance. One man in a mixed marriage reported that when he got married, his godmother said, "You shouldn't ever let anybody call you a mixed marriage, and frankly, the only mixed marriage that people are ever worried about is one between a man and a woman." Seconding his godmother, this man added that, in his experience, "there is a bigger, more fundamental, more cosmic empathic gap between men and women than there is between any people of two wildly disparate cultures that you care to put together in a room."

Where acceptance does occur, either from the outset or over time, connections in an interracial family can sometimes be closer and more significant than in many ethnically homogeneous families, because to have a relationship at all requires real emotional engagement. It takes real effort and compassion to understand the alien "other" or others, and to appreciate their essential humanity and capacity for love.

GAY RITES

Straight society's acceptance of gays and lesbians as "virtually normal," in gay essayist Andrew Sullivan's wistfully ironic phrase, has come a long way in just a decade. Even so, most heterosexual parents still have fairly conventional expectations for their children: they will complete their schooling, grow up into accomplished adults at their chosen professions, get married to a suitable partner of the opposite sex, and have children of their own.

Even for parents who consider themselves tolerant, having a child turn out to be gay or lesbian is usually a shock. And even if parental bigotry is not at work, fears about grown children being discriminated against or being at risk of contracting HIV, or not producing grandchildren, may come into play. Parents are lifelong worriers, often to excess. As a generation of gay literature has made poignantly clear, adolescents coming to terms with the reality of their homosexuality face multiple forms of anguish, not the least of which is whether, when, and how to tell one's parents. Indeed, the profound desire for parental acceptance on the part of gay and lesbian teens and young adults is only a more intense variation on the need of all young adults simultaneously to achieve their own personhood while retaining parental love and approval.

Betty Fairchild and Nancy Hayward, leaders of the organization PFLAG (Parents and Friends of Lesbians and Gays), in their now classic book, *Now That You Know: A Parents' Guide to Understanding Their Gay and Lesbian Children,* recount innumerable coming-out stories. Some have happy endings in which parents and gay and lesbian children come to know and respect each other more deeply. Others do not. But what all have in common is the taking of great emotional risks for the sake of love, connection, and affirmation. And, almost by definition, it is the teenager or young adult who takes the first risks.

"If we truly want to understand our children," Fairchild and Hayward write, "we must stop *explaining* them to themselves and listen to what they have to say to us." They quote from a letter a man named Jeff Moses wrote to his mother:

> Look at this for a moment from the perspective of the gay child. . . . The gay child sees no healthy gay people, as such. He/she hears the locker room humor. . . .

I lived in the closet for years. I know a lot of people who are still in the closet. It's HELL. Imagine a world where you and Walter had to hide not only your relationship but the possibility of your relationship. Imagine not being able to hold hands in a public place for fear you'd be told you had to move out of your apartment. Imagine to pretend you hardly knew each other when your children came to visit, or your friends. . . .

Jeff's mother told Fairchild and Hayward, "It was not until Jeff wrote me the letter that a flood of understanding came. . . . My heart ached for my son and other gays."

Another man in his early twenties, Lou, resolved to tell his parents of his homosexuality. He composed a very thoughtful letter, which he hoped would raise issues that might be cut short in his initial conversation. He began:

Dear Mom and Dad:

By the time you read this I will have told you that I'm a homosexual. I know this must be a difficult situation for you. Undoubtedly all kinds of negative thoughts are running through your minds. Will our son be happy? Why is he "different"? What will relatives and neighbors think?

There are many who have advised me never to tell my parents I'm gay. "Why create problems and tensions and maybe even lose the love of your parents forever?" they ask.

I think it's to your credit that I can't do this. I just can't, and won't, live a lie. What's more, I believe deeply it would be an insult to you had I concluded that you were incapable of looking beyond the generations of erroneous information, slander, and downright silliness that have molded the prevailing opinion of homosexuals. . . . I truly believe that once you have made an honest and sincere attempt to examine the situation objectively, you will come to view homosexuality as being just as healthy and natural as heterosexuality, and as just another variation in human sexuality and love.

In the meantime, how will we relate to each other?

I wish I could honestly answer that question. I can only say I'm through pretending.

But despite this very thoughtful and sensitive letter, Lou's emotional bravery was rebuffed, at least initially. His parents did not take the news easily. They begged him not to tell relatives. And it took years before they could accept him for who he is, to feel comfortable when he brought friends home. But eventually they did.

Truly accepting parents who reciprocate the courage of their gay and lesbian children, however, can achieve something that most parents of grown children want and seldom get—an emotionally rich and trusting lifelong connection. Actual relationships, of course, run the gamut from complete cutoff to tense, simulated connection, to genuine emotional acceptance. Moreover, life is full of surprises. Relationships seldom stay put. Parents of gays and lesbians may have gamely accepted the reality of sexual preference, only to swallow their disappointment at the choice of a partner, or more than one partner.

One gay couple, Frank and Gene, moved into a suburban subdivision, complete with dogs, SUV, and barbecue. Frank, the more conventional of the two, found the house. Gene, who misses their apartment in the city, likes to live closer to the edge and delights in baiting straight society.

Frank and his parents have worked very hard at a mutually respectful relationship. One Sunday, he invited his parents, George and Anna, his sister, her husband, and nephew Joey, over for a cookout to see the house, which had been decorated mainly by Frank's partner. Everything went well until his mother asked to use the guest bathroom. Gene had papered the walls in a highly inventive photo collage from sexually explicit gay men's magazines, complete with spotlights.

Frank's mother was appalled, and even more aghast that Frank would expose his nephew to this material. She said nothing until they got home, and then complained bitterly to her husband, George. Whatever Frank and Gene did in the bedroom was their business, but how could they expose Joey to this filth?

George had been more bemused than upset at the time; he figured that Joey had seen worse. But now he was angry that Frank had so upset his wife. This led to a tense father-son phone call that ended in a rare shouting match.

Gene and Frank also quarreled. From Gene's viewpoint, he and Frank were expressing their lifestyle. This was what gay men did. Frank's parents could accept it—and him—or not. For Gene, Anna's disgust was proof that she hadn't truly accepted the reality of their homosexuality, much less their relationship. Frank actually had never thought the wallpaper a great idea, certainly not in the first-floor guest bathroom.

Acceptance is a two-way street. Grown children who rub their parents' noses in the details of a lifestyle that is hard for the parents to embrace are raising the bar of acceptance. They may need to do some of this, to test the limits of their families' love, but they should do so knowingly and not scapegoat the parents. And gay couples of course have disagreements, just like straight couples. Frank's relationship with his own family may be more comfortable than Gene's. Gene may need to constantly test straight friends and family who come to his home. Gene may unconsciously experience Frank's family as rivals and he may need to relentlessly test them, too.

Given the contempt with which straight society has treated homosexuality, the impulse to test and retest alleged tolerance is not hard to understand. Indeed, if society is finally more accepting of homosexuality, it is only because of the courage of millions of individual acts of coming out, some of which were necessarily confrontational. These, in turn, have put a human face on homosexuality. They have forced heterosexual Americans to come to terms with the fact that someone in their family or circle of friends is very likely gay or lesbian. Sometimes, these acts have had to be in-your-face, because often that's what it takes to challenge entrenched bigotry. One national gay organization has as its slogan, "We're here, we're queer, get used to it." Revolutionary social change is rarely polite or linear. All of this sometimes militant set of demands for inclusion has been part of the process of the normalization of homosexuality, which in turn has made it safer for the next generation of gays to come out, which in turn has reduced bigotry all around.

That said, when it comes to the process of connection and reconnection within a family, in-your-face tactics can sometimes backfire and both parties do well to proceed with some delicacy. As always, it is important to keep in mind that inevitable setbacks need not, and should not, lead to permanent cutoff. Renewed efforts at repair are always worth the trouble. The stakes are just too high to let missteps become lifelong ones.

Few young adults in their twenties force the kind of direct emotional encounters with parents that gays and lesbians must do. One of the uplifting paradoxes of the pain that gays and lesbians often endure to connect with their families is that, to succeed, everyone works harder at the project, and reaps rewards. The lovely book, *A Member of the Family*, in which gay men write about their families, is mostly not about the ordeal of coming out or painful distances but about common journeys of exploration. One of the essays, by Darrell Schramm, describes his apprehension about finally telling his father, a somewhat austere and wrathful parent, that he was in love with a man. But that turned out to be the beginning of a series of conversations that led not only to mutual acceptance but greater mutual curiosity and closeness between father and son, as well as an acceptance of Darrell's partner, Chris. "Seeing Chris as an extension of myself [Dad] gave Chris as much attention and affection as he gave me." Though all such stories don't have this happy ending, straight society's increasing acceptance makes them less the exception.

THE HUMAN FAMILY

This book cannot possibly exhaust all special situations that confront families. Other than an examination of intermarriage in the United States, we have not attempted a discussion of how parents and grown children separate and reintegrate in different cultures. Nor have we addressed in detail families where the primary caregiver is a grandparent. And if parents with gay children represent a special variation on our theme, so do children of gay parents. Sometimes, a father concludes that he is gay or bisexual after years of marriage. His taking of a gay partner comes as a shock to his children. Mutual acceptance requires extra effort. Yet, as in the case of homosexual children of straight mothers and fathers, the additional work can yield uncommonly close connections.

Still another special situation involves children given up for adoption, who in recent years have won the right to learn the identities of their biological parents. The experience of adopted children seeking reconciliations with birth mothers runs the full gamut. Some mothers have built new lives, borne other children, and are embarrassed by the prospect of any sort of relationship. Others welcome the chance to reconnect with a lost son or daughter. Here, too, the challenge is to set aside assumptions and endeavor, compassionately, to know the other as a person. Reunion with birth parents also has its own testimonials and growing literature, and we suggest some resources in the bibliography.

The human family has almost infinite variations. It may be, as Tolstoy famously wrote, that each unhappy family is unhappy in its own way. Yet our review of a broad range of families reveals remarkably similar issues and patterns in very different family situations and a wide variety of roads to affirmation and acceptance. In all but the bleakest circumstances, efforts at compassion, repair, and reunion are rewarding. Even if not always requited, such initiatives are healing and liberating for the one who makes the effort.

Chapter 8
Revisiting Our Families

A memory of Bob's: *When I was a twenty-year-old student in London, I bought a beat-up motor scooter, for my thirty-minute daily commute from my flat in North London down to the London School of Economics near the banks of the Thames. I drove it in the drizzle of damp, slippery rush-hour mornings and back through dark and foggy winter evenings, driving on the English "wrong" side of the road. I had several near misses.*

My mother managed to keep her own counsel. My stepfather had wisely observed that raising objections and expressing fears would not keep me from the Vespa; it would just make all of us anxious. I only learned this story decades later. At the time, the hidden message in that maternal silence communicated trust. Perhaps I drove more prudently, not having to experience my Vespa as an act of defiance.

I was well into my twenties before I began to appreciate my stepfather. When he married my mother, I was not quite eleven. My own father, whom I missed terribly, had died a little more than a year before. During that year I was, briefly, the man of the house. My stepfather was, simultaneously, displacing my beloved father and displacing me. He was a man without much formal learning but with a good deal of emotional wisdom, comfortable with himself and deeply kind to my mother. He was also concerned about the adjustment of his own son, just seven months my senior, who had recently lost his mother. My new stepbrother, sharing my room, further displaced me from the entitled role of only child. We occupied the same physical space, but not the same emotional space.

The two of them, father and son, were aliens in my house. The new family script called for me to make them feel welcome. I did not. The cruelty of a child can be breathtaking. I looked for every possible flaw in my stepfather, comparing him uncharitably with my own father. One of my joys as a precocious small boy had been learning things from my father, who had a lively wit and was a wonderful dinner-table teacher. I had delighted pleasing him with my burgeoning knowledge of facts—the names of the planets, the capitals of states, the batting averages of Dodgers and Yankees. I decided my stepfather was not very bright. I relentlessly tested his factual knowledge, and found it wanting. For a short while, until my mother firmly put a stop to it, I decided that my nickname for him would be "Stu"—short for stupid. In retrospect, his patience and resilience must have been almost biblical.

A few months after meeting Sharland, when we were both twenty-five, I introduced her to my mother and stepfather, who I still considered sort of second-rate. She noticed that my stepfather was terrific—easygoing, warm, funny, friendly, and deeply patient and loving to my mother. I was flabbergasted. It was only through her eyes that I could take a fresh look at him as a person, and, belatedly, develop a kinder and closer relationship with him.

In retrospect, my own hostility to my stepfather was a transparently childish overreaction to my father's death, almost a caricature of an Oedipus complex. As a young adult, using my well-advertised intellect, I might have noticed this. Yet my juvenile misconception of my stepfather carried over into an adult blind spot. My mother, seeking to leave well enough alone, did not push me to give my stepfather a second look, only to rein in my more destructive overt behaviors. It took a new member of the family constellation—my bride—to change this particular dynamic.

A revision of family myths took even longer for my step-brother and me. We had kept in touch, but it was not until we were both in our forties and comparing notes about my mother, now approaching eighty, that we were able to move beyond our assigned roles from childhood to a compassionate understanding of who we were as people, to appreciate our common history, and to feel like brothers.

While stepchild/stepparent relations in blended families can be particularly charged, all grown children need to take a second look at their parents through their own adult eyes—whether at thirty or at fifty. Otherwise, they are likely to get stuck, developmentally, in the adolescent task of separating and thus forever keep their parents at bay to signify their own adulthood.

As we suggested in Chapter 4, a great many adults never give their childhood myths about their parents a second look, never really come to know them as people, and thus keep their parents locked in mythical family roles that neither generation likes. Developmentally, it is not easy for newly launched adults in their early twenties to cultivate enough imaginative empathy to begin seeing their parents as people. Most are too preoccupied with the necessary business of separating.

At first, the task of keeping doors open, and permitting autonomy to coexist with connectedness, either now or in the near future, falls largely to parents. As mothers and fathers of twentysomethings, unless our families are seriously pathological, we have it in our power to treat our young adult children respectfully while still being able to express love and give (carefully selected) advice—or to drive them away by infantilizing them. Later on, the initiative passes to grown children, especially when it is the parents who are stuck.

GETTING UNSTUCK

A recurring theme of this book is that *a change in any element of a system can alter the whole system and its other constituent parts.* This can be both opportunity and threat. In the short run, it can trigger conflict. As the family therapists Ivan Nagy and Geraldine Spark have written, "[E]very move toward emotional maturation represents an implicit threat of disloyalty to the system." Yet, often, the system that commands our tacit loyalty is one that none of us really likes; we wish it allowed us different roles and try to break free in order to attain those roles. By "rewriting family scripts" in the phrase of another family therapist, John Byng Hall, we can have it both ways—we can become the person we really want to be, without throwing over our family in the process. But this takes empathic skills on both sides of the generational divide, whose cultivation is richly rewarding for both.

Unexamined, assumed loyalties or obligations toward the previous generation prevent children from becoming true adults, and then often lead to resentments and conflict or distance. Some of these obligations are explicit, others are imagined— mere projections on the part of the young adult. "Many of the rules governing family relational systems are implicit, and family members are not conscious of them," Nagy writes. As long as subconscious "family scripts" and imagined localities are buried, people will tend to get stuck in old roles. By making explicit these unacknowledged felt obligations, one can allow constructive change to occur. Nagy observes, "My father will always remain my father. . . . [E]ven when I rebelled against all that he stood for, my emphatic 'no' only confirmed my emotional involvement with him."

A related theme of our book is that *any part of the system can initiate change.* A midlife parent, with newfound maturation and emotional wisdom, can let go of old parental roles and invite a more comfortable adult relationship with newly adult children. A grown child, even in the twenties, starting a career, perhaps with a new romantic partner who sees things differently, can also take steps to break out of old roles. Sometimes this emerges out of crisis; sometimes out of new insight and compassion. Either way, it takes time, discernment, and empathy. The therapist Lee Headley calls upon adult children to cultivate a capacity for "detached curiosty." Too few grown children spontaneously manage this enterprise in their twenties, and too few adults of separating children spontaneously invite it.

However, a further theme of this book is that *life offers many second chances.* The aforementioned Philip Roth, writing in the persona of Alex Portnoy in his early thirties, could depict his own father as emotionally stunted, literally and metaphorically constipated, dutiful and distant. The portrait of the "weary, afflicted" and inept father was almost cruel. Roth/Portnoy, at age thirty-three, recalled from childhood a father who was, if anything, overinvested in his son's success, but who could not manage much emotional contact. "In that ferocious and self-annihilating way in which so many Jewish men of his generation served their families, my father served my mother, my sister Hannah, but particularly me. Where he had been imprisoned, I would fly. That was his dream. Mine was its corollary: in my liberation would be his—from ignorance, from exploitation, from anonymity."

This passage is a nice rendition of Nagy's concept from family systems theory that children, even when pushing parents away, feel a sense of loyalty—an obligation to be the bearer of their unfulfilled dreams. At the same time, the felt obligation also engenders resentment of the imagined filial duty that cramps a young man's style. Roth/Portnoy's early adulthood was marked by not much empathy for his father; his project was to liberate himself, not just from ignorance but from his father's influence. Yet a quarter century later, when Roth was fifty-eight, he could write a touching, endearing memoir, *Patrimony*, deeply cherishing his father and recounting their close connection later in life. Describing his devotion to his aged father, whom he nursed with a fierce attachment, Roth wrote: "And had I, as his son, received devotion any less primitive and slavish? Not always the most enlightened devotion—indeed, devotion from which I already wanted to be disentangled by the time I was sixteen and feeling myself beginning to be disfigured by it, but devotion that I now found gratifying to be able to requite. . . ."

Adam Hochschild, in his autobiography *Half the Way Home*, writes of the longing he felt as a child for a more authentic connection with his formal, distant father, a mining magnate. Looking back, nearing age fifty, Adam wrote that his mother "was sensitive enough to know there was something wrong between her husband and her son, but she dared not look too closely. She almost seemed to hope that if she would just act as if Father and I were the best of friends, sooner of later we would be." She, too, was playing her part in the family script; to attempt change would have invited unacceptable conflict.

Writing about his college years, Hochschild recalls:

> "If the story of Father and me were a play, it would call, at about this point in the action, for a scene of dramatic conflict . . . I pound my fist on his desk and say: Lay off! Stop telling me how to run my life. . . . It's *you* I'm rejecting. I don't want to be like *you*. . . . But all this never happened. . . . We fought not like wrestlers but like diplomats. . . . Thus, there was no pivotal episode to our play, no catharsis, no release. Instead, I could cope with the pressure I felt from him only by putting thousands of miles between us. In the end I asserted my independence not by a scene of violent confrontation but by exiting from the stage."

Only in his eighties, after Adam's mother has died, does the father begin softening somewhat. There is a bit of sweetness yet to be reclaimed, but it doesn't compensate for a lifetime of distance. Adam, a self-consciously devoted father, asks: "Will my children feel towards me as I did toward Father and as he did toward [his father]? Or have I broken the chain at last?"

Sissela Bok, the daughter of the distinguished Swedish social critics Gunnar and Alva Myrdal, wrote a biographical memoir, *Alva Myrdal,* in an attempt to come to terms with her parents, especially her mother, Alva. Both of her parents were extremely strong-willed; and in order to carve out a life of her own, Alva at times separated herself from both her husband and her three children, at one point living apart from Gunnar, at another point leaving her children with Gunnar's mother while she joined Gunnar in America. Gunnar, like many great men, gave himself mostly to his work, and not much to his family. Of her mother, Sissela Bok writes: "I have found layers and variations in my own memories and in my diaries concerning the complicated woman whose depth and many-sidedness I only gradually came to understand." By the time she composed this book, Bok could acknowledge complex feelings, including regrets that her mother sometimes subordinated family to career, but she had learned enough about who her mother was, as a person, to understand her charitably. Children of exceptionally gifted and powerful parents, she writes, "live in fields of force that can draw them in and risk turning them into hapless satellites. . . . or self-pitying, bitter antipodes. . . . How can they share in the energy and richness of such lives without being undone as individuals?"

OUR PARENTS AND OUR SELVES

In recent years, we have noticed the appearance of memoirs by sons such as Adam Hochschild and James Carroll expressing regret that they never were able to attain desired closeness with fathers, even as mature adults. A number of women writers, ranging from Sissela Bok to Sara Lawrence Lightfoot, Alice Walker, and Doris Kearns Goodwin, have written books attempting to grasp more about the lives of their mothers and fathers. There have been several other works of grown children making an honest effort to demythologize their parents and figure out who they were, as people. This is no mean feat. The popular 1989 baseball movie *Field of Dreams*, based on the W. P. Kinsella novel *Shoeless Joe*, is an elaborate fantasy that is in part about a son's desire to know and vindicate his father. There is an electric moment in a dreamlike sequence when the son encounters his father on a ball field as a young man about his own age. This must be every son's fantasy—what was my father really like at my age? In real life, of course, none of us gets to do this. But we can know more about who they were, and are. Coming to know our parents as people rather than as powerful mythic presences requires effort, compassion, and precisely "detached curiosity."

Grown children frequently find themselves at odds with their parents, often over choices of career, political values, marital partner, lifestyle, and so on. Often, these ostensible "value" conflicts, though legitimate and real, are also proxies for deeper conflicts over authority, hierarchy, respect, and loyalty. In later life, sons and daughters who were unable to heal old divisions may experience profound regret. The counterpart emotion, in the older parent, may be proud, bitter distance—regret of a different sort.

To be a mature adult, capable of both autonomy and connection, is to pursue a mature relationship with one's parents, and with one's intimate partner, and often, in time, with grown children. If such a relationship is just not attainable, one at least needs to come to terms with that painful reality and mourn what was not to be.

Robert Karen writes that staying angry with one's parents well into adulthood "is a way of staying enmeshed. If a man repeatedly sticks the knife of rage into his mother for what she did to him when he was little, it's not the past that's killing him but the knifings themselves, whether they come out in actual encounters with the mother, in bitter complaints to others, in restaging his mother dramas with his wife, or only in his fantasies."

Even in situations that are not pathological or overtly conflictual, revising childhood conceptions of parents is often difficult. One woman whom we interviewed, Allegra, who is an African American surgeon, tells a particularly poignant story— with a universal ring to it. Her parents, both immigrants to the United States from the Caribbean, divorced when she was twelve. She adored her father, was much more distant with her strict, disciplinarian mother. Of her mother, she says, that "her loving me was buying me the proper clothes, the proper shoes, making sure I had the right books for school. When I moved out of the house to go to college, she called on the phone and she was by herself for the first time and she was in tears. I had rarely ever seen her cry. . . . And she said to me on the phone, 'I just want you to know that I love you.' I don't think I had ever heard her say that. I had to be away from home for her to finally break down her defenses, and let me know that she loved me and probably for me too, to be able to say 'I love you too' back. For a long time, growing up, I didn't like my mother. We never saw things the same way. And today, finally, we've gotten our relationship straightened out. I think it's because of my having children. She's a great grandmother, openly adoring and affectionate."

In contrast, Allegra's relationship with her father when she was young was entirely positive. "You always knew if you were going to fall, Daddy would catch you." She describes her distress when her father remarried. She declined to go to the wedding. "It was silly," she says. "I was, like, twenty-five years old. I was a big girl. But I thought there would be someone more important for him." Inevitably, the relationship changed. "He would tell me things about his relationship with his wife. I really didn't want to hear it. To be honest with you, I listened and tried to be a friend, but I did not like the role reversal in the least. And that's the problem I've had with my dad, that after many, many years of him being the ultimate Daddy, now when he turned around and wanted to be my friend, I was unable to be a friend to him, because I could not make the transition."

A parent, even in close and loving relationships, is not exactly just a good friend. The legacy of one's childhood lingers, as does a residual parental authority. But in fortunate families, parents and grown children do experience each other as friends. They respect each other's opinions, cherish the common history, and enjoy each other's company. To attain this requires a mutual letting go of the roles of childhood.

Making that transition—abandoning the lines of hierarchy and reaching for a measure of moral and emotional equality—is critical in completing the task of emotionally leaving the parental home and achieving personal authority in living. If a parent remains the psychological parent (in terms of protecting, nurturing, guiding, etc.), then the offspring, as in Allegra's story, is still psychologically a child.

It is astonishing, and a little depressing, to realize how many accomplished and thoughtful adults, well into late middle age, are still recapitulating patterns from childhood or adolescence in which their sense of self requires distancing from parents.

One man in his early sixties, a college professor and himself the parent of grown children, explained how all of his life he has kept himself safe from feeling suffocated by an overbearing mother by just not sharing very much about his achievements with her, or letting himself show much emotion in her presence. This pattern, of course, reinforces the overfunction/underfunctioning dynamic that we discussed in Chapter 3. This mother is now ninety years old, frail, and in and out of nursing care. She still tries to foist food on David. It still makes him physically ill when she asks him to eat off her plate. This pattern of distancing from parents almost inevitably, spills over subconsciously into distancing in other relationships.

One as wise as the psychotherapist Sophie Freud Loewenstein, wrote, not long after her own mother had died, about the difficulty she had expressing compassion: "I did not gladly hold her old hand. I could not find the words of comfort that I might have found in my heart for almost anyone else. I sat next to her bed with an icy and armored heart, and waited. . . . until I could flee, in terror, lest her spirit would invade me and defeat my life-long struggle to be separate and different. . . . I dreaded any intrusion on my boundaries from her, to the extent that I could not tolerate her asking me the most trivial question. . . . I believe my exaggerated need for independence is still related to my dread of being invaded by mother."

The point is not that we need to revisit our aging parents out of duty, or guilt, much less pity. It is in our own interest to build more authentic connections, to make ourselves whole people. And sometimes, parents need to take the initiative and let their children in on painful or shameful secrets.

Another family whom we interviewed—call them the Millers—had reasonably cordial if cool relationships between the parents, now in their late fifties, and their grown children. The Miller family was not in the habit of sharing emotional information. Anne Miller, the mother, had had a very rough childhood. Her parents had divorced when she was young. Her own father had started another family. He didn't bother to come to her wedding. In this family, the style was to sweep painful matters under the rug, even to disdain family ties. Anne had not been told of the deaths of two grandparents in time to attend their funerals. After a second divorce, her mother became depressed and then increasingly needy, dependent, relentlessly critical and demanding. She did not like Anne's husband, and made that clear to Anne. "At that point, the only good contact was no contact," Anne told us.

Anne shared little of this bleak history with her daughter, Emily, who seemed baffled by the distance between her mother and grandmother. In our interview with her, Emily said: "There's a lot of tension between my parents and their parents. It's kind of a hands-off topic. A little information comes along now and then . . . I can only guess there's unresolved issues. Or that it's just too painful. Sometimes it's like Vroom! It's like a neon sign goes up: Do Not Enter."

She added that when her grandmother telephoned, "It was okay for me to say my mom's not here. Nobody told me to do that, but it was okay for me to lie on the phone because my mom wouldn't want to talk to her. It was like, it's okay to just disrespect this person. . . . In some cultures, respect is inherent and implicit, but not in my family."

Anne had just not felt comfortable sharing with Emily much about her painful childhood or her conflicts with her mother. So her daughter saw only the baffling end product—the bitter, guilt-ridden cutoff. Because she had never been entrusted with much of her mother's story, she tended to judge her mother harshly rather than compassionately. She said, wistfully, "I wish I knew them more as people. I never will know them as people." And Anne, a little wistfully too, confirmed: "We don't really sit down and have big intimate talks, with any of the children. I don't seem to know how." But either generation can take the initiative to break the emotional silences.

FROM HIERARCHY TO EQUALITY

Donald Williamson, the family therapist who coined the term "former parent," explores how parents and grown children can pursue relationships of genuine equality. For this to occur, young adults need not abandon their parents, but rather shift to appropriate relationships based more on adult equality rather than hierarchy. By overturning the implicit assumption that parents are still in charge of their lives, young adults are substantially freed of parental ghosts. "Leaving home," in this sense, "means taking emotional responsibility for one's life" and "no longer being programmed by the transgenerational script. The adult is no longer compelled to work upon the unresolved problems of previous generations. . . . 'Leaving home' means the [younger] adult generation no longer yearns for validation from the older generation, as far as appearance, job, marriage, children, values, and life style are concerned. Perhaps toughest of all to negotiate, 'leaving home' means that the adult is no longer controlled by nor required to make restitution for parental 'goodness' or 'badness,' or for the more tragic aspects of parent vulnerability and failure, whether past or present, real or imaginary." Children can still appreciate real-world parents for what they have done, but not treat them as figures of mythic power to be venerated or slain.

This insight is easy to misinterpret. As adult children, we can enjoy the respect and appreciation of our "former parents," but by letting go of the hierarchical relationship we no longer make decisions *in order to* seek that respect. We are freed to follow our own hearts. We are less whipsawed by real or imagined parental expectations. It is that self-confidence and mutual respect that creates the possibility of an adult kind of trust and intimacy.

This task may be premature for people still in their twenties, because few people under thirty have lived long enough to have given up their romantic myths, positive or negative, about life and about their parents. Most newly separating adults do not yet have children of their own, an event that forces a reappraisal of the previous generation as well as the succeeding one. And few people in their twenties have thought seriously about death, a task that Williamson believes to be a precondition for attaining "a genuine compassion for the people who used to be [one's] parents." He adds: "Children do not 'know' parents except as 'parents,' and have no direct knowledge of the inner world of experience of the man and woman who used to be 'mommy' and 'daddy.' Knowing the man and woman behind the parental roles is the essence of the change process."

Such insights and changes can occur via life experience, via deliberate efforts to gain dispassionate understanding of one's parents, or through psychotherapy. As Ivan Nagy suggests, "relational integrity" is realized when the younger generation attains a kind of psychological equality with the older. This recalls the distinction in political science between *power* and *authority*. The former is based on command; the latter is consensual. As adults, we still enjoy the unique ties of family, based on a common emotional and genetic history. But in a family where hierarchy no longer rules, the authority accorded parents by adult children, the respect for their life experience, their wisdom and achievements, is earned and freely given rather than simply a felt obligation based on nominal status or mythic role.

Our own belief is that the shift from a hierarchical relationship to one of greater equality and compassion is a gradual and lifelong process and, above all, a reciprocal one. Older parents who are overly invested in the parent role can contribute to conflict and pained distance in their offspring, regardless of the chronological age. Conversely, wise fifty-year-old parents of a college freshman can encourage the process of healthy separation which allows true self-knowledge and adult friendship to emerge.

The intuitive sense in a family of loyalty and obligation can be functional or dysfunctional. We may honor it or resist it, in ways that make us feel good or bad about ourselves. Ivan Nagy uses the compelling metaphor of the family as a multigenerational account book, a complex system of obligations incurred and debts repaid over time and across generations. According to Nagy, we may have an accumulation of unpaid family debts, which we transfer into later intimate relationships. A "symptom" in a particular individual, for example, might be a sign that the family's emotional ledger is unbalanced.

For instance, a son who has lost a father may become an overly involved father to his own son, in an effort to compensate for the loss by giving his son (and himself) the fathering that he never had. His over-engagement with his son may perplex and alienate the child's mother, who was not part of the father's original family system and who considers herself the primary parent. The tension around appropriate mother and father roles may leave the son feeling responsible for parental conflict; the son may well end up bearing symptoms, while the parents "triangulate" and define the problem as residing in the son rather than the intergenerational family. Yet the source of the problem is not some defect in the son but an unacknowledged imbalance in the family system. This pattern can be disentangled, either with therapy or through individual growth, when the father backs off and allows his son to become his own person and his wife and their son to have their own authentic relationship. As the son comes to understand something of his father's experience, he can assert his own needs charitably rather than angrily.

A mother who has always felt rejected by her own mother may attempt to balance the family account book by being (at least overtly) devoted to her daughter, who in turn is implicitly asked to make up for her mother's pain, giving her the love and attention she lacked in her childhood. As the family therapist Lynn Hoffman observes, the daughter may harbor inexplicably negative, hostile feelings toward her "devoted" mother, who is really tending to her own needs in the guise of caring for her child.

Children may be well into adulthood before these under- and overpayments get sorted out, if at all. The daughter can perhaps, by knowing her mother's story, understand that her mother's unintended exploitation of her was motivated by the mother's own deprivation. Perhaps she can then forgive her mother, Hoffman writes. Or perhaps the mother can come to see that she has unwittingly used her daughter to make up for her own mother's limitations and change her behavior and expectations. But both will need to let go of their roles and view each other, compassionately, as people.

Nagy sees patterns like this as not invariably destructive, but as sustaining of intimate family ties, though sometimes awkwardly. His work attempts to shift the focus to resources rather than pathologies, and to acknowledgment and acceptance rather than blame. Nagy invokes the philosophy of Martin Buber, especially Buber's concept of "healing through meeting," in which protagonists come to see each other empathically as an "I" and a "Thou." Nagy believes that there are intrinsic opportunities in every significant relationship for "meeting"—discovering new opportunities for refreshing connections. Any member of the family system can initiate a process of restoring meaning and viability to a relationship, even in the midst of injustices and mistrust. Forgiveness is key to halt the cycle of reactive blaming and hurting process, which Nagy calls "the chain of displaced injustices." All of this requires that we cultivate a capacity for flexibility and intergenerational compassion. Few endeavors in life are simultaneously so empowering and so ennobling.

KNOWING OUR PARENTS, AGAIN

If we find ourselves in midlife with awkward or strained connections to our parents, it's possible to make reconnection into a kind of personal research project. Family therapists working in the tradition of Murray Bowen encourage middle-aged sons and daughter to pursue projects similar to genealogical histories with extended families. These efforts can help to dissipate conflict and lead to more authentic connections all around. Letters, e-mail correspondence, and visits to long-lost relatives can be part of the strategy.

Monica McGoldrick, who is trained as a family therapist but who has invented far-flung applications, has written a lovely book titled *You Can Go Home Again*, using family-systems techniques to better understand famous families and, by extension, ordinary ones. McGoldrick writes: "By learning about your family and its history and getting to know—over several generations—what made family members tick, how they related, how they got stuck, you can consider your own role, not simply as victim or reactor to your experiences but as an active player in interactions that repeat themselves. Learning about your family heritage can free you to change your future."

By pursuing a kind of family history project, it is possible to transcend assigned roles. You can learn to pose questions, and adopt a posture of genuine and nonjudgmental curiosity that you are unlikely to achieve in the course of ordinary daily intercourse. Bowen advised his students to begin with just the facts. Emotional issues are too loaded for a first conversation. But in asking about facts, one invariably elicits emotional information that emerges in the way personal and family histories are described. Some family members may feel pleased and flattered by your interest. Others may be extremely wary, at least initially. But in the course of pursuing such a family project, it becomes possible to ask respectful questions about loaded subjects that would otherwise seem impertinent. This can open up forbidden topics in a context that feels uncharacteristically safe. Simply the act of pursuing such a project changes the usual family dynamics. But, as the family therapist Peter Titelman cautions, "Family of origin work should not be undertaken as a way to change one's family. Rather, it is something done for self."

The technique includes constructing a special kind of family tree known as a *genogram*. This diagram indicates not just births, deaths, marriages, and lineages but also disruptions and cutoffs. It indicates whether relationships were close or conflictual. As you learn more about your family, going back at least to your grandparents' generation, you can fill in these blanks, both literally and empathically. Having gained greater insight about the struggles faced by earlier generations in your own family, you can come to understand your own parents and siblings with more compassion and thereby defuse emotional tripwires. Sometimes, people can benefit from some coaching from a family therapist before embarking on such a project. Some people manage it spontaneously.

The very process of undertaking such an enterprise transforms how you imagine yourself in relation to your family. It forces you to step out of role. It is empowering. It also shakes up well-worn assumptions about how you and other family members are "supposed to" interact. People who undertake such projects often find that their curiosity gets engaged, and their reactivity gets damped down. For those of us trying to come to terms with parents who have died, these conversations can yield new information and insights.

This process also yields family secrets—things that many people in the family actually knew, but which were not to be spoken of. The very process of carrying around such a secret takes energy and slightly warps other relationships. Sharing such secrets, especially with a younger family member, can be a relief and can invite closer and more authentic connection or reconnection. Sometimes, family secrets are just blurted out. If we have our radar on, this can be an opportunity for greater exploration and understanding.

Bob recalls: *When we were in our mid-forties, we found ourselves on a long car trip, chatting about longevity in our respective families. From the backseat, my mother chimed in:* "Well, your great-grandmother lived to be ninety-six."

She did? What great-grandmother?

"Grandpa Kuttner's mother, Amy," *she replied,*

"But you always said that Grandpa was an orphan."

Awkward pause. It gradually came out that my grandfather and his young mother had been abandoned by his father, while my grandfather was still an infant. The father apparently fled to Mexico and was never heard from again. This was in 1880. Amy, the young mother, shamed and humiliated, fell into a state of melancholia. Eventually, she was sent to New York's public asylum at what was then called Welfare Island. Today, she would have been put on Prozac or referred to a therapy group. At Welfare Island, they decided nothing was seriously wrong with her, and they put her to work helping out in the kitchen. By then, the family, mortified by the desertion and uneasy about Amy, didn't want to take her in and there was no place for her to go. So she remained on Welfare Island—for seventy years!

My grandfather, meanwhile, was raised by two aunts. He, and later my father, my aunt and uncle, would visit Grandma Amy on Sundays. She outlived my grandfather, and died at

Welfare Island in the 1950s. Seventy years at a public asylum. No wonder nobody told us about Great-grandmother Amy. As the Jews say, this major family skeleton was nicht for the kinder. My generation was just told that Grandpa was an orphan. After my cousins and I grew up, no one got around to setting the record straight. In our forties, we were still kinder.

A few things began to fall into place after hearing this story. My grandfather had always struck me as a nervous and austere man, but he also wrote sentimental poetry. How had this history affected him and the kind of father he tried to be? My aunt, the oldest of his children, was a lifelong rebel. She eloped at age eighteen. All three of his children worked for my grandfather's small accounting firm at one time or another, but their relationship with him was not easy. An accountant and a frustrated poet! What sort of compensations was my grandfather trying to make in his relationship with his children? How did this affect the way my father connected with me? What did he and my grandmother give each other? After hearing this story, I sought out my aunt, the only child of my grandfather then living, and started putting together pieces of the puzzle. This was the beginning of my effort to understand my father's family just as people.

Exploring one's family of origin, almost as an anthropologist with an attitude of detached curiosity, one often grasps that different members of one's family have different "truths." Different siblings in the same family have very different childhoods and different experiences of what it is like to be a member of the family. By adopting, temporarily, the role of chronicler or biographer, we can partially let go of our own hang-ups about our family and view family members more dispassionately, and hence more compassionately.

This work should not be undertaken casually. It should never be undertaken if the real motivation is to settle a score. The more alienated and dysfunctional the family, the more care is required. Simply the resolve to put aside old grudges and wounds and the project of approaching your extended family with dispassionate respect and curiosity will feel empowering, and will help put others at ease. McGoldrick adds, "If you want to reconnect with your family, you will need to develop a kind of empathy which recognizes that you and your family belong to each other. . . . The grown-up child who truly has an individual identity can be generous to a critical, distant father without becoming defensive, even when that father continues to be critical."

Either party to a difficult or distant relationship can initiate change. But it is the initiator who needs to change his or her behavior rather than mounting a crusade to change the other. As we have suggested, by changing your own routine you change the dynamic of the system.

"Imagine," suggest family therapists Barry Dym and Michael Glenn, "interviewing a parent who had hurt you badly when you were a child. For years you keep your distance but eventually you want to know more about the story of your life; and the only way to find out is to reacquaint yourself with this feared or hated parent. After a series of interviews and with time to think about them, you don't exactly adore the parent, but a fondness, a sense of having shared a common history, emerges and becomes more important. You even look forward to meetings despite the fact that he or she will continue, in some way, to hurt your feelings."

Jack LaForte, as a family therapy intern, pursued his own project to develop more authentic one-on-one connections to each family member. He began by learning more about them and by taking a dispassionate look at family patterns.

His family, like many overly entangled families, was characterized by bouts of conflict alternating with periods of distance. The pattern included a great deal of "triangulating," in which other family members butted in to try and mediate between those having the conflict: "My mother would be stressed by my absence. She would complain to my father, who was in a more passive position. He would eventually agree with her and become active; then they would both attack me for not writing or calling. I would become defensive, then reactive, and a big argument would result. The cutoff would last one to two months, until some . . . event or holiday would open things up again. My sister, who had her own family and who was in a more outside position, would help to smooth things out by encouraging each 'camp' to understand the other 'camp's' feelings." Over a period of fifteen years, LaForte reported, little had changed.

LaForte made an afford to change his own role on the family dynamics, reversing his usual behavior, becoming more emotionally available, and initiating instead of avoiding contact. He stopped relying on his sister as mediator. Instead of getting defensive, he used paradox and gentle humor. Food was a big issue in his family. His parents, from a large Italian family, were always urging him to eat more. During one visit, instead of his usual routine of asking his parents to please stop offering food that he didn't want, he announced that he was really hungry. "At each meal I had an excess of at least one course, such as meat or dessert. Before the main meal, I asked my parents why we were having only one entree instead of two." His parents "finally commented that I might get sick if I ate so much." LaForte adds, "Since that weekend, my parents have backed off a lot in offering me food when I do not want it."

Arguments about food, of course, are rarely about food. They are about love and about power. By seeing the humor in a situation and disarming an old pattern, it's possible to turn food back into just food. By learning more about who each of his family members were, and working to develop one-on-one connections with each, LaForte gained the insight and courage to change patterns that nobody really liked—not by forcing others to change but by changing what he did. His family, in turn, became a lot easier to take.

Another therapist, Ellen Benswanger, reports on her efforts to reconnect with a branch of her immediate family, after decades of cutoff. Her mother was her father's second wife. His first wife had died of a brain tumor, leaving him with a grown son and two teenage daughters. The other children resented their father's second marriage. After Benswanger's own mother died, there ensued bitter fights and misunderstandings over a will, and the two branches of the family just stopped communicating.

Many years later, in middle age, she initiated contact by writing a kind letter to one of her half sisters, now seventy-two. She visited the family cemetery and placed flowers on the grave of her father's first wife, a gesture that her half sister appreciated. After several exchanges of letters, the half sisters decided to meet. Benswanger reports:

> Needless to say, my anxiety level was exceedingly high. . . . In the initial meetings with my sisters and their families, I tried to maintain a position of curious detachment. I asked questions about their children, grandchildren, family milestones and moves. . . . I noted the warmth and ease with which one sister greeted me and the coolness and apparent suspicion in the other. I tried not to react emotionally or to form premature conclusions about either response. . . . I had brought a collection of family pictures, some dating from before the cut-off had occurred. The photographs evoked a range of reactions from my sisters, from nostalgic reminiscences to angry questions ("What happened to our mother's dishes? Who took the figurines that used to sit on the mantel?"). They also led to detailed descriptions of parallel events, disappointments, and frustrated ambitions. For the first time, I was able to empathize with their sense of grief and loss and I began to see some portions of family history from their point of view.

Benswanger concludes with some thoughts about how this project affected her as a person: "I am learning to ask more appropriate questions and to direct my curiosity to other events and people in the extended family. . . . The process of reconnecting has generated some vivid insights and clarified certain patterns in my personal as well as professional relationships. I have been made aware of my tendency to dichotomize 'good' and 'bad' qualities in others, my readiness to assume the role of rejected child, and my chronic ambivalence about expressing anger."

Revisiting our families of origin is not easy work. Sydney Reed, a Bowen-trained therapist who coaches people in revisiting their families, recounts the story of teaching a course for pastoral counselors. Attendance was almost perfect until the day the class was asked to each describe their own families. Reed recalls pointing out to those who made it that half the class was not there, that perhaps this assignment was creating some anxiety. "I'm so glad you said that," one woman commented. She added that on the way the class she had had to pull the car over three times, to vomit. "This can really be a gut-wrenching process," Reed observes.

One of the most remarkable family chronicles of recent years is James McBride's 1995 bestseller, *The Color of Water*. McBride, a journalist and jazz saxophonist, is the son of an African American musician and preacher-father, and a mother who was the daughter of racist Orthodox Jews in the Deep South. McBride only learned about his mother's history in the course of a series of taped interviews with her that resulted in his book.

The mother, Rachel Shilsky, was in flight from an abusive father, a shopkeeper and part-time rabbi who was brutal to both his wife and children and vicious to his black customers. As a teenager, young Rachel found comfort and acceptance mainly in her black friends. At fifteen, she already had a black boyfriend, had become pregnant and had an abortion. At twenty, she left her family for good and never came back. Eventually, she married Andrew McBride, began going by the name Ruth, and became for all intents and purposes part of the black community. "Rachel Shilsky is dead as far as I'm concerned," she told her son James in one of several extended interviews. "She had to die in order for me, the rest of me, to live." Until James succeeded in persuading her to recount her history, she had never told any of this story to her children. Asked about her race, she would say, "I'm light-skinned."

After several such conversations with his mother, James took a trip south to see what else he could find out about his abusive Orthodox Jewish grandfather. In a small town in southern Virginia, next door to the address his mother had provided, he found an elderly black man named Thompson who remembered the Shilsky family well. James recounts:

I told him my business: Mother used to live here. Name was Shilsky. A little store. He fingered his glasses and stared at me a long time. Then he said, "C'mon in here."

He sat me down and brought me a soda. Then he asked me to tell my story one more time. So I did.

He nodded and listened closely. Then his face broke into a smile. "That means you ol' Rabbi Shilsky's grandson."

First he chuckled. Then he laughed. Then he laughed some more. He tried to control his laughing but he couldn't, so he stopped, took off his glasses, and wiped his eyes.

Eventually, James McBride asks more detailed questions about his grandfather. Thompson uneasily replies: "You won't find anyone around here who liked him enough to even talk about him."

"Why so?"

"His dislike for the colored man was very great."

"How so?"

"Well, he just disliked black folks. And he cheated them. Sold' em anything and everything and charged 'em as much as he could. If you owed him five dollars he'd make you pay back ten. He shot ol' Lijah Ricks in the stomach. . . . He was a hateful one, Old Man Shilsky. His own wife was scared of him."

McBride began seriously exploring his family history after realizing he was stuck professionally, having walked away from one good journalism job after another. He was torn between pursuing his music and his writing. "There were two worlds bursting inside me trying to get out. I *had* to find more about who I was, and in order to find out who I was, I had to find out who my mother was."

"It was a devastating realization, coming to grips with the fact that all your life you had never really known the person you loved the most. . . . It sent me tumbling through my own abyss of sorts, trying to salvage what I could of my own feelings and emotions, which would be scattered to the winds as she talked."

For James McBride, the project of learning his mother's real history was complicated by questions of race. The exotic story she told only made the exploration more intense. Yet all of our families are potentially fascinating, since they are our own history; and all such explorations help us come to know our families as people.

You don't have to be a psychotherapist or a gifted biographer, or to have a family story as remarkable as James McBride's, to undertake a fresh exploration of your own family. The enterprise of finding out more about your family is a very democratic one; just about anyone can do it. Some grown children, like Rachel Shilsky, require a total cutoff from their own parents in order to survive. But most, like her son James McBride, find reconnections with parents emotionally liberating.

Over the course of a lifetime, we grow up and our parents often grow. By acknowledging each other's growth, we grow. Adult children who lack the maturity to engage parents constructively at thirty may have new reserves of insight and compassion at forty or fifty.

Bob recalls: *I'm in my office, at age fifty-seven, on deadline. It's January, and outside snow is lightly falling. My mother, still alert at eighty-seven, telephones. "I hope you're planning to leave the office early," she is saying. "They're forecasting a blizzard."*

"I think I can make it home okay, Mom," I say.

"But the roads are really supposed to be terrible," she persists. "You haven't been listening to the weather reports like I have."

At an earlier time, I might have felt irritated and belittled. I'm fifty-seven years old and she's still treating me like a little kid. And I might have kept it all inside in order to protect her from my wrath. But I reflect for a minute. I'm not really angry, I'm bemused. After all, she's alone. She worries. But there's not much harm or threat to my self-esteem in her behavior any more. Still, it's constructive—and conducive to a more authentic connection—to let her know she's a little out of line. "Mom," I say gently, "you know, I travel all over the world. It almost sounds like you don't trust my judgment."

"Of course I trust your judgment," she replies, backing off. "I guess I'm just being a mother." In twenty-five years, we've

both learned a few things. She is still capable of reverting to Jewish mother. But we both see the humor in it. And I am able to let her know, respectfully, when she's overdoing it. It's okay to push back gently; she won't break. The flip side is: my manhood is no longer tied up with keeping her at a safe distance. Because I've changed my routine, we're better friends. Most important, I don't mind that she cares about me.

Chapter 9
From Parents to Grandparents

In a few short years, separating young adults find themselves in early midlife—often marrying, having children, advancing or shifting careers. And their parents are now in later midlife, becoming grandparents and on the verge of retirement. The train has moved on.

For the purposes of our narrative, this evolution presents new opportunities—for distance or reparation. As we suggested in the last chapter, people in their twenties, who, in Donald Williamson's terms, lacked the life experience to see their parents as people, may have gained new emotional capacity—or new needs for support. Their own odysseys may have revived issues and questions that they assumed were long buried or moot. Conflicts may turn into crises that produce either painful distance or satisfying resolution. Older adults, becoming grandparents, may have softened and attained a new level of wisdom, or they may have grown "set in their ways" and embittered.

The shift in role from parent to in-law and then from parent to grandparent can often shake up family patterns in a constructive way. It can be a time of second chances for older parents, of emotional growth and greater compassion for the new mother and father. In some our families, the words, "Someday you will be a parent and you will understand," were uttered more as a frustrated curse than a promise of future blessing. But this declaration contains a large germ of compassionate truth if it is understood as empathic rather than retributive.

The role of grandparent can be sweetness itself. The psychologist Mary Pipher wisely observes that "Parents and grandparents have very different roles. Parents have the job of socializing children and of raising them to be emotionally sturdy, responsible and independent people. Grandparents mostly have the job of loving them for who they are." Grandparents are quick to pull out photos of their grandchildren, in part from the sheer joy of the relationship but also because fresh, new life in the family represents continuity and renewal at a time when older people are conscious of the shortness of time.

There is a joke told among the Florida retired set about the group of grandmothers who just could not stop crowing about their grandchildren. After a while, they all admitted the conversations were getting a bit tedious, so they agreed on ground rules. Each grandma with a new grandchild was entitled to just three words of description. One new grandma, just back from a visit to see her first grandchild, looked absolutely blissful and for a moment was speechless. Then she spoke, eyes shining dreamily: "You could *die!*"

Jokes, as Freud pointed out, often have unintended double meanings. This joke is funny because it expresses the exaggerated emotions that grandmothers often indulge. This grandmother evidently means: you could die of joy, you could just die because the baby is so beautiful, so precious, so lovely. But consider the literal words. The family lineage is continuing and life is complete. Now you could, with a clear conscience, die.

Arthur Kornhaber, a psychiatrist who specializes in the grandparents' role in the family constellation, observes: "The basic biological urge to assure the survival of the child is something that grandparents and parents have in common. From there on, however, grandparents have a very different experience with children, and frankly, grandparents have the best of it." Why? As every grandparent knows, you are not the one primarily responsible, and visits are usually time-limited. You are rarely the disciplinarian and it is okay to be a little indulgent.

One grandma interviewed by Kornhaber said, "I was much shorter with my own children. I know I was. And with your own kids, you're always worrying about their schooling and whether they get along with their friends and whether you can afford to give them every advantage. It's not that I don't have concerns about my grandchildren. I'd do anything for them. But I don't have to! That's the point. The parents are the ones who are in charge. I'm off duty on that score. So when I'm with the kids, it's practically a holiday."

Many grandparents see their new role as a gentler reprise of parenthood, reflecting increased wisdom and increased availability of leisure time, to do right by young children. Pipher quotes a professor friend, who cherishes his role as grandfather. "When I had my own kids I was always exhausted, overworked, worried about money and stupid things like tenure. I had papers to grade. This time around I am present." Grandparents, as Pipher observes, grew up in a slower time, they slow down as they age, "and they are the only adults in America who have plenty of time for children." In a landmark survey by Kornhaber, fully 68 percent of grandparents interviewed reported that they tended not to make the same mistakes with grandchildren that they had with children.

Being a grandparent, seemingly, is all the sweetness with none of the pain. That is the popular image, anyway. But a lot of grandparents don't get to have that experience, and so feel doubly cheated.

NEW PARENTS, OLD PATTERNS

The birth of a baby, like a marriage, is a life event that triggers primal issues of loyalty, autonomy, control—issues that can blindside even seemingly well-adjusted families. Adult children may grow up to be parents who are self-confident—or anxious and tentative. We really have no clear idea how we will adjust to the role of becoming a parent until we become one. Until the birth of children, a young couple may be doing well enough, only to have a new baby trigger all sorts of latent conflicts. A couple that adjusted nicely to marriage may find, to their bewilderment, that they have entirely different tacit working models from their own families about how a mother or father is supposed to behave—or not behave. The task of raising a child rekindles long-buried, unfinished emotional business from one's own childhood, and in the marriage.

By the same token, the birth of a child alters what seemed to be tolerably stable relationships between an adult couple and each set of their parents. That seeming stability may or may not be built on solid foundations. As we have seen in earlier chapters, it may just be polite distance, with hidden regrets or resentments. When a mother and father have their first child, they are usually thrust back into a more intimate connection with their own parents. Grandmothers are famous (or notorious) for wanting to swoop in and "take care" of daughters, and even daughters-in-law who are new mothers, and of course to make a happy fuss about the beautiful new baby.

Sometimes this help is entirely welcome, sometimes less so. Sometimes it dovetails beautifully with what the new mother and father really want, sometimes not. Often it is genuine compassionate help. Other times, it is more about the older person's emotional needs—to be loved, appreciated, and to feel relevant. This new intimacy, whether invited or not, immediately rekindles often submerged issues between grown daughter and grandmother, for better or for worse.

Grandma's new presence also complicates the marriage. A generation or two ago, new fathers were mostly absent from the birth tableau, nervously pacing outside the delivery room, passing out cigars, feeling uncommonly virtuous when they occasionally changed a diaper or performed a 2:00 a.m. feeding, and otherwise largely not part of the drama. That, mercifully, started to change thanks to the feminist revolution that began in the late 1960s. Today, fathers typically participate in childbirth classes, and spend far more time with infants than their own fathers did.

However, older adults, who grew up in a very different era, often have an entirely different conception of gender roles. Grandma, in arriving to "help" the new mother, may just take it for granted that the new father is disinterested and incompetent at the tasks of the nursery. This is, after all, women's business. That mentality, in turn, can trigger unwelcome conflicts in the marriage at a time when it is already stressed. A new mother, in addition to struggling with everything from joy to exhaustion to hormonal swings to keeping her employer at bay, has to mediate between the powerful emotions of her mother and her husband.

How a new grandparent taps into this system can produce new opportunities for intimacy, or new conflict and distance, and often both. Sometimes, it is a grandparent who is acting like a child, and the adult child who needs to initiate constructive change. The common thread here is that a young couple, who have often kept their distance from their parents during early years of marriage, is suddenly and intimately thrust back into an extended family, at a time of adjustment and vulnerability.

Psychotherapist Harriet Lerner, in her classic book *The Dance of Anger*, recounts the story of Maggie, a twenty-eight-year-old new mother whose parenting is relentlessly criticized by her own mother. "Margaret," her mother complains, "I cannot stand to hear that child cry. When a child needs to be picked up, I just can't sit here pretending I don't hear her screaming." Arguing with her mother about the particulars made no headway; something deeper was at work. The mother had never really let go of her daughter, and, paradoxically, Maggie kept giving in, in a misguided effort to protect her mother's feelings. At length, with a lot of coaching from the therapist, Maggie kept her own anger in check, stopped debating the pros and cons of picking up the baby, and changed the subject to the real issue—who is the adult. "You know, Mother," she said calmly and without anger, "Bob and I have our struggles as parents. But I think we're pretty good at it and that we'll get better. I'm confident that we won't ruin Amy."

In the short run, this just made the mother assert more control. Eventually, in this particular episode, her mother angrily slammed the door and retreated to her room. Lerner commented: "Both Maggie and her mother were experiencing 'separation anxiety.' Maggie was leaving home."

There is seldom an epiphany in which both parties to conflict recognize the need for new patterns of relating and then live happily ever after. As Lerner observes, real, durable change will take more than one such encounter, a lot of loving persistence, and an appreciation for the paradox of autonomy. Lerner comments: "Maggie needs to show (for her own sake as well as her mother's) that she is at last declaring her independence from mother but that she is *not* declaring a lack of caring of closeness. *Independence means that we clearly define our own selves on emotionally important issues, but it does not mean emotional distance.*"

Perhaps Maggie and her mother were carrying around very old patterns of insecure attachment from childhood, in all likelihood reflecting patterns that Maggie's mother had had with her own mother. But these patterns could be changed. Either mother or daughter could take the initiative (in this case it was daughter).

Some men and women in late midlife are going through emotional upheavals that are only complicated by the arrival of grandchildren. This is especially true when relationships with their children are already frayed. While they take vicarious pleasure in a new birth, and look forward to the sweetness of the role of grandparent, subconsciously they may above all want to be wanted; to have their life wisdom acknowledged, and to be a major part of the new drama.

A woman whom we interviewed, now in her mid-sixties and fairly recently divorced, was still burdened with unfinished business with each of her three children and leftover pain from the breakup of her marriage. When we spoke with her, her youngest daughter, in her early forties, unmarried and living on the other side of the country, had just had a baby. A tender, tumultuous time. The mother had flown west to be with her daughter when the baby was born in the late spring, and then had persuaded her daughter to bring this new grandchild east, to spend several weeks with her in her house in a tiny beachfront community in New England.

For the mother, the visit was massively disappointing, leaving her with hurt feelings and lingering anger. "I don't want to be a mother anymore," she said. "I poured everything I had into being a mother. Maybe it was too much." Mother and daughter had entirely different expectations for this visit. The daughter yearned to be taken care of so she could devote herself entirely to her new baby. Her own mother felt left out of this exclusive, mother-infant dyad, and resented being relegated to errand-runner and laundress. "I couldn't do anything right," she said. "The fact that I had any needs of my own, apart from her and the baby, my daughter perceived as hostile."

Had they tried to process this? Talk about it? No. Will they? Probably not. "She'll have to be the one to initiate it. She'll have to apologize." But the daughter was consumed with her own adjustment to motherhood.

Yet life presents countless second chances. A new grandmother with exaggerated expectations for her new role, followed by disillusionment, is making a tragic mistake if she writes the relationship off. Either woman can take the lead in trying to rebuild these bridges. A little magnanimity goes a long way. However momentous the occasion for the new grandmother, it is more so for the new mother. New grandparents are wise to hold their own feelings in check, at least for a while, and to recognize that the drama belongs to the new parents.

One of the most poignant themes we have encountered is a relationship with an older parent as a kind of negative role model. Psychologists Barbara McFarland and Virginia Watson-Rouslin quote Carol-Ann, a married mother of two: "My daughter sees how I am with my mom and hopes it won't be that way with us. My daughter and I talk openly about our feelings, and she'll tell me if I'm intruding in her privacy. She is in her twenties. I think if I had done this much when I was her age, I wouldn't be resenting my mom so much now."

Denise is a thirty-five-year-old daughter of immigrant parents, and a stay-at-home mother of a son and a daughter. Her own childhood memories are not happy ones. Denise's parents split up when she was twelve, and she rarely saw her father. After the divorce, her mother became controlling and moody, bordering on cruel. She limited Denise's social life, and communicated a deep mistrust of men. Denise, however, married young, and was very relieved to get out of her mother's house.

Her own solid marriage and experience as a parent have gradually transformed her relationship with her mother. Denise says that her own childhood made her determined to be a conscientious and caring mother. She refuses to believe that children of abusive families are destined to grow up to be abusive parents themselves. As she has matured into a compassionate adult, Denise has also managed to appreciate her mother's story, which included a harsh childhood in poverty, a destructive marriage, and a bitter divorce. She has forgiven her mother—and her mother in turn has softened and become an affectionate grandmother.

Victoria Secunda, in a generally depressing book (*When You and Your Mother Can't Be Friends*) that mostly offers survival advice for grown women with hopelessly poisoned relationships with their mothers, concedes that "[M]any mothers are able to be loving to their grandchildren in ways they never could with their own children." Mothers who feel a sense of remorse about their own inadequate parenting or unsatisfying connections to their grown children have a kind of second chance to make up for it as grandmothers. But there is more to it than that.

Secunda quotes one woman, Kitty, who was intimidated by her domineering and short-tempered mother both as a child and a young adult. Kitty has resolved to keep her distance from her mother, but she is amazed at how tender and gentle her mother can be with granddaughter Julie.

"Julie is the only person my mother has ever loved unconditionally—they have a wonderful relationship. My mother is able to see how terrifying her behavior can be to a child. Once Julie dropped a glass of milk, and my mother screamed at her, just as she used to scream at me, and Julie burst into tears. My mother dropped to her knees and said, 'Oh, Julie, I'm so sorry, please forgive me.' My mother could never see *my* terror when I was a kid, but she's able to see Julie's, whom she adores and whose adoraion she wants." Kitty, according to Secunda, is somewhat ambivalent about this turn of events. She wonders why her mother could not be so empathic when she was a child; she is still wary. But the kinder face that her mother shows to Julie also opens the door to some repairwork with Kitty, if Kitty is ready for it.

For adult daughters who have had even tolerably close relationships with their mothers, the arrival of a new baby can be a wonderful time. A grandmother can function not just as a babysitter but as a source of nurturance and affirmation to a new mother. For mothers and daughters whose own relationships have been tense, a grandchild can be an opportunity for a grandmother to have a second chance, not just by interacting with a young child, but by using the time for mother and grown daughter to improve their own relationships.

Most of us really do acquire a measure of emotional wisdom as we grow older. It isn't just that grandmothers like Kitty's mother are trying to make up for having been bad mothers by showering affection on grandchildren. A woman in her sixties very likely has more self-knowledge and patience than she did in her twenties or thirties. A new mother may know little about raising children; she has never raised one. But by the time her children are grown, even if times were often difficult, she has learned a lot—about life, about parenting, and about herself.

A mother and daughter interacting with a new grandchild can begin a whole set of dialogues about how hard it is to be a new mother, or about regrets the older woman may have about her own inadequacies as a mother, or about any of the myriad emotional crosscurrents triggered by having a child. But this opportunity requires a measure of compassion on both sides of the relationship.

A SPECIAL RELATIONSHIP

As sages ancient and modern have noted, there is something quite special about the connection between grandparent and grandchild. Sometimes, a connection between a grandparent and grandchild can bring a whole family closer together. It can help bridge distances between parents and adult children.

However, the early years, when grandchildren are infants and the experience is new to both parents and grandparents, are likely to be the time of most serious adjustment. Grandparents may have their own ideas about everything from breast-feeding versus bottle-feeding to whether a crying child should be picked up to how warmly a child should be dressed. The grandparent, after all, is the experienced expert. A grandparent may use her new role to reassert authority over a grown child who has long since separated. New parents are still insecure about their own competence and still figuring out their roles as a couple. Even just a year later, however, the child is old enough to have his or her own relationship with grandparents. There are a wide variety of ways to play with a fourteen-month-old, all of them tolerably acceptable. Once a child arrives at an age when grandparents can have a one-on-one relationship, the issues of how best to keep the baby safe begin to recede and everyone can relax a little. Like every other relationship in the larger family constellation, the key to happy connections is a series of authentic one-on-one bonds, even between a seventy-year-old and a one-year-old. The beginning of trouble is the triangle.

We had a wobbly beginning as new parents, and ties with in-laws were sometimes frayed. But Bob's mother, Polly, soon developed a strong relationship with both of our kids, and for more than two decades the role of grandmother became her primary identity. As a relatively young widow living in our community, she spent a lot of time with Jess and Gabe when they were growing up. Gabe, now an actor and producer, has much in common with her first husband, Bob's father Arthur, who died at forty-one. Arthur Kuttner was an amateur actor. He and Gabe's grandmother met as teenagers, doing theater productions. Arthur, like Gabe, had a quick-witted, gentle sense of humor. Gabriel also physically resembles the grandfather he never knew. And Gabe seems to have the same knack that her husband endearingly had, to draw Polly out of herself with sweetly teasing humor.

This wonderful relationship took nothing away from us as Gabe's parents, and allowed us to see and appreciate Grandma in a new light. As a mother and mother-in-law, Grandma conveys her life wisdom, not by giving direct advice but by showing how to interact lovingly with a child.

At the same time, because of her own mother's relatively early death, observing the loving interaction between one grandmother and the kids while the other grandmother was absent sometimes caused Sharland pangs of loss. Sharland knew that this was not Grandma Polly's "fault," but the loss was nonetheless real and poignant. What is critical here is to be alert to one's own feelings, to let a relationship between child and grandparent be what it is, and not a set of issues and symbols.

If mothers and fathers remain stuck as insecure parents, or have lingering issues with their own parents, or still have emotionally loaded and unacknowledged issues in the marriage fought out through the kids, then the role of a grandparent can be an emotional minefield. On the other hand, because the grandparent-grandchild connection can be so loving and nurturing, parents are wise to take it as the gift that it is.

Rachel Naomi Remen, in her book *My Grandfather's Blessings,* vividly recalls her relationship with her grandfather, who died when she was just seven. He was an immigrant from the old country, an Orthodox rabbi. Her parents were secular and socialist. Rachel Remen grew up to be a physician and fiercely gentle healer. Judging by her career and her writings, Remen carries with her something of both her parents and her grandparents. She begins with a story, at age four, of being confused and somewhat disappointed when Grandfather told her he was giving her a present. It turned out to be a little paper cup full of dirt. "If you promise to put water in it every day, something may happen," he said mysteriously.

For three weeks she faithfully, if somewhat skeptically, put water in the little paper cup, and all but gave up expectations of anything special happening.

> But I did not miss a single day. And one morning, there were two little green leaves that had not been there the night before.

I was completely astonished. Day by day they got bigger. I could not wait to tell my grandfather, certain that he would be as surprised as I was. But of course he was not. Carefully, he explained to me that life was everywhere, hidden in the most ordinary and unlikely places. I was delighted. "And all it needs is water, Grandpa?" I asked him. "No, Neshume-le," he said. "All it needs is your faithfulness."

That was perhaps my first lesson in the power of service, but I did not understand it that way then. My grandfather would not have used those words. He would have said that we need to remember to bless the life around us and the life within us. He would have said when we remember we can bless life, we can repair the world.

Wise parents might also have given a four-year-old such a wonderful gift. But there is something about this story that seems particularly grandfatherly, never mind rabbinical. Grandparents are often the ones who have the time, and the wisdom, and the sweetness, to offer this kind of gift to a child. Parents, as well as children, should be receptive to such gifts, even if the grandparent's way is not their own. Young children are little receptors of wisdom, and it comes from multiple sources.

Reading between the lines, Rachel's parents and her grandfather must have had serious disagreements about values—an Orthodox rabbi and secular socialists. It may have been very painful to her grandfather that his grown children had their own strong views, so different from his own, about how to repair the world. But those differences did not interfere with a lovely connection between grandfather and granddaughter, who quite evidently absorbed something precious from each generation.

Of course, it is easy to appreciate the sweetness of being a grandparent in families where adults and their own parents have decent relationships. What about families where they don't?

TROUBLE IN PARADISE

Often, the idealized picture of sweet grandparenting is less easily attained today, in part because so many extended families no longer live in the same community. America was always a more mobile society than most, but fifty years ago more grandparents lived in the same communities as their children and grandchildren. Sometimes this felt confining, especially when three generations lived in the same house or on the same street. But when Grandma and Grandpa live down the block, it is less of an emotional big deal to send the children off to Grandma's to make cookies, or to have Grandpa come over to help fix a bike, toss around a ball, play a game, or just baby-sit. There is no high drama, no complex scheduling.

However, when aging parents live in Florida or Arizona, and fly in for occasional brief visits, everything is more compressed and emotionally charged. Children are expected to be on best behavior, parents are also dealing with the logistics of a visit, grandparents are living out of suitcases and fighting jet lag, and too much often gets crammed into a short time period. The result is often raised expectations, frayed nerves, disappointments, and sad relief when the visit ends. Even so, the real problems, and their solutions, are often more emotional than logistical.

Dr. Arthur Kornhaber, in a study with Kenneth Woodward of grandparents in families, found that a surprisingly large number of people who had retired to Florida experienced their retirement as a kind of exile from their families. A few had just had it with family obligations, and thoroughly enjoyed the new independence. But a larger number, usually the women, felt pained distance from families, especially from grandchildren. One women, seventy-six, told him: "I don't know what happened. We retired to this lovely place in Florida. I have eight grandchildren and I do see them a couple of times a year. I guess I don't do much of anything. I mean, I enjoy myself, but sometimes think, 'Is this what I want, to be a grandparent who is not involved with her grandchildren?'"

Divorce can lead to even greater distance between grandchildren and grandparents, who are innocent bystanders to the breakup. Even though joint custody is becoming more common, the mother is still usually the primary custodial parent. If a divorce is bitter, the mother and father often fight over the last details of visitation rights and there may be very little time to spare for parents of the non-custodial parent. When a mother remarries, the grandparents of her former spouse can seem like part of a former, no longer relevant family constellation—even though they remain biological and emotional grandparents. Courts have generally held that grandparents have no legal rights to visitation. It is up to the grandparents, sadly, to try to keep relationships alive and to wait for the grandchildren to grow old enough to begin making their own decisions, which sometimes is too late.

A divorce can also reopen wounds between parents and grown children, especially when the older parents put their own needs first and are not fully cognizant of their motivations. As in the case of the blessed event of a birth, the poignant event of a marriage breaking apart is also one that belongs to the couple. Older parents, concerned about everything from the immediate well-being of their child, to financial and domestic ramifications, their connection to grandchildren, and how it looks to relatives and neighbors, may try to intervene to patch up the marriage. Or they may, out of intended compassion, demonize the departing spouse. Neither intervention is likely to have constructive effect. What is needed is love, support, compassionate listening, and often short-term help.

The last thing a child going through a divorce needs is lectures about how parents managed to stay together through difficult times, or how divorce is a sin. Nor does a divorcing young adult need his or her parents to collude in making an ex-spouse a unique villain. Managing a divorce is hard enough, especially when there are children, without having to manage parents in the bargain.

Emily had gotten pregnant her freshman year in college. Her mother was appalled. It was her father and mother-in-law who initially provided the emotional support. Emily and her boyfriend decided to marry, and kept the baby. Her mother soon softened, and became a devoted grandma. But after five years it was clear that they had married too young. Emily was miserable, depressed, and physically ill from the stress. Again, her mother, a devout Catholic, was initially so aghast that she found it hard to be supportive. But after the divorce, both parents gave her loving help, both emotionally and financially, and became especially close to their grandchild. Mother, daughter, and grandson formed a very strong bond.

Years later, Emily's older brother, a successful man close to his father, and in a seemingly storybook marriage with beautiful children, suddenly announced that he and his wife were splitting up. His father, who had been close to his son, never got over it, and remained somewhat estranged until his death, both from his son and his son's children. Evidently, he could comfort his daughter when she made a youthful mistake, but not forgive his middle-aged son for shattering the image of a perfect family. Perhaps midlife reconnection is generally easier between mothers and daughters than between fathers and sons. Perhaps men are more likely to be tripped up by pride. But adult children of both sexes will invariably do things, serious as well as trivial, that disappoint their parents. How much better if crises are moments when we can depend on each other.

Divorces, however painful, are a time for parents and grown children to renew connections, with compassion. The stakes are even higher when there are grandchildren. Parents looking to minimize the damage to their children in divorces are wise to have some respect for the connection between children and grandparents, who may represent a more reliable and stable connection to children whose parents are in a period of emotional turbulence.

While some grandparents suffer the loss of connections because of a divorce, the opposite problem can occur. A newly single mother who is the custodial parent after a divorce may be overly reliant on her mother. The older woman, looking forward to the long-awaited, sweet, but not overly demanding role of Grandma, may suddenly find herself the primary "parent." Instead of enjoying occasional visits, she becomes the main baby-sitter. She may find herself having to parent both her grown daughter and her grown daughter's child. Over time, however, adjustment and maturity can set in, and this situation may also lead to new closeness between mother and grown daughter. We interviewed Yvonne, an African American divorced mother who has an eight-year-old child and a very demanding job. Her mother moved, to be closer to her and her grandson. "I couldn't do it without her," Yvonne told us. "We used to fight a lot when I was younger, and we still have our differences. But since David was born, we appreciate each other more. She always said I would understand once I had children of my own, and there's truth in that."

NANNIES AND GRANNIES

When President Clinton's first two nominees for U.S. Attorney General, both high-powered career women with children, got into political trouble after it was revealed that they had not paid full Social Security taxes for their children's nannies, the Reverend Jesse Jackson quipped, "In the black community, we don't have nannies, we have grannies." Here is one stereotype that contains some truth. Because of the lower median income in the black community and the higher prevalence of young unmarried mothers, grandmothers are often the backbone of the African American family.

Another landmark study of grandparenting, by the sociologists Andrew Cherlin and Frank Furstenburg, found that 44 percent of the black grandparents in the survey reported that they lived with grandchildren for three months or more, compared to 18 percent of whites. And grandparents tended to view themselves as the disciplinarian in families that seemed to them lacking in adequate authority. Eighty-seven percent of black grandparents, compared to 43 percent of white ones, reported that they often or sometimes moved to correct behavior in a grandchild they considered problematic.

One black grandma, who prided herself on brooking no nonsense from her grandchildren, told the interviewers that she was known at the local day care center as "the Sergeant." Another bought a house with four apartments for her extended family after her own husband died and her daughter was alone raising a small toddler. She said, "This child, when he came to us, he was a small child. He's fourteen now. Now that he's fourteen, I'm going to tell you right now, he's no angel. You hear me? He calls me the worst grandmother in the world, the meanest one. Because this child doesn't have a father there with us, and I was raised in a family without a father's image. So this means I've got to be a little stronger . . . he can get around his mother, but he can't get around me so well."

Particularly in poorer families generally, where rates of single parenthood are higher and the financial toll of divorce more devastating, family survival often depends on grandparents. When a young person, often not yet out of her teens, becomes a mother, she is still in many ways a child. There may be an extended period when the grandmother is the primary parent of both a daughter and a grandchild. These extended families range from entirely loving to tense and full of rage. It takes exceptional forbearance for a woman just on the verge of ending the child-rearing years to find herself starting all over again with an infant because her daughter became pregnant as a teenager.

Describing families in which grandparents serve as surrogate parents, the authors of the study comment that this "is not a style of grandparenting freely chosen; rather, it is a style adopted under duress. It is rooted in past and present experiences with hard times. . . . At the turn of the [previous] century, when family life was less stable and predictable for white and black families, this may have been a much more common way for American grandparents to behave. Black grandparents may represent the last holdout of a form of grandparenting in which companionship can sometimes take a back seat to authority."

In a sense, lower-income and African American grandparents are less likely to experience the easy, pure "sweetness" of grandparenting because they are too busy holding the family together. Even so, as Cherlin and Furstenberg report, black grandparents like white ones tend to find the experience gentler than the relentless stress of primary parenting. Grandparents, one black grandma told the interviewers, "have love to spare."

At the same time, a family in which a child shuttles between parent and grandparent is one in which the child is at risk of getting mixed signals. This can be compounded if the grandmother feels resentful at the additional burden she has had to take on, or if the daughter feels resentful at being again dependent on her mother, and these conflicts are fought out through the child.

Grandparents are often inside the nuclear family not just out of love but out of common need. Unless parents and grandparents take the time to work through the emotional aspects, relations can be tense. Arlie Hochschild, looking at how working parents juggle child rearing and paid employment, coined the term "appreciation gap." Each parent feels he or she is contributing more than they bargained for, and not getting full appreciation in return. The same can be true of parents and grandparents when a grandparent has a major role in child rearing. Sometimes this role is far more than the parent wants. Having a child may bring a young adult back into closer connections with parents than she sought, because the emotional connections were never solid and satisfying, and adulthood represented nothing so much as escape.

To pick up again on Harriet Lerner's story of Maggie, the new mother whose own mother wouldn't stop second-guessing her, a happy ending required a brave blend of persistence, firmness, and love on Maggie's part. As Lerner observes, a person in a family system who is wedded to an old pattern of interaction will at first resist the other person's attempts to alter the pattern and demand, in effect, that the other person "change back" to familiar ways that are comfortable, even if conflictual.

Over more than a year of therapy, Maggie, with coaching from the therapist, gently but firmly resisted her mother's relentless backseat driving about the baby. As she gained a greater sense of self-confidence and mastery, she was able, paradoxically, to establish a closer and more authentic connection with her mother. They "began to talk about topics that had been previously eclipsed by their endless years of fighting. Maggie began to ask her mother more about her past life. . . . Maggie talked with her mother in a way that neither of them had previously done, since their interactions were so heavily based on silence, sarcasm, outright fighting, and emotional distancing. As they talked more and more often in a new way, Maggie was able to see her mother's old 'obnoxious' behaviors in a different light. . . . Maggie also learned that her mother had had much the same kind of relationship with *her* mother, maintaining closeness through constant squabbling."

In this case, although it took a radical change in well-entrenched behavior patterns, the birth of a grandchild was the catalyst that eventually led to a more authentic relationship between mother and adult daughter. This grandmother had a lot to be thankful for. Another daughter might have dealt with the relentless disparaging advice by just writing the relationship off.

Further conflict occurs when a child and grandchild are living in the grandparents' house. Psychologists Jean Davies Okimoto and Phyllis Jackson Stegall tell of one young mother, Jillian, who had a bout of serious depression after her marriage fell apart and she couldn't cope with the stresses of being a single mother working in a demanding job. After three weeks in a psychiatric hospital, where she got excellent care, she came to live in her parents' house, where her six-year-old son, Matthew, was already staying. When his mother returned from the hospital, Matthew, confused and displaced, sought her attention. But she was too depressed to do much mothering. The grandmother gradually stepped into the role of primary parent, and after some resistance ("You're not my mother! I don't have to listen to you.") Matthew gradually "almost completely shifted his requirements for mothering to his grandmother." As Jillian recovered from her depression, Matthew resisted shifting his attention back to her, and Jillian found herself resenting both her mother and her son. Only with some therapy did mother and grandmother work out a common strategy to allow grandma to gently and gradually withdraw from the role of primary parent so mother and son could return to a normal bond. Rather than just pursuing her own emotional needs, the authors write, "Jillian's mother never forgot whose child he was."

In emotionally charged situations, not everyone is this lucky or this wise. A grandmother less clear about her own feelings and her own role might have resisted giving up a cherished new connection with a child. Far from facilitating her daughter's recovery, this would have aggravated a difficult situation.

As we have suggested throughout this book, families keep separating and reintegrating, as people move through the stages of the life experience, perhaps acquiring greater insight and wisdom. The moment when a family adds a third generation can be a propitious moment for reintegration. Young adults in their thirties may be mature enough to begin to see their parents as people. The experience of having a child may give new parents some appreciation of what their own parents went through as young adults. And the new grandparents, having had a period of respite from young children at home, may acquire the wisdom both to give their adult children some support, to cut them some slack, and to know when to do which.

The role of grandparent is part of the process, as the final decades of life unfold, of trying to make sense of it all. That is not just an individual enterprise, but a family one. It is this process to which we now turn.

Chapter 10
Life Reflection and Reunion

BOB RECALLS: *After my mother turned eighty, my friends marveled at how spry and alert she still was. But I noticed that more and more of the conversation was small talk: minor family news, accounts of domestic expeditions, medical reports. I sadly concluded that this narrowing must reflect the inevitable loss of cognition and short-term memory that often accompanies aging; that Mom was giving up livelier conversation out of anxiety that she could not keep up; that she was lonely; that old age was making her depressed. It made me feel sad, guilty, and dutiful. I found myself sinking into a mild depression of my own during visits with her, and letting her fill up the spaces with familiar monologues. Visits became polite but a bit strained.*

Others with aging parents reported the same pattern. In our interviews and informal conversations, each of several people, describing the quality of their relationships with elderly parents, spontaneously mentioned the Bill Murray movie, Groundhog Day, in which a man is condemned to relive the same day and repeat the same conversations over and over.

In working on this book, I began wondering whether I was selling my mother (and other aging parents) too short. I was.

Almost by accident, I stumbled on the fact that my mother's intellect, cognitive capacity, and emotional insight all were sur-

prisingly alive and well, even if her short-term memory was a bit shaky. I first grasped this when we began including her in social occasions with our friends. In many modern families, middle-aged people have one social life for friends and another for relatives; the idea of mixing peers and parents seems embarrassing, if not inconceivable. I'm a little chagrined to report that we were no different. One year Sharland suggested that we include my mother in more social occasions with our middle-aged friends. This brought out a whole new side of her. Stimulated by new people, she couldn't rely on familiar scripts. There was a lot more to her than we were giving her credit for. Our friends liked her, and vice versa. We began to get out of what was becoming a mutual rut. While memory loss is not uncommon, old people, especially those who live alone, suffer from nothing so much as understimulation.

An even more surprising realization came when I began sharing with my mother my experience dealing with a wife facing a fatal illness and some of the issues in this book. One day, thinking both about a chapter I was working on and my own issues regarding financial help to my grown children, I surprised myself by phoning my mother, then in her mid-eighties, and saying, "Mom, I need some advice. I'm not sure whether it's good for Gabe that I'm continuing to subsidize his acting career."

What followed was a startlingly good conversation. My mother asked thoughtful questions and offered perceptive suggestions. She listened. We stayed on the phone at least forty-five minutes, playing out various scenarios and likely results. She raised several points I hadn't thought of. We continued the conversation over several dinners.

Only afterwards did I realize how far I had departed from the usual script—and thereby invited a much richer conversation. For much of our adult life, the tacit script had called for us to avoid conflict by avoiding too much intimacy. As the only child of a mother who had lost two husbands, my implicit job was to live up to her dreams for me and to avoid causing her further heartache. But as the same only child of a mother who

had lost two husbands and who had a lot of emotional investment in me, I also needed a degree of healthy distance from her,
in order to become my own person. Ours was a dance of
approach/avoidance, though it was never unkind. I have friends
with more extreme versions of this dance; they oscillate
between dutiful, exaggerated, but superficial fealty to a parent
coupled with deep ongoing resentment.

In our case, the implicit bargain was that we'd have a cordial relationship, but also one somewhat at arm's length. I
didn't tell her more than I wanted her to know. She tacitly
trained herself not to probe or backseat drive. Unconsciously, I
was trying to protect her from knowledge that I was less than
the ideal son she imagined, as well as protecting myself from
the maternal domination I had needed to escape at age eighteen. Without quite acknowledging what we were doing, we
had negotiated a respectful emotional distance. We both continued to assume that the consequences of violating this tacit
pact would be pain, conflict, or greater distance. But the emotional distance came at a price.

By explicitly asking for advice, I unintentionally but radically changed the script. (I could almost hear my mother saying
incredulously, You want what?) Instead of skating on the sur-
face of a relationship and simulating intimacy, we could have a
real conversation about something important. Instead of the
polite and patterned chitchat that both of us actually found
boring, we could discuss something real. Without quite meaning to, I had signaled that I was ready to change the pattern. I
was no longer the eighteen-year-old who needed to keep his
mother at a distance. As a more self-confident adult, I no longer
found it threatening to let my mother in on some real concerns.
I could admit that I didn't have all the answers. And she
amazed me by being all there cognitively, as well as all there for
me emotionally.

When Sharland died, I began asking my mother what losing
a mate had been like for her. What it was like melding with a
second family, bringing a stepfather and his son into our house
just a year after my father died? Had she worried about how

this would affect me? How had she and my stepfather dealt with issues of divided loyalties? How much had she tried to keep memories of my father alive, for herself and for me? I also wondered aloud why she had been unwilling to open the door to any further relationships for herself, after she had lost her second husband at a youthful age sixty-four. Having just lost a wife of twenty-six years, I found myself letting down my hair emotionally far more than I ordinarily did with my mother. Without quite meaning to, I was modeling comfortable intimacy.

This was not my usual style with my mother. Looking back on it, I think I subconsciously pushed myself to change my ordinary behavior by rationalizing it as good material for this book. Paradoxically, I became a more emotionally accessible person by reverting to a familiar and safe professional role—reporter. But the fact is that I was also lonely, grieving, and in need of emotional support from the other woman in my life, my mother, someone who had been through a similar ordeal. Playing reporter and co-author of a book on families gave me an excuse to admit that, at age fifty-four, I needed to turn to my mother, and that she had something to give me. Asking about her own experience reflected the stance commended by the work of family therapists—constructive detachment, allowing compassionate curiosity, which in turn yields new and more comfortable intimacy.

I was rewarded with stories and insights about her, and about my family and my own childhood, many that I had never before heard. The old, patterned anecdotes did not reflect my mother's limitations, it turned out. Rather, they were the stunted fruit of a narrow, patterned relationship. They were covering over a much richer inner life, waiting to be tapped. I began sharing some of my own concerns about how a second marriage would affect my grown children. Again, my mother offered real wisdom. Our relationship became richer, closer and more relaxed. We became pals again, the way we were when I was nine, before my own development into adolescence and then manhood required me to push her away. I could put aside

*the mythic figure from my childhood from whom I needed to
escape, and be curious about her as a person, trusting that if
anyone in this unreliable world loved me, she did. And in the
process of this emotional reconnection, in her mid-eighties, she
"became" a much more interesting person.*

Older people with moderate short-term memory loss may em-
barrass themselves and annoy their children by repeating anecdotes they told only yesterday, or by dredging up the same family
stories we've heard a hundred times. But our elders are also fonts
of wisdom—if we can break through stale patterns that nobody
really likes, to access that wisdom. We are one of the few societies that conventionally fails to honor that role. This is not
about filial duty. If we can bring ourselves to broaden our expectations for our aging parents, relationships can become sources of
enrichment rather than irritation, resignation, or regret.

A great many older people live alone. People who live by
themselves are deprived not just of the comfort and love and
common history that an intimate partner provides. They also
lack an outlet for both the mundane domestic chatter that married couples take for granted—I picked up the cleaning, the car
has a funny noise, the supermarket is having a sale, I'm going to
the dentist—and they also lack an outlet for more intimate emotional connection. Facing the end of their lives and attendant
worries about declining health and physical stamina, old people
are often mildly depressed. They can seem tedious to be around.
But a lot of what they are suffering from is just understimulation
and underconnection.

Grown children who have made implicit bargains with parents based on their preconceptions from early adulthood often
sell their aging parents—and themselves—short. By the time
aging parents are in their seventies and eighties, they should no
longer be treated as powerful ghosts from childhood. The adult
who risks real intimacy with aging parents is likely to be
rewarded with a relationship that is much richer, and, paradoxically, less burdensome.

So much of what has been written recently on old age deals

with the medical and custodial aspect of an aging population. As more people live into their eighties and nineties, they fear losing autonomy and dignity; they don't want to be resented burdens to families. Often, children experience aging parents, a little sadly, as a necessary duty. While dependency in old age is a real and growing social problem, an equally significant new reality is how many people reach advanced age in relatively good health—how many people in their seventies and eighties are vigorous and alert. An equally important challenge is attaining emotional wholeness and connection to family. This process ought to begin long before an elderly person is at death's door.

To be sure, many elderly people are very frail toward the end of their lives. And their connections with their extended families are based mainly on concerns about finances and physical condition. But only 5 percent of Americans over age sixty-five are in nursing homes and only 10 percent of Americans will ever be in nursing homes.

HELLO IN THERE

The bluegrass singer and composer John Prine has a haunting song whose refrain goes:

> Old trees just grow stronger
> And old rivers grow wilder every day
> Old people just grow lonely
> Waiting for someone to say
> Hello in there, hello.

When we were in our twenties, we attended a conference that included an encounter-group session. One of the exercises called for everyone in the room to share a concern that they would not ordinarily tell to a stranger. One man, well into his seventies, talked about an existential puzzle that frustrated him. He had spent most of a lifetime thinking through what his values were, how to integrate his work with his family and other aspects of his life, how to be a worthy human being. "I've finally pretty much figured it out," he said, "and now it's almost time to die."

It dawned on us that older people just might have some wisdom worth paying attention to. Sometimes this is hardest to appreciate in our own families. We get stuck in well-worn routines. We are doubtful that our parents will ever change. We experience them as limited.

Age can soften the early parent–grown child ambivalence, or it can harden into a new rigidity, only with roles now reversed. An elderly parent who expects to be taken care of by adult children can be hurt and outraged when those expectations are dashed—and also feel a sense of embarrassment and shame at being dependent at all. In families where the idiom of intimacy is reproach, it is painful to listen to adult children in the role of caretakers patronize their parents and scold them for repeating anecdotes or missing medications. Sometimes, however, age can liberate long-suppressed feelings. The ensuing honesty can be cleansing and enhancing of the relationship.

Old age can be a time of emotional integration and ripening wisdom. It is scarcely necessary to remind ourselves that some of the most influential world leaders of the past century took office at an age when most people retire—Churchill at sixty-five, de Gaulle at sixty-eight, Reagan at sixty-nine, Adenauer at seventy-three; "Der Alte" was still chancellor at eighty-six. Monet and Picasso executed some of their most stunning paintings in their eighties. However, it is one thing to acknowledge the contribution of older people to politics, literature, and the arts. It is another to give aging a second look in the context of the family.

Many midlife adults have had the sobering experience of noticing, with weary resignation, that their parents, at age seventy-five or eighty, are still hard to take in all too familiar ways. And as elderly parents age, there is the gnawing sense that the death of an aging parent will soon foreclose, irrevocably, the possibility of a richer relationship. With every passing day, as cognitive capacity in the aging begins to diminish, the task seems more difficult, and many midlife adults defer it until it is too late. Yet often, even the very elderly are surprisingly resilient and receptive to new compassionate overtures. By the same token, older people are also capable of taking emotional initiatives, as well as being their compassionate object. The common insight here is that people into their seventies, eighties, and even nineties are still capable of remarkable personal growth. This reality has long been accepted in literature and in folk wisdom, and in the role of elders in traditional societies. Oddly, until a few decades ago, the wisdom of age was almost forgotten by modern psychology and cast aside by modern medicine.

Lately, a growing literature by older people has challenged society's tendency to ostracize and pathologize the old. Betty Friedan, who pioneered modern feminism, recently contributed a magnificent, encyclopedic work celebrating the vitality and human potential of old age, appropriately titled *The Fountain of Age*. She wrote, "We need to evolve new ways to sustain the ties of human intimacy and love . . . new ways of working and learning—no longer defined by career—to give purpose to our days and keep us part of the human enterprise."

Erik Erikson, in his last book, written with his wife, Joan, when he was in his mid-eighties, said that elders "endeavor to remain independent, despite increasing needs for various kinds of assistance. In an effort to balance stubornness with compliance, they seek to make some kind of personal peace with societal expectations of the aged, without surrendering the sense of self-determination that is essential to the sense of autonomy throughout the life course." Mary Pipher, at age fifty, looked at her elders and saw "another country," the land of the old who are often needlessly isolated from the young and middle-aged. One's "last years can be difficult, but also redemptive," Pipher wrote. "As we care for our parents, we teach our children to care for us. As we see our parents age, we learn to age with courage and dignity. If the years are handled well, the old and young can help each other grow. . . . I encourage adults to seek out older relatives and get reacquainted."

In America, with its obsession with youth, we squander one of our culture's greatest resources, the wisdom of age. We trundle off even the vigorous elderly to age-segregated leisure villages, which include every amenity but the comfort of family. We have all but abandoned the rich tradition of storytelling in favor of television, a medium that reinforces the stereotypes of old age. All of these shifts have reinforced a national prejudice against the old.

The pioneer of a different, more supple view of aging is Dr. Robert Butler. For four decades, Dr. Butler, a distinguished geriatric psychiatrist, has been a crusader for the idea that normal human development extends well into old age, and that quality of life for the elderly is a major social and personal challenge. Butler, embellishing Erikson, holds that the natural developmental task of old age is not just nurturance but to try to make sense of it all. In 1961, Butler wrote a now-classic paper about what he termed "life review." It is natural and healthful, he declared, for people in their later years to look back on their lives. He observed, "The life review is a normal developmental task of the later years characterized by the return of memories and past conflicts, which can result in resolution, reconciliation, atonement, integration, and serenity. It can occur spontaneously or it can be structured." He also designed an interview to help older people begin the process of systematic reminiscence. As Butler observed, one of the most poignant lingering regrets in the aged is a sense that one never achieved the connection that one hoped for, either with one's parents or one's children.

Dramatically breaking with geriatric psychiatry as it was then understood, Butler observed that older people were frequently discouraged from actively taking stock of their lives. "Often the older person is experienced as garrulous and 'living in the past' and the content and significance of his reminiscence are lost or devalued. . . . The prevailing tendency is to identify reminiscence in the aged with psychological dysfunction and thus to regard it essentially as a symptom." In contrast, Butler, then a young psychiatrist specializing in older patients, saw the life review "as a naturally occurring, universal mental process characterized by the progressive return to consciousness of past experiences and, particularly, the resurgence of unresolved conflicts." Butler added that "these revived experiences can be surveyed and reintegrated. Presumably this process is prompted by the realization of approaching dissolution and death . . . the more intense the unresolved life conflicts, the more work remains to be accomplished toward reintegration."

For one thing, old people are probably the only large group of adults with spare time on their hands. For another, the nature of memory seems to change in old age. Short-term memory sometimes weakens. But as the mind is less crowded with frenetic daily tasks, long-term memory often sharpens. Many older people report a near-photographic ability to recall detailed events from sixty or seventy years ago.

In his life review exercise, Butler turned the widely recognized tendency of older people to look back on their lives into a kind of therapeutic technique—not for the clinically depressed but for everyone. Butler wrote: "Only in old age with the proximity of death can one truly experience a personal sense of the entire life cycle. That makes old age a unique state of life and makes the review of life at that time equally unique."

Bob's aunt, Adele Kuttner, who died at ninety-two, was our favorite older relative. She demonstrated that one could combine joyous rebellion with great dignity. As an impulsive eighteen-year-old, she and her boyfriend made off with his parents' car, drove five hundred miles to Niagara Falls, and eloped. Adele worked for most of her life as a travel agent, and was able to take exotic trips all over the world. She had many love affairs; she was married three times. She was the first relative we knew who had lots of gay friends. She had a superb repertoire of dirty jokes. She also dressed impeccably, corrected everyone's grammar, saw the humor in daily life, and was a grand New York lady. Adele scandalized the family, but the family recognized that a little of Adele's sort of scandal in a slightly uptight family did us all a lot of good. She was deeply loved because she was the most generous person any of us knew. Her generosity with gifts was legion, but a small part it. Her real gift was generosity of spirit. Although she had a wicked tongue, she never used it at other people's expense. She was not one to gossip and she invariably interpreted the actions or motives of others with charity.

Countless Adele expressions and stories became part of our family folklore. Adele was the oldest of three children. The children's favorite family meal was roast duck. Their mother would protest, "But there's so little to eat on a duck." Young Adele piped up: "Did you ever hear of two ducks?" In our house, two ducks became a family term for Adele-style generosity. Set an extra place at the table. Pick up another ticket. Think outside the box. Adele was the only living sibling of Bob's father, and she outlived him by almost forty years. Getting to know Adele, Bob got to know something of his father. Observing and listening to Adele and watching their parents interact with her, our children learned more about their origins, about the grandfather who had died before they were born, and they learned something about family feeling and generosity.

Then something unusual happened. In her ninety-first year, as her eyesight was failing, Adele, a hardy and independent soul, became uncharacteristically depressed. Having outlived most of her friends and spending a lot of time alone, Adele began brooding on her past. One day, Adele asked Sharland if she could come talk about her lingering concerns. Adele, the free spirit, was wracked with regrets. Her wildness, she said, had taken a terrible toll on her mother. She wanted forgiveness and absolution. At ninety, she also had new curiosity about her sex life. Did her promiscuity as a young woman, perhaps, have something to do with her emotionally distant father? Did people really love her for herself?

Sharland was astonished, and cherished these conversations. What Adele was doing was pure life review, as characterized by Robert Butler. By having an outlet for it, in this case with a family member who happened also to be trained as a therapist, Adele could make better sense of her life, achieve a sense of peace as she approached the end of her life, and also achieve a closer connection to her extended family.

Robert Butler's work was a pioneering part of a revisionist trend in psychology which also revolutionized the study of adult development. In the 1970s, developmental psychologists began focusing on development and emotional growth as a lifelong process. The psychologist Paul Baltes defined what he termed life span developmental psychology, or lifelong human development.

In the early 1980s, the MacArthur Foundation announced a twenty-year program of support for research and writing on "successful mid-life development." A MacArthur-sponsored summary of more than two decades of research, *Successful Aging* identifies social connectedness as a key ingredient of physical and emotional health in old age. The MacArthur research put a social science imprimatur on common sense: "People who have a great deal of social support are healthier, on average, than people who lack such support. . . . The more older people participate in social relationships, the better their overall health." It is not that the aging need, as many younger people misperceive, to "be supported." They need to be part of reciprocal relationships, to give as well as receive. Indeed, just as children need a large measure of self-reliance, so do the elderly. "Unwanted or uneeded support," the researchers observe, can backfire by leading to dependence, passivity, depression—and resentment on the part of the caregiver.

Indeed, in our own interviews we found that some of the distance between grown children and their aging parents is caused by chasms of false assumptions regarding what the older generation expects. These guilty projections on the part of the middle-aged regarding parents' demands then breed guilty resentments, and further emotional distance, which is the opposite of true reciprocal support.

THE RICHNESS OF ORDINARY LIVES

The movement in geriatric psychiatry to encourage life reflection and review is closely related to the genre of oral history and memoir, and memoirs need not be the exclusive properties of literati or statesman. Ordinary people lead lives just as fiercely and intensely as celebrities. As Butler observes, "Autobiography is one literary genre that potentially gives everybody the opportunity to become 'someone.'"

Our dear friend Carolyn Goodman, now in her mid-eighties, decided about four years ago to write a memoir. She wrote it not so much for publication as for herself. Carolyn has had a remarkable life. A lifelong political activist and student of families, she was something of a role model for Sharland. In her mid-thirties, as a parent of three young children, Carolyn went to graduate school, got a graduate degree in psychology, and founded a path-breaking community psychiatry program in the Bronx for poor women with serious mental illnesses. These women, in addition to battling mental illness, are consumed with worry that they are failing their children. So Carolyn built the entire therapeutic enterprise around mothering. The program combines treatment for the mother with group activities and coaching centered on parenting skills. Carolyn, a civil rights pioneer, lost a son, Andy Goodman, who was murdered in Mississippi while working in a voter registration drive in 1964. Much of her later life has been devoted to bridging gaps between the generations around political issues. She also has lost two husbands. One of her two living sons is an environmentalist/entrepreneur. The other is a Hasidic Jew and musicologist in Israel.

Carolyn's memoir is about sorting it all out, the two marriages, the children who pursued such different courses, her own parents, what effect her political and professional dedication had. The exercise makes her more accessible to herself and her children. She is pursuing it, in a sense, in anticipation of her death, even though she has no serious illness.

The extensive literature of autobiography is another sign that as human beings come to terms with approaching death, there is a universal need to make sense of our lives, not just in a bid for posthumous immortality but to achieve a sense of integration and wholeness in the days remaining to us on earth. Memoirs, journals, and oral histories can be part of that project, yet making sense of one's life is rarely a solitary enterprise.

Indeed, review of one's life can entail a reconnection with other family members, especially grown children. In this sense, it is the flip side of the process described in Chapter 8, of revisiting our parents as adults. Older adults can also undertake the process of revisiting grown children, not just through journals and memoirs, but through letters, extended visits, e-mail correspondences, and taped conversations. This sort of extended family project can be a two-way street to greater integration, resolution, and wholeness. Grandchildren, armed with the latest technology and a less emotionally loaded relationship with grandparents, can be a key part of this process.

Oral histories have been a part of the American experience for better than a century. They are a variant of timeless rituals in traditional societies, where traditions were handed down through storytelling. In America, oral history got a big boost with the invention of the wire recorder. During the New Deal, the WPA Writers Project and kindred enterprises began systematically sending out interviewers to record the reminiscences of old folks. This effort preserved for future generations details of regional subcultures, reminiscences of Civil War veterans, and narratives of former slaves. However, oral history takes on a deeper meaning when it is part of a deliberate enterprise of self-reflection and reintegration within a family.

If we have spent much of a lifetime tiptoeing around real feelings, this kind of reconnection takes effort. Carol Shields's novel *The Stone Diaries* is the chronicle of the richness of an ordinary life, that of Daisy Goodwill Flett. Late in Daisy's life, her daughter Alice comes to visit her in the nursing home.

> On the plane coming over, she had invented rich, thrilling dialogues for the two of them.
>
> "Have you been happy in your life?" she's planned to ask her mother. She pictured herself seated by the bedside, the seat folded back in a neat fan, her mother's hand in hers, the light from the window dim, churchy. "Have you found fulfillment?"—whatever the hell fulfillment is. "Have you had moments of genuine ecstasy? Has it been worth it? . . . Has it been enough, your life, I mean? Are you ready for—? Are you frightened? Are you in there? What can I do?"
>
> Instead they speak of apple juice, gravy, screams in the corridor, the doctor, who is Jamaican. . . .

These reconnections need to begin well before an aging parent is at death's door, and sometimes it is the parent who is the initiator. A number of therapists whom we interviewed for this book mentioned that for their elderly patients, one of the great sadnesses was a sense of distance with their grown children that seemed unbridgeable. For families where relationships are distant and conflictual, reconnections initiated by older people need to be particularly well thought out, and structured. Letters are often a good place to begin. These, in turn, can lead to meetings and extended conversation. In families characterized by embittered distance, the usual idiom is often one of blaming. Parents and adult children vie for the role of who is the more badly misunderstood and maligned victim. This style of discourse is a dead end.

If the older adult wants to take the initiative, often an initial letter needs to start with a candid expression of regret. Shauna Smith, a clinical social worker who works with older parents seeking reconciliation with their estranged adult children, writes that such children, especially when a history of abusiveness is behind the estrangement, want several things: to be listened to; to have their statements and feelings affirmed; to know how their parents felt; to have their parents express regret for their adult children's undeserved pain and struggle; and to have their parents make amends by being willing to work on their relationships, in the present.

Psychologist Robert Karen writes of one patient whom he calls Norman. This man was emotionally torn apart by the fact that his three grown sons were "combative, distant, or openly rejecting of him." Norman, it turned out, had been raised by a father who verbally abused him. He was determined not to repeat this behavior with his own children. But occasionally, "when one of his sons displeased him, he could not tolerate the threat this posed to [his] fantasy of goodness and superiority." He was an emotional perfectionist who occasionally just "lost it." So Norman's sons experienced him as emotionally unreliable. Eventually, Norman was able to speak of his own fears to his sons, and abandon the image of perfection that in turn led to his rage and his sons' estrangement. (It was Willy Loman's tragedy that he could not.) Karen writes that Norman could "speak from the heart to his disparaging, contemptuous, rageful sons and say, without indictment, 'Can you allow me my flaws?'" A little humility can go a long way in transforming blocked relationships.

Seemingly, the stakes are higher for parents than for children. The younger generation wants to forge its own way, into the future. Our parents seem to represent the past—childhood and dependence. As parents, we consider children one of our crowning achievements. When they are grown, we want them finally to stop behaving like self-absorbed adolescents and affirm who we are and what we did for them. It is often parents who have to work harder at this process of staying connected than grown children do, because it often means more to parents. Yet kids who casually put parents out of their emotional lives are missing something. Grown children also need their parents' affirmation (if not their meddling). As James Framo observed, though many of us seek emotional safety in distance, no one ever gives up the yearning for love and acceptance by parents.

As people approach their own demise, some face it with a sense of wholeness and integration; others are filled with regret. "The most tragic situation," Robert Butler writes, "is that of the person whose increasing, but only partial, insight leads to a sense of total waste: the horrible insight just as one is about to die that one has never lived. . . ."

A number of works of fiction and theater underscore this dread. Henry James's classic novella *The Beast in the Jungle* recounts the story of a man who spent his entire life resisting intense experience, because of a premonition that something profound was destined to happen to him. He rejected the love of a woman because it did not seem profound enough. After she died, when he was well into old age, he realized, too late, that he had been resisting life itself. Some in old age give in to their fears that their children are unappreciative or disloyal, and these fears are often fantasies. Shakespeare's Lear, like many of the bard's tragic protagonists, faces advanced age and death not with reconciliation and integration, but broken and embittered. In Samuel Beckett's play *Krapp's Last Tape*, a very old man is surrounded with a collection of tape-recorded diary entries that he has accumulated in order to make sense of his life. But the tapes are a jumble of incoherent ramblings. He is absurd, and alone.

It isn't always easy making room for reconnections between elderly parents or other relatives and middle-aged adults. In midlife, nothing seems so scarce as time. But the problem isn't just a lack of time. Often, we lack both the motivation and the emotional vocabulary for family reconnections. Consider the phenomenal popularity of the inspirational bestseller *Tuesdays with Morrie*. The book is Mitch Albom's reconstruction of his weekly visits to a remarkable and wise former teacher, mortally ill with one of the most cruel of wasting diseases, ALS. Morrie is a font of life wisdom and spiritual optimism. The book obviously touched a national nerve. In a sense, Morrie is a surrogate for the reader's own father, experienced at the emotionally safe distance of two removes, through Albom's appreciation of Morrie Schwartz. Morrie's own beautiful book, *Letting Go: Morrie's Reflections on Living While Dying*, did not sell nearly as well as Albom's book. The reader, experiencing Albom's experience of Morrie Schwartz, is vicariously connecting with an aging and dying parent.

EMBRACING MORTALITY

Until fairly recently in America, death was a taboo subject. For the most part, people were denied the emotional reality of the last great journey of life, and their children were deprived of a final opportunity to restore connections and heal wounds. Even as late as the 1970s, although for a generation the popularization of Freud had rendered sex a fit subject for drawing-room conversation, death was avoided. If the occasional memoir dealing with mortal illness appeared, as when the columnist Stewart Alsop, dying of leukemia, wrote *Stay of Execution* in 1973, it was seen as brave, unconventional, and a little bit odd. In his introduction, Alsop wrote very wise words that he felt he had to couch almost apologetically:

> This is, in short, a mixed-up sort of book. But I have led a mixed-up sort of life, and no experience of that life—not even when an American colonel almost had me shot as a German

spy after I had parachuted behind the lines in France—has been more mixed up than the peculiar hell-to-heaven-to-purgatory existence I have had since I was first diagnosed as an acute leukemic. In a way, no experience has been more interesting than living in intermittent intimacy with the gentleman W. C. Fields used to call "the man in the white nightgown." . . . Death is, after all, the only universal experience except birth, and although a sensible person hopes to put it off as long as possible, it is, even in anticipation, an interesting experience.

Society's cultural permission for us to engage death has changed dramatically in three decades. The cultural radicalism and human potential movement of the 1960s helped blow open the door. The work of people like Elisabeth Kübler-Ross, though some of it spilled over into fringe spiritualism, had a very constructive effect on the mainstream. The growing interest of ordinary Americans in yoga and meditation connects to traditions in which death is less fearsome and unspeakable. Books like Norman Cousins's works dealing with serious illness and Max Lerner's *Wrestling with the Angel* lifted the emotional shroud that kept the business of confronting mortality hidden and almost shameful.

Perhaps the most important influence of all has been the hospice movement, which has allowed people to take back from medical technology the experience of approaching death. Though the hospice movement, for the most part, has been an effort to change medical practice, it also irrevocably alters the emotional experience of the end of life. Before hospice, approaching death was the business of doctors, punctuated by the occasional visit from a clergyman. Bereavement was a process that occurred after death. The medical imperative was to keep the patient alive as long as possible, and to deny the imminence of death in order to "keep the patient from giving up hope."

The hospice movement was a radical challenge to the arrogance of modern medicine. It was founded by a remarkable English nursing student named Cicely Saunders, who had seen terrible pain and suffering in World War II. She eventually got degrees in both social work and medicine. Many doctors undermedicate patients when it comes to pain relief. Dr. Saunders wanted to combine the best pain relief available with a setting in which the terminally ill could do what she called "the real work of dying," namely, an encounter with the meaning of one's life. She roughly modeled her own hospice, founded in 1967, on preexisting hospices, which were refuges run by religious organizations mostly for the indigent dying. She imbued her own work with the mission of radically transforming how medicine treated mortality.

By forcing the system to acknowledge that incipient death was inevitable in some circumstances and that quality of life was as important as deferral of death, the hospice movement emphasized what came to be known as palliative care—making the patient as comfortable as possible and encouraging a capacity to take whatever richness was still available from being alive. But along the way, inevitably, other revolutionary changes were set in train. At first, a hospice was a physical place—a special, homelike facility for the dying in which comfort and pain control, rather than medical heroics, were paramount. But over time, "hospice" came to mean a whole dissenting philosophy of end-of-life care. Once they were empowered to decide how they wanted to die, most terminally ill people working with hospice programs, not surprisingly, resolved to spend their final days at home. The hospice movement provided both the home-care and ideological supports to make that choice possible.

Several foundations have embraced the movement for death with dignity, including the most influential of the medical foundations, the Robert Wood Johnson Foundation, as well as George Soros's Open Society Institute. Soros, who recoiled from the ghastly medicalized deaths of his own parents, has underwritten a whole program on death in America. The Johnson program is run by another pioneer in the movement for death with dignity, Dr. Ira Byock, author of the book *Dying Well*, who was a hospice medical director. Dr. Byock, who trained at the University of

Denver, where Kübler-Ross had taught her celebrated seminar on death and dying, and who also studied Tibetan Buddhism, writes, "[T]he phrase, dying well . . . expresses what I have witnessed most consistently: that in the very shadow of death one's living experience can yet give rise to accomplishment, within one's own and one's family's system of values. Over the years, I have met a number of people who were emotionally well while their physical body was withering and, for some, literally rotting. Logically, if even the most emotionally whole of us will eventually die, it follows that a certain wellness in dying must be possible. My experience in hospice confirms that this is true. Even as they are dying, most people can accomplish meaningful tasks and grow in ways that are important to them and to their families."

The real hospice revolution was not palliative care; it was that people facing terminal illnesses were given back control over their own dying. This, in turn, invited families into a new process of acknowledging that death could be, and needed to be, addressed. Patients and their families were given cultural permission to plan the circumstances of an approaching death.

As the hospice movement has become part of the American mainstream, few family members who have been part of this process will approach their own final years in denial of death. And, as more of us experience it, this new candor about the fact of mortality can have a further spillover. Even before the diagnosis of a serious illness, this new cultural acknowledgment of mortality invites more authentic connections between elderly people and their children. In our final chapter, we turn to our own experience with this unwelcome yet rich odyssey.

Epilogue:
Terminal Candor ·

This is, of course, not the last chapter we imagined. We have chosen to include this Epilogue about our own experience, not because this book has turned into autobiography, but because it ties so much together. The prospect of death, which we all face, is a final separation. Yet engaging with that reality can bring life-affirming reunion.

As we wrote in our Introduction, we began thinking about the project of family reunion when our son, Gabriel, was already in college, and our daughter, Jessica, was in her sophomore year of high school. Like many couples in our early fifties, we were anticipating the empty-nest phase of our lives with both eagerness and dread. We considered ourselves devoted and conscientious parents. Though we both felt grateful for good friends and for work that we loved, much of our definition of who we were was bound up with being the parents of a daughter and a son. Like most parents, so many of our rituals as a couple had become rituals as a family.

We each counted ourselves lucky to have spent many of our children's early and middle years working at least partly at home, Sharland as a graduate student and then a clinical psychologist, Bob as a writer and editor. At a time of escalating tension between parents' work and family roles, we felt blessed that more often than not, one of us could be present to greet a child coming home from school and be available for after-school activities. We were something of a throwback, and proud of it. Our kids made fun of us for insisting that we all sit down at the dinner table to eat the same meal at the same time, with the TV off. And we had come through our son's turbulent odyssey a stronger and more closely knit family.

As the conflicts of our children's early adolescence began to dissipate, we had also become better friends in our marriage. We felt we had gained a measure of wisdom as parents, as a couple, and as individuals beginning the passage into late middle age. So, as our daughter's final year of high school approached we contemplated life without children at home and the hope of close bonds with our young adults. The ruminations about such a future prompted this book.

It was less than a year into the work on the book when Sharland learned she had metastatic cancer. What followed was surprising and uplifting, as well as wrenching. Nothing had prepared either of us for it. As we all dealt with Sharland's illness and then her approaching death, we found ourselves living more vividly and coming together as a family. Although Sharland will make frequent appearances in this last chapter, in quotes from her interviews, talks, and journals, the narrative that follows, necessarily, is mainly Bob's.

In October 1994, Sharland began having pains that were initially dismissed as associated with menopause. After several weeks of misdiagnosis, a scan revealed advanced metastatic cancer in her liver. In a moment, we were transformed from ordinary, normal people into a family dealing with a fatal illness.

The journey that followed was partly medical, partly emotional, partly spiritual. Medically, we first needed an oncologist. We were extremely fortunate in that our family doctor referred us to Lowell Schnipper, the chief of oncology at Boston's Beth Israel Hospital. Dr. Schnipper, in addition to being a gifted clinician, is a deeply humane person and a leader in the movement for death with dignity. He is as dedicated to working on an emotional level with people facing terminal illness as he is to treating and some-

times curing cancers. Above all, he is committed to the proposi-
tion that the patient is in charge. Even as late as 1994, the idea
that patients rather than doctors should take control of their own
deaths was relatively new. Many if not most oncologists saw their
jobs as simply doing battle with the cancer, and persuading their
patients to endure gruesomely heroic treatments in service of possible cures, right to the end. So if this was to be an unusual engagement with a fatal illness, we had an ally in Dr. Schnipper.

Medically, at the time there was just one real option, a well-
established chemotherapy protocol that combined the drug 5-
fluorouracil and a metabolic agent called leucovorin. The side
effects were described as "not too bad" as chemotherapy goes—
nausea, diarrhea, mouth sores, and fatigue. Sharland, petite and
meticulous about her appearance, would not lose her hair.

At our initial conference with Dr. Schnipper, Sharland was
characteristically direct. What was the prognosis? "This cancer
cannot be cured, but it can be treated," he said carefully, using
words he had doubtless spoken many times before. How long
would she likely live? Sharland asked. There are no guarantees, he
said, but with this type of cancer perhaps six months to two years.
Does anybody beat this cancer? she asked. That would be most
unusual, he said delicately. What about experimental treatments,
we wanted to know. There were some, but only so-called stage-
one clinical trials, human experiments in which there is no evi-
dence yet that the chemical agent does any good. The purpose of
the early testing is simply to establish a safe dose level for a possibly beneficial new drug. And these experimental chemotherapy
agents had worse side effects than the proven one.

So the strategy was very limited: Keep Sharland alive and
well as long as possible using available treatments, in the hope
that there might be some medical breakthrough that would then
prolong her life. In the meantime, we would all endeavor with
Sharland to make her remaining time on earth as rich and vivid
as possible.

We met with Jon Kabat-Zinn at the University of Massachu-
setts Medical Center. By an eerie coincidence, I had just finished

taking his stress reduction course, which relies on meditation and yoga. The course is intended for people facing chronic pain and chronic illnesses, for health professionals, and ordinary overstressed people who wish to take back their own lives. I had had a health scare the year before, some gastric distress that mimicked a heart attack. I took this as a signal to slow down. I felt I got a great deal out of the course, and I was now in the habit of doing a yoga routine daily. Mediation and yoga help one gain a sense of proportion; they encourage a posture of engaged responsiveness, as opposed to reactivity.

Jon had developed the course, as he put it, to help people facing chronic illness gain access to "their deep inner resources for healing," to calm the anxious mind and thereby make illness or pain less fearsome. The instruction program, which ran for eight weekly three-hour sessions, included one final private session in which each participant was to spend an hour with Jon discussing the classes, the insights gained, questions about the meditation practice, and personal goals. At the end of the last class, I asked to have a word with Jon. "I'd like to bring a guest to our private session," I told him. "My wife has just been diagnosed with metastatic cancer." The following week, he and Sharland and I had a long conversation, and she enrolled in the next session of his course. Jon's book is called *Full Catastrophe Living*. The premise is that life is a kind of daily catastrophe that we need to engage mindfully, and that we need to be vividly present for our own lives. This thought became a kind of mantra for us and our children in dealing with Sharland's cancer.

Sharland's experience doing yoga and meditation also led us, a year later, to Commonweal in Bolinas, California, which operates a weeklong retreat for cancer patients and their partners. The Commonweal Cancer Help Program gives people a wide variety of medical information, but it mainly endeavors to empower people with serious illness to take greater control over their own lives, whether or not their cancer is considered likely to be terminal. Michael Lerner, who conceived and directs the program, observes that it is the emotional and spiritual business of everyone in the second half of life to come to terms with the reality of their own mortality.

People at Commonweal spend their week doing yoga and meditation, working in small group sessions, comparing experiences, writing poems, going through a variety of exercises to help them and their partners acknowledge that impending death can be the last great odyssey of one's life. Our yoga teacher, a poet named Waz Thomas, let us know, after we had come to know him a little better, that he had been HIV-positive for twelve years. The effect of the Commonweal retreat, and programs like it, is often a greater receptivity to life, even in dying. The very fact of taking control of one's own dying can be empowering, at a time when one feels nothing so much as powerless.

Rachel Remen, the medical director at Commonweal, calls people with serious illnesses who gain strength for themselves and others "wounded healers." Perhaps the most important task at Commonweal is to give people dealing with cancer the courage to break through conspiracies of denial signaled by nearly everyone around a person with a potentially fatal disease. Remen, who has been living with Crohn's disease for four decades, has edited a book of poems from Commonweal. One of her own poems is:

Mother Knows Best. . . .

Don't talk
about your troubles.
No one loves a sad face.

O Mom.

The truth is
cheer isolates,
humor defends
competence intimidates

control separates,
and sadness. . . .

sadness opens us to each other.

At Commonweal, Michael Lerner introduced us some concepts we had never encountered before. One was the distinction
between illness and disease. Disease is the malady that afflicts
the body. Illness is partly subjective, Lerner writes. It has to do
with one's attitude toward one's disease. Attitude cannot "cure"
disease, but it can change the nature of the experience. A person
struggling with a medical condition can feel, to a greater or
lesser degree, in a state of dis-ease. Different people with similar
clinical diagnoses can have very different experiences of illness
or healing. One participant in a Commonweal retreat, Carole
Munson, wrote this poem:

> Steven Levine says a person can be healed and still die
> I feel relieved to know that.
> Thinking that I absolutely have to stay alive
> feels like a great burden on my shoulders.
> With that one removed,
> I feel I can get on with my living.

We learned about people whom Lerner calls "exceptional cancer patients"—people who, for no explicable medical reason, suddenly find themselves free of cancer. It is possible to be entirely
realistic about one's condition, yet to live as if there is the always
the possibility of a miracle, even if one doesn't come. We learned
about "healing circles," a kind of extended support group for people with cancer and their friends and loved ones. We also learned
the phrase "the well cancer patient." A great many people dealing with cancer, even people who will eventually die of it, spend
several productive years in relatively good health. These can be
years of physical distress and escalating gloom. But even if they
include pain, they can also be years of intensified presence. In an-

other of the Commonweal poems, Suzanne Lipsett, dealing with a breast cancer that would be terminal, wrote:

> It took years for me
> To learn we were a garden
> And finally hear
> The music of the sea.

In this sense, living with a terminal diagnosis is only an intensification of the human condition itself. In the end we all die. We can use that knowledge to live a vivid life, or we can stay in denial of death, and consequently often in denial of much of life. This is, above all, a message and a mentality about living, not about dying. Each of us can come to this insight in our own way. It is a sensibility, not a cookbook.

A disclaimer: Nothing in life is stranger than death. There is a lot of New Age material about death and dying, and a lot of well-intentioned people (and a few outright frauds) giving dubious advice. Nonsense comes bundled with profound insight. Elisabeth Kübler-Ross, one of the pioneers of the movement to acknowledge the emotional reality of death, eventually decided that she could communicate with the dead. Before she got to that point, she wrote several very useful books.

As much as I came to admire how Sharland dealt with her cancer, sometimes with a wonder bordering on awe, my purpose here is not to glamourize death. Nor was that the way Sharland went about dying. To be clear-eyed about one's mortality is not to make dying a romantic experience. Sharland was a very discerning and practical woman. She read widely, and when she became a cancer patient she explored books about healing, about alternative cancer treatments, about religion and spirituality, and about dying. In Sharland's odyssey, we never got weird about death. Although we explored diet, exercise, and made good use of yoga, Sharland never abandoned mainstream medicine for extreme diets or folk cures. Those we respected most, like

Michael Lerner and Lowell Schnipper and Jon Kabat-Zinn, never saw medicine and inner healing as rivals, but as complements. We never bought into the claim advanced by some alternative medicine gurus that people somehow "cause" their own cancers by negative thinking. And we certainly did not become infatuated with the idea of death or mystify the process of dying beyond the inherent profound mystery of our mortality.

The three years of Sharland's illness were simultaneously a period of vivid living and of deep sadness. Much of the time, cancer was merely a terrible ordeal, medical crises to be dealt with, diversions from activities we both loved, and the random cruelties of serious disease. Like any family, we had our arguments and moments when we just wanted it all to go away. As Gabriel later observed, we had to remind ourselves both to engage and to back off, because constant engagement would have been unbearable and inhuman. Sharland's journals are filled with pages that reflect her efforts to maintain dignity amid daily struggle. She wrote:

> I am so tired of having to deal with cancer. But what's the alternative? My eyes are puffy from the 5-FU, prone to tearing. I look at my face in the mirror. It feels like a "not-me" experience. Who is this sad, puffy-eyed woman? And what is in her heart? Putting it into words sometimes feels unbearably difficult. This is my work, after all, getting other people to "put it into words." I feel overwhelmed by the task of taking the measure of this experience, to allow myself to feel it all, at least part of the time. I must not be paralyzed by it. I will shout at it, laugh at it, cry about it, and dance with it for as long as there is time.

Sharland's courage and spiritual journey coexisted with unsentimental daily trials: frustration that she felt sick on the day of our daughter's high school graduation; rage at a catheter that kept clogging and a pump that kept beeping; misery that came from sitting in her office with a sobbing patient, knowing that more than anything she needed to use the toilet.

Yet Sharland's illness also became somehow enriching and heroic, because she somehow found the strength to embrace fully the deeper reality of impending death: as she often said, to be "fully present." She would quote a folk song we learned at the summer camp where our daughter worked, with the refrain, "right here, right now." She would take joy where it was available. It was this posture that gave our family the courage both to grieve and to embrace life while she was fully alive, and that made her illness into something inspiring and even transcendent. As friends expressed wonder, I often quoted John F. Kennedy's remark, when he was asked how, as the young commander of a naval patrol vessel in the Pacific, he became a war hero. "It was involuntary," he replied. "They sank my boat."

In a long conversation which we tape-recorded about two months before she died, Sharland said: "It's taken me a long time to realize how much I love my life. Now, at the end of my life, I realize how much of my life I took for granted. More often than before, I'm able to be intensely present, in the moment. I'm conscious of the shortness of the future. There are times when it's very frightening to imagine not existing any more, but I feel a curiosity about what comes next because I don't really believe it all just ends. So I'm not really afraid of death. My life has been too short, but it has been very rich."

Sharland's presence and the way our family dealt with her dying was in some respects a conjuncture of accidents. Looking back, it feels as if all of our prior life was a preparation—her work as a therapist, my avocation as a poet, both of our experiences with our own parents, and our early travails with our son. We were also lucky, if one can use that word, in the course that this particular cancer took. Diagnosis of a fatal illness does not always leave one with three years of relatively good health. The onset of ultimately fatal illness sometimes leads to extreme physical incapacity and may come on with terrible abruptness. Yet the majority of us alive in midlife today will reach our seventy-fifth birthdays in basically intact health. Most of us will not die of a sudden heart attack, or in an instant accident. So it is indeed the business of all of us, whether or not we have yet been officially "diagnosed" with the human diagnosis of mortality, to take stock of what it means to have a limited tenure on this planet. This can begin well before one begins the process of wrestling with a terminal illness. The process of exploration, being mindful of one's mortality, can lead to a final and affirming reunion between parents and children. It is not morbid or narcissistic to believe so.

LOSING AND FINDING A PARENT

When we first learned about Sharland's condition, we had several immediate fears. One was that Sharland would be so sick so soon that there would be too little time to do much of anything, because she would just be consumed with the physical ordeal. A related fear was that she would be too sick to keep working; that she would not have adequate time to complete her clinical work with her patients, whom she would feel she was deserting. Another was that Sharland's entire being would become defined by the role of patient and the mind-set of patient; that she would just withdraw into a depression and become emotionally alone. Mercifully, none of this occurred. Instead, her temperamental stoicism, far from isolating her, served Sharland's physical bravery, while her curiosity about relationships and the human condition allowed mortality to be an intriguing engagement rather than a death sentence.

We both come from families of deniers. When I was young, the very word *cancer* was something not to be spoken aloud. A generation ago, it was commonplace for doctors and families to collude in a usually vain attempt to keep the dreaded news from the patient. Most patients, of course, knew all too well what they had and the likely outcome. Indeed, it was the very fact that cancer was usually both so gruesome and invariably fatal that made it such an unspeakable word. But, with the best of intentions, families tried to spare patients grief and pain, and patients reciprocated by trying to spare loved ones. For the most part, this mutual conspiracy of denial mainly spared both the kind of intimate love and consolation that both so desperately needed. Both ended up being more alone than they might have been.

After Sharland got sick, my mother and I began more candid conversations about my father's illness and death. I was stunned to learn that she and my father had never discussed the fact that he was dying. He was sick with Hodgkin's disease, a form of cancer that had no effective treatment when he died in the early 1950s. During the year that he had an illness which both knew to be fatal, he and my mother never directly acknowledged to each other that reality. As my mother explains it, each was trying, out of great love, to protect the other. I have no doubt that this is true. They had a close and good-humored marriage. They had survived poverty in the Depression and my father's horrible months in a German prison camp during World War II. I don't remember either of them ever saying a harsh word to each other. But half a century ago, the idiom of love in the face of disease and death was largely one of conspiracies of mutual denial.

At the same time, my mother had been surprisingly candid with me. In response to a direct question that I asked as a boy of nine, she did tell me that my father could die of the illness he had. And we had talked about what our lives might be like after he died. I have always been very grateful for those conversations. They must have been the model for the candor that I felt our children deserved, and could handle. Children are not stupid. The fear of abandonment is one of the most primal, and even as we think we are sheltering our children, they are already imagining the worst.

My mother did tell me the realities of my father's condition, but in their eagerness to protect me, my family explained that I couldn't visit my father in the VA hospital where he lay because children under twelve were not permitted on the ward. Pop and I visited on the phone, and in the rare weekend furloughs they permitted him during his several months in the hospital. When he died, I was not permitted to go to his funeral, which was deemed not something suitable for a nine-year-old child. My mother made these decisions out of love, yet she denied something important to herself, my father, and me. Later, numbed against feeling, I found it hard to recall his voice or memories of things we had done together.

Sharland's father, a taciturn scientist, had a tender side that he seldom revealed to his children. He died, at seventy-two, of emphysema. The week before he went for the last time into the hospital, where he knew he would be put on a respirator that would make it impossible to talk, he had a long, urgently compressed conversation with us. In far too short a time, using an unfamiliar vocabulary, he tried to convey the love for his family that was in his heart. He gave his children copies of a book-length journal he had been keeping, which was deeply sentimental and seemed out of character with his exterior. His family had not thought of him as a man with a rich inner life—but everyone has an inner life. Sharland wished that he, or she, had initiated such conversations earlier in his life. Recalling his long weeks on a respirator, gradually weakening in the hospital, Sharland was determined that she would die at home, surrounded by friends and family.

Sharland had a close relationship with her mother. She watched the tenderness with which her mother had cared for her father during the years of his emphysema. Her mother was a very active woman, and an international bridge grand master. Sharland imagined that as a fairly spry widow of sixty-nine, her mother would grieve for a time and then begin a new active life. But within just a few months of her husband's death, Sharland's mother was herself suddenly in a rapid downward spiral, with both lupus and cancer. Life during her remaining weeks was mainly about medical urgencies, not spiritual ones. She died with Sharland feeling that much had been left uncompleted and unspoken.

The first death of a close friend that we faced together occurred in the first year of our courtship, when Bob Ockene, a New York editor and former colleague of Sharland's, died of leukemia at thirty-five. Bob was the editor for several Beat poets. At his memorial, one of his poets read a composition that closed with the line, "I wish I had been kinder to you." It made a powerful impression on both of us. We did not want such regrets either when our loved ones died or when one of us died.

Having had this experience with three of our parents, we

hoped our children would be fully present for the last years of Sharland's life. This was not something that could be coerced, only modeled. We would live our own lives in a way that made clear that all could be spoken of, that any questions could be asked, that grief, fear, need—and love—could be openly expressed. I wrote this poem, thinking of my father:

Deaths

The first death was hushed voices and dry eyes
whispered discussions, well intended
to protect self and other
from deepest grief.
The first death was
a quiet conspiracy
of shared solitude.
And death prevailed.
We can't quite stare down this death
but we look it in the eye
saying the unspeakable
making some meaning
taking from death
what death
can't take
from us.

In retrospect, I am making it sound almost as if we had a deliberate plan. Of course we did not. We were improvising, even as we were reeling from the experience. Rather, several things about our prior lives had come together to make it possible for Sharland to deal with impending death the way she did— our separate and common histories, issues from our families of origin, her strong friendships with women, her work as a therapist, my poetry, the struggles and sometime triumphs of our marriage and our parenting. Without our planning it, we found ourselves treating candor as an act of defiance. It became our pact, against the cancer.

When Sharland was diagnosed, there was the immediate,

awful question of how and what to tell our children. Gabriel and Jessica were still relatively young, too young to have to face this ordeal, and far too young to lose a mother. But, given that Sharland was almost certain to die of this illness, we could hardly protect them from that ultimate reality. They needed to be fully present, as Sharland and I did, for what was unfolding. How to be present was their choice, but what could possibly be gained by trying to spare them the truth?

The evening that we received the test results, we asked Jessica, then seventeen, to join us in the living room for a serious talk. At the time Jessica's best friend, whose mother had just moved to another town, was temporarily living with us so she could graduate with her senior class. Jess was concerned that we had some problems with the arrangement, and she suspected that her friend was the subject of this particular hasty family conference. If only that had been so. We sat down on the living-room couch. "I would give anything in the world not to have to tell you what I'm about to say," Sharland began. "It's very likely that I have cancer." We all had tears in our eyes as we went over what would be happening in the coming weeks, and the likely course of the disease and treatment.

The next day, we had a similar conversation, by phone, with Gabriel in London. It was his second year of theater conservatory. The news was devastating to each of us. But we now had something of a family pact that we would all be present.

With the knowledge that she had an illness that was very likely terminal, Sharland considered, among other things, how she should deal with her patients. They ranged from seriously depressed people in long-term therapy, some of whom had been suicidal, to people having temporary difficulties with life's stresses. Everyone in psychotherapy, like everyone alive, deals with issues of loss, real losses through death or divorce and symbolic losses of what might have been. The potential loss of a therapist is wrenching: it taps feelings about every other loss, including long-buried issues with parents and premonitions of one's own eventual death.

Disclosure of details of a therapist's personal life is an appropriately controversial topic in psychotherapy. Keeping good "boundaries" between the therapist's own personal issues and the treatment of the patient is considered the mark of a competent therapist. Also, there is almost no professional literature on how psychotherapists deal, or should deal, with their own serious illnesses in the course of their patients' therapy, and many therapists keep their own medical conditions totally confidential. Some reveal nothing until they are at death's door. How much of her illness to divulge? How would this awful news affect the therapy? Should she just refer patients to other therapists? Not discuss her illness at all?

A week after she was diagnosed, Sharland consulted with a senior colleague, Dr. Gerald Adler, who had been her clinical supervisor. They spent an entire day reviewing all of her case files and discussing her patients. At length Sharland and Dr. Adler concluded that she should candidly answer their questions, but not foist unwanted information on patients by telling them more details than they asked to know or were ready to hear. Different patients should be treated differently, as appropriate, and would very likely react differently. One patient soon decided she would be better off working with another psychologist. A second terminated therapy. But the rest of her practice, about fifteen patients, elected to continue with Sharland. For them, the likelihood of her death became central to the therapy process; the mutual permission to explore deepest fears became enriching both to therapist and client. Sharland was eager to contribute a scholarly paper on how a therapist's impending death affects the course of the therapy, but she died before she could write it.

Sharland observed, "Every loss evokes every other loss. Sometimes, I'd spend the hour listening to how angry or how sad the patient was that I was dying on her. Inevitably, it allowed patients to go deeper into issues that had been taboo. It also allowed me to be braver about facing my own mortality. And I soon realized that if I could be totally, unflinchingly candid with my patients and myself, I also needed to be completely honest with my husband, and my brother, and my close friends, and my children. People don't know how to behave around someone with a fatal illness. They take their cue from the ill person. If the person signals that this mystery can be spoken of, that questions can be asked, it is a profound relief. It opens new doors."

One of Sharland's close professional colleagues and a dear friend, Orli Avi-Yonah, wrote:

> Over the course of three years, most of Sharland's patients gradually terminated therapy with her. She struggled with the complexities of treating patients while dying with the same honesty she brought to other relationships. She continually wrestled with the question of whose needs were being served. She worked to be attentive to her patients' relational needs as they were saying good-bye to her while continuing with their own lives.
>
> Her core belief as a therapist was always in the healing power of relationships. Her decision to continue to see patients, as unique individuals, was based on her respect for their decisions to work with her, or not, as long as she was able. She often spoke about her wish to help her patients make the decision when to leave therapy with her, without feeling guilty or burdened that they had abandoned her. She loved her work, but when the time came, she felt the best gift she could give her patients was to let go.

Over the course of three years, most of her patients gradually concluded their therapy. Sharland was still seeing patients until just weeks before she died, and she went to great lengths to work to plan transitions to another therapist whom both she and the patients trusted.

Sharland was also blessed with a close circle of women friends, some of whom were professional colleagues as therapists. All were committed to being with her and all were put at ease by the way she engaged not so much her battle with cancer but her engagement with her life and death.

A close friend of Sharland's, Jenny Mansbridge, was interviewed by Ellen Goodman for Goodman's book written with Patricia O'Brien on women's friendships. As Jenny recalled it for Goodman, her casual friendship with Sharland deepened after Sharland became sick, because they both knew time would be short. "Death trumps the datebook," Jenny put it. Jenny experienced Sharland as a remarkable listener. At the end of one long and heartfelt conversation, Jenny found herself thinking about how many people Sharland was responsible for—patients, friends, husband, children. Jenny impulsively took both of Sharland's hands into hers and said, "It's okay with me if you die." For the next several days, she felt appalled that her line was tactless and would be misunderstood. Arriving for a visit several days later, Jenny began to apologize. Sharland said, "I knew exactly what you meant. You meant you could be there for me, but that I didn't have to worry about you."

Sharland referred to her experience of deepening friendships during her illness as "time out of time." This is not a state that comes easily, especially because death is such a taboo subject for both the dying persons and the well-wishers. Another friend, Alexandra Marshall, sent Sharland an early novel of hers, *Gus in Bronze*, loosely based on her own mother's death. The character Augusta, or Gus, dying of cancer, grows weary of the bedside ritual, the tiptoeing around what is going on, the lack of real conversation, and the narcissism of a sister whom the novelist has aptly named Mimi (me-me.) In the novel's a climatic scene, several people are in the sickroom. The dying Gus asks one of those present, Jackson, to read aloud a long and brutally candid poem about one's own dying, by the nineteenth-century British poet Matthew Arnold. The poem includes the lines:

> Spare me the whispering, crowded room
> The friends who come, and gape, and go;
> The ceremonious air of gloom—
> All, which makes death a hideous show!
>
> Thus feeling, gazing, might I grow

Composed, refresh'd ennobled, clear;
Then willing to let my spirit go
To work or wait elsewhere or here.

This dialogue follows:

"Well," Gus said, "I rather liked that poem once I read the whole thing. Mimi, did you?"

Mimi gasped. "No," she blurted out, "how could you?"

"How could I like it?"

"Do that! God, Gussie!" Mimi buried her head.

"I thought it was time."

"And what if it was hard already?"

"Now, it's harder, that's all." It did hurt Gus to see Mimi weep, but she said anyway, "You were sapping me. I had to."

Jackson felt he would be sick but didn't dare move for fear Gus would notice. It was the most pitiful sobbing ever, Mimi's wretched guttural sobbing sounds.

"Gus said, "Now, you see, we can talk about it. I've wanted to."

This kind of brutal reversal, late in the process, did not become necessary for Sharland. From the beginning, she was determined to embrace the experience and to invite friends and family to embrace it with her. In our reading, we found that nearly everyone whose work we respected encouraged a candid engagement with mortality that may seem almost brutal or morbid. Dr. Sherwin Nuland, another pioneer in the movement for death with dignity, writes that "The dying themselves bear a responsibility not to be entrapped by a misguided attempt to spare those whose lives are intertwined. I have seen this form of aloneness, and even unwisely conspired in it, before I learned better."

After she was diagnosed, Sharland and I began reading a lot of poetry, and I began writing more poems. Long ago, I found that the discipline of poetry could enable me to focus on the essence of something important that I might otherwise miss. Poems demand candor. The poems we read and those I wrote became part of our pact that everything could be faced, that the way to deal with her mortality was to stare it down, to name it and defy it. They also became ways of expressing to our children how we were experiencing what was unfolding. Here is a poem written early in her cancer.

                              You

    What is it like for you?

    I can tell you what it's like for me.
    I am ashamed that it is almost romantic
        sometimes,
    looking hard at love and death.
    It is changing priorities
    making resolutions, writing poems
    being kind.
    It is loving you in new ways
    taking better care of myself
    learning to jettison what doesn't matter.
    It is appreciating friends
    seeing life more vividly.

    I am ashamed that sometimes it is feeling like
        a hero.
    It is thinking bravely about the next months
    thinking about all we have built
    thinking about what I may lose
    thinking, even, about life beyond your death.
    It is horrible, exotic, virtuous.
    It is valor and dread,
    love and loss.
    I am sometimes ashamed of being well
    of finding charity
    getting extensions
    coping bravely, bearing up.

And then I think harder
And I think,
my God,
darling
What is it like for you.

Jessica later remarked that the poem titled "You" got her attention. As a seventeen-year-old in her senior year of high school,
she had been naturally thinking of her mother's illness and possible death as a horrible tragedy for herself, which it surely was.
But what was it like for her mother?

The family therapist Donald Williamson, as we have noted,
holds that newly separating grown children ordinarily don't
have much empathic curiosity about their parents until well
into midlife. But an exception is a parent facing a fatal illness
with the courage to invite that curiosity.

Jess and Gabe were increasingly there for Sharland. When
they were small, we used to joke on family trips that our children, who fought constantly and could not keep their hands off
each other, were like some impossible couple that we unac-
countably kept taking vacations with. Now, I wrote this poem,
taking off from a well-known Jewish prayer said at every sabbath
and holiday service:

Couples

The other couple
sharing our house
is different
from the bickering couple
of years past.

This other couple
laughs easily
plays lightly,
lives generously,
knows life.

Praised be thou,
Lord our God,
King of the Universe,
who has allowed us to live
to see this day.

The poem, I realized later, had a double meaning. The "other couple" also described Sharland and me earlier in our marriage, before the prospect of her death had uncluttered our minds and compelled us to pay attention to what really mattered.

In a variety of ways, we were making it clear to our children that they were, irrevocably, part of this. It was nothing any of us had volunteered for, but we would all do it as well as we could. We were doing this, I think, partly for ourselves and partly for Gabe and Jess. Sharland did not push them, much less try to make them feel guilty, about what tasks they were supposed to perform or how they were supposed to behave. Rather, by inviting presence—her own and that of others—she was demonstrating an emotional availability that those around her were free to embrace.

As soon as she had recovered from the initial surgery and got established on a chemotherapy regimen she could tolerate, Sharland got in touch with a local hospice program. A representative of the program came to the house and spent a few hours with us, answering questions. Sharland, having recently recovered fully from colon surgery and not yet suffering any visible effects of either the cancer or the chemotherapy, looked crisp and fresh. She was entirely composed as she went over exactly what services the hospice program offered, how many hours a week of care the visiting nurses provided, whether there were any circumstances that would require dying in a hospital rather than at home. Jessica joined us for the meeting and listened intently. Sharland would not become incapacitated with the illness for nearly three more years. But she was engaging with her mortality. At the time, it was almost surreal, serving tea and cookies to a compassionate representative of hospice as we calmly discussed how a Sharland seemingly in robust health hoped to go about the enterprise of dying.

A HEALING CIRCLE

For about fourteen months, into early 1996, the treatments gradually worked to shrink the cancer in Sharland's liver. Sharland did not quite have her normal energy level, but she kept up her clinical practice, conducted research for this book, continued to take long brisk daily walks and do yoga. Except for the last two weeks of each chemotherapy cycle, which played havoc with her digestion, she felt surprisingly good. Our daughter graduated high school and went off to college. Our son completed theater conservatory and became engaged. We visited him in London. We took a trip to Italy.

We settled down to a kind of quasi-normal, but strangely enhanced routine. Once a week, we would meet at the outpatient chemotherapy unit at the Beth Israel Hospital. I would pick up sandwiches and coffee, and we would have another of what we came to call our chemotherapy picnics. One of the two nurses who regularly took care of Sharland would hook her up to an IV drip, and the treatment would take about two hours. Sometimes, Jess or Gabe would join us, occasionally one of Sharland's close women friends. Often, it was just a time for the two of us to be together and to encounter the eternal.

But by mid-1997, it was clear that the treatments were no longer having effect. In June, Sharland was still feeling well enough to plan a wedding for Gabriel and his fiancée Kate, and to host a festive reception. But time was running out. She would die within a few months, we all knew.

We planned to spend an extended summer at Cape Cod. Gabriel and Kate spent the summer with us. Jessica went on a month-long Outward Bound trip, and when she came back and rejoined the family on Cape Cod, she found herself better prepared to deal with what was coming. Though she was about to enter her third year of college, and had been considering spending a semester or year abroad, Jessica decided instead to take time off from school and live with us at home. Gabriel and Kate, who had just moved into a new flat in London, also decided to come home for the duration. Sharland's brother, John, moved in with us, too.

A stream of close friends and well-wishers visited with us as the summer wore on. One Sunday afternoon, we had resolved to keep some precious time for just the family. But two dear friends, Paula Rayman and Rob Read, asked if they could drop by. In the course of the visit with them, Rob and Paula mentioned a healing circle they were participating in with Pat Farren, another close friend of theirs who was dealing with incurable cancer. We had heard the healing circle concept mentioned the year before, during our weeklong retreat at Commonweal, but hadn't pursued it.

Healing circles are a modern variation of religious supports for the sick and dying used by a variety of traditional peoples. More recently, they have become a variant of cancer support groups. They have been particularly prevalent in the gay community, where people often find several friends and loved ones simultaneously dealing with terminal HIV/AIDS, something that is both emotionally and logistically overwhelming. Feminists have organized support groups for women dealing with breast cancer, sometimes as healing circles. To a degree, healing circles are a formalization of what goes on spontaneously, if an ill person is prepared to let others in. They connect what can be a horribly lonely experience to a loving community. They also anticipate what goes on in many religious faiths after a person dies.

In some healing circles, where a person struggling with a fatal illness needs material as much as emotional support, much of what occurs is logistical—meals, child care, giving immediate caregivers some respite, a community taking turns running errands and visiting. In other cases, the support is emotional, both for the dying person and for the ones grieving. Sometimes, the support works both ways. The dying person is able to comfort those who are already grieving, and people are able to say good-bye. I often felt that Sharland took strength from making things easier for people who were already missing her.

Rob and Paula had brought with them a copy of a short piece Pat Farren had written on the healing circle that his friends and family had organized on his behalf, which had been meeting monthly for nearly a year. He wrote:

> It's spiritual without being sectarian; communal without being narrow; low-key, nurturing, touching, and fun. Our circles are intended to "heal" if not to cure—that is, to bring us closer, to allow us to use the time we spend together to deepen our relationships and to say what we want to say, and to get better at being full human beings without necessarily having strong hope that the course of the illness may be transformed into wellness. On the other hand, there is an openness to miracles. . . .
>
> At a time when community is relatively rare, a circle can be most welcome. This has been an easy way for us to receive a profound amount of support, while knowing we were fostering community. One need not even be ill to reach out and build this kind of bridge.

We thanked Rob and Paula for telling us about their experience with Pat Farren's healing circle. They were hardly out the door when the four of us could read each other's minds. This was something we all wanted to do, for each other. "I wanted to make it ours," Gabe told me, looking back. "I didn't want to follow somebody else's script."

In the healing circle, we recognized an echo of Commonweal. We also recognized a similarity to groups that often come together after a person dies, in Catholic wakes, in the general custom of bringing food to the family of the bereaved, and in the Jewish tradition of sitting Shiva, in which the grieving family receives well-wishers at the home for seven days after a death. But why wait to grieve together until death occurred? In a moment of black humor, Sharland referred to our healing circle as "pre-Shiva."

We carefully considered whom to invite. We included our children, Sharland's brother John, my mother, and several close friends who had already been part of the process of Sharland's informal healing circle. With the exception of Rob and Paula, nobody in the group had ever been in anything like this.

We organized the healing circle to meet once a week, late on Sunday afternoons. Neither Sharland nor I were members of a formal religious congregation. She was a lapsed Congregationalist, I a not terribly observant Jew. As her illness progressed, however, Sharland found herself dealing with spiritual questions. At Harvard's Appleton Chapel, there is a tradition dating back more than three hundred years of having Morning Prayers on weekdays, an ecumenical half hour of worship and reflection at which a guest gives a brief talk. Sharland, in mid-1997, spoke on the subject of "Wrestling with the Angel," taken from the biblical story of Jacob.

There is part of what she said:

> It feels both strange and familiar to be here, for although I grew up in a religious family, I stopped going to church about the time I started going to college, and in the 30-odd years since then, I have not much missed it. If I thought about God at all, it was fleetingly. My life was too busy, too rich and full and complicated. God seemed like an abstraction, not a profound mystery with intense personal meaning.

> Illness and healing, living and dying are a form of wrestling with the angel. If we avoid engagement with the angel, whether it's the angel of death or the angel of life, we flirt with a kind of frozen death-in-life, while the pervasive denial of death, of our own mortality, becomes in the end a denial of life itself. Dealing with a life-threatening illness, I've discovered, presents a paradoxical task: to fight death without denying its reality, and at the same time to assert life as fully and as forcefully as possible.

> For me, the assertion of life has primarily taken the form of discovering how deeply I am connected to other people—to my family, to my friends, even to the strangers I've met in the course of interviewing for a book I'm working on. I am bathed in the love of other people, and I am blessed. I have never before felt such moments of intimate communion, and of joy. At the same time, I have experienced moments of unutter-

able loneliness, felt keenly the invisible barrier that divides the sick from the well. It is at these darkest, most alone moments that I find myself absorbed in the mystery of God, have felt Him both as a comforting presence within me, and as a force outside of me. No longer an abstraction, He has become personal and real—realer than hospitals, doctors, nurses, needles and procedures, realer at times even than the love and support of those with whom I am most intimate. I have come to think of God as a negotiator, mediating between me and my illness and sparking the self-healer in me.

There is another dimension to the mystery of God, and that is the idea of the sacred in life. When you are fighting for life, it is for the preciousness of each moment. I notice things more intently, and more deeply: the wind blowing through the sea grasses in Truro, where my family and I spend a part of each summer, the waves cresting on the shore, the early spring sky in Boston and, after months of struggling to eat, the simple pleasure of relishing food. Give us this day our daily bread, and let us enjoy every morsel. The places where I feel most comfortable and at peace I think of as sacred spaces that invite meditation or prayer. The sacred resides in things both large and small, mundane and extraordinary, that hold life's deepest meanings.

My images of the sacred, and of God, are bound up with images of life and death. He represents both, transcending the apparent contradictions. He has held out his hand, and asked me to dance. And so I have, learning the intricate steps of the long slow dance of death, rejoicing in the rhythms of life. This dialectical dance of life and death is one of the great and surprising gifts that a life-threatening illness can bestow.

As our pastor for the healing circle, we turned to another dear friend, Jim Carroll, who had been ordained as a Catholic priest. Jim had left the priesthood, and was now a novelist, newspaper columnist, religious historian, social critic, and the married father of two children. He remained the most deeply spiritual person we knew. We were still improvising, with a deep sense of presence and mindfulness. The whole experience was still a profound paradox that combined the most intense emotion and sadness with a "detached curiosity" and invitation to community.

At the first meeting, we distributed a one-page description of what a healing circle was and what we hoped to accomplish. We quoted from Pat Farren's piece, and added:

> We've been blessed with a large community of friends who have been an informal healing circle. We hope that coming together weekly will deepen these bonds, and allow all of us a time of mutual comfort and exploration of eternal questions.
>
> We hope these meetings can include periods of meditative silence, music, poems, stories, and a chance for all of us to speak about our own concerns, burdens, and joys. Nothing is more important at this time than to give voice to what is in our hearts.

The members of the circle included people with diverse backgrounds and professions. Perhaps a third were observant members of diverse religious faiths. A few were therapists. Some were professional or amateur writers, or teachers. One was a former priest, another a near rabbi, another an organizer, another an architect, another a restorer of public sculptures, another a judge. Except for our children and my mother, most of us were in our forties and fifties. All were friends of many years standing. Some had been present twenty-five years before at our wedding.

At times, the healing circle resembled a Quaker meeting. At times, it was a discussion group. Other times it was raw, emotional and cathartic. We learned surprising things about each other. People brought and read favorite poems, either by published poets or of their own composition. Two of us played banjo and guitar, and we always sang songs. "Amazing Grace" became the anthem of the healing circle. It would be the closing hymn at Sharland's memorial service.

After a couple of sessions, people began asking probing, even intimate questions. Did Sharland believe in an afterlife? What regrets did she have? What was she going to miss? What was it like to imagine imminent death? Sharland herself had set the standard. There was nothing that could not be spoken of. For the most part, our children did not talk a lot. But they listened. What they heard was a group of adults struggling to make sense of the ultimate mystery, with candor, bravery, integrity, and love. This was another intergenerational connection. There were also times when we had doubts, when we just didn't know what to say. And the silences were part of the reality, too.

As we read more poems, the poet Mary Oliver became the unofficial poet laureate of Sharland's healing circle. Sharland's favorite Mary Oliver poem, "When Death Comes," also read at her memorial, summed up how she took from death enriched life.

When Death Comes

When death comes
like the hungry bear in autumn;
when death comes and takes all the bright coin from his purse

to buy me; and snaps the purse shut;
when death comes
like the measle-pox;

when death comes
like an iceberg between the shoulder blades

I want to step through the door full of curiosity, wondering:
what is it going to be like, that cottage of darkness?

And therefore I look upon everything
as a brotherhood and a sisterhood,
and I look upon time as no more than an idea,
and I consider eternity as another possibility,

and I think of each life as a flower, as common

as a field daisy, and as singular,

and each name a comfortable music in the mouth,
tending, as all music does, toward silence,

and each body a lion of courage, and something
precious to the earth.

When it's over, I want to say: all my life
I was a bride married to amazement.
I was the bridegroom, taking the world into my arms.

When it's over, I don't want to wonder
if I have made of my life something particular, and real.
I don't want to find myself sighing, and frightened,
or full of argument.

I don't want to end up simply having visited this world.

Probably the most moving moment came when Susan Linn, the psychotherapist and ventriloquist whom we met in Chapter 2, agreed to bring her favorite puppet, Audrey Duck. Our family first encountered Susan and Audrey in 1979, not long after we moved to the Boston area, when Susan was performing at the local Puppet Showplace. We were immediately smitten. Audrey, who has the personality of a curious and precocious six-year-old, became a favorite guest at our children's birthday parties. Two years later, beginning graduate school, Sharland was pleasantly surprised to find that one of her new colleagues among the first-year students in psychology was none other than Susan Linn. A ventriloquist since childhood, Susan had gone on to study theater, and had begun using her talent with puppets to work with cancer patients at Children's Hospital. She had virtually invented puppet therapy—a form of projective therapy intended to help seriously ill children give voice to fears that adults were trying to keep bottled up—and she was now pursuing a clinical degree.

At the healing circle, Susan, as always in her routine, began by taking Audrey out of the bag where she reposes. As always, Audrey, coming to life, was benignly bewildered and Susan had to explain things.

"Susan?" asked Audrey. "Where are we?"

"We're at Bob and Sharland's, Audrey."

"Ohhh. Is it Gabriel's birthday?"

"No, Audrey."

"Is it Jessica's birthday?"

"No, Audrey, it's not."

"Well, why are we here?"

"Audrey, we're here because Sharland has cancer."

All of us were holding our breaths, as Susan and Audrey continued this dialogue. Presently, Audrey turned to Sharland and began asking some innocent and profound questions. Sharland answered each one tenderly, as "Audrey" raised deeply affecting issues that even Susan wouldn't raise. Audrey told Sharland how angry she was that Sharland was dying. The conversation ended thus:

"Good-bye, Sharland."

"Good-bye, Audrey."

We were, as they say, blown away. As often, there were tears, laughter, hugs, and wonder. We were all sixties kids, pushing at limits, even in the face of death. Susan, out of role and always impertinent, quipped: "Our generation is going to do for death what we did for sex."

So captivating and believable was this tableau of Audrey talking with Sharland about life and death that, as the gathering was breaking up, I turned to Susan's husband and blurted out, "Clifford, Audrey is amazing." Clifford looked at me oddly. "No, Bob, Susan is amazing." The healing circle enabled everyone present to reach new places of insight and compassion, to become larger than the people we had been.

BEYOND THE DEATH TABOO

A few months after Sharland died, I happened to be at a conference where Dr. Sherwin Nuland was leading a discussion. As he often does, Dr. Nuland was criticizing his own profession for stressing the purely clinical aspects of death and depriving patients of choices that are properly theirs to make. I have long admired Dr. Nuland's work and learned from it. Raising my hand, I thanked him and suggested that perhaps things were changing for the better. I recounted our good experience with the hospice people, with Dr. Schnipper's team at Boston's Beth Israel Hospital, with the Commonweal Cancer Program, with Jon Kabat-Zinn's mediation wisdom, and I described the healing circle. No one, I said, had taken from Sharland control of how she chose to live her final years, and many in the medical profession and elsewhere had facilitated her journey. In fact, society now offered a variety of very different models of how to die. He agreed that, thanks largely to hospice, things were slowly getting better, but that most people still died in hospitals hooked up to wretched machinery; that too many oncologists still denied people informed choices.

But increasingly, we do have the power to take control of our own dying. More than the medical system, it is our own sense of taboos that precludes choices. All of us—most of us, anyway—are capable of the kinds of connections and insights that occurred in Sharland's healing circle. It may require a gifted spiritual leader, like Jim Carroll, to animate a support group. It is easier if the dying person offers something of Sharland's grace. But nearly all of us have inner lives and are capable of profound emotion. This is a self that can be cultivated, whether through formal religious belief, meditation, support groups, or one's own unique spiritual odyssey. In the case of our family, none of us began the process with this sensibility. Yet each of us is capable of deciding that, in the course of dying, we want to stay vividly connected to life. Our communities can come together to affirm our decision. We are all cowardly lions about our mortality, capable of great fear and great courage. We each, potentially, can find that self, for ourselves and our children.

In early October, several of my cousins announced that they wanted to plant a tree for Sharland. Come while I'm alive, Sharland said. My whole extended family arrived early on a Sunday afternoon, bearing a Kousa dogwood, and we invited them in for coffee and cake. After about twenty minutes of awkward small talk in groups of twos and threes, I realized with a sinking feeling that nobody knew quite what to say, that nobody felt they had the permission or vocabulary to speak candidly; and that people would soon be drifting away.

Everyone was ignoring the elephant in the room. Emboldened by the healing circle, I tapped a glass and heard myself say something like, "Excuse me. I need to drop a small bomb. Sharland and I appreciate that you've come today. And I suspect all of us will feel terrible afterwards if we let this moment pass without saying what is in our hearts." A long moment passed. Then Linnie, who is married to my cousin David, began recalling how hard it had been when she first "came into the family"; how grateful she was that Sharland, herself a veteran in-law in this sometimes baffling and turbulent family, had been very welcoming; what a role model Sharland had been as a woman professional and a mother, and now, as someone facing death. Soon, everyone had something to say to Sharland and to the group, much of it deeply moving. My cousin Jim remarked that he had never been in anything close to this kind of conversation with a dying person. Heads around the room nodded. There were tears and hugs as everyone present became a larger person. My own extended family, which I often sold short, had joined the healing circle.

It was a time of uplift and deep sorrow. The house often felt chaotic and invaded. Even in our gratitude to family and close friends, we could say that, too. We could say anything. I wrote:

Circle

As death dawns,
we have returned,
weirdly,
to the commune of our youth
a sixties collective
of drop ins
pot lucks

and pot smokes
this time, medicinal for real.
and, as our own younger selves,
our grown children.

In one sense,
it is community
as we always imagined it
back when we were too young
to do it properly,
a loving adult communing
of learned compassion and tact;
gourmet tables, this time
and clean kitchens,
a danse macabre
feasting in the teeth of death.

Sometimes, though,
community comes bundled with
missed signals
dishes put in wrong cupboards
glasses chipped in friendship
systems trampled and space invaded
with the best intentions
community means queuing up for a turn
to lie with you in my own bed,
grief magnified
in the sorrowing faces
of dear friends
pounding on the door;
my halo slips.

Mostly,
the circle is healing
but I miss
our community
of two.

In the conversation that we taped two months before she died, Sharland reflected on how she had gone about living and dying, and where she had found the strength to approach her death with such remarkable presence. She remarked: "I gave my own mortality very little thought until I was diagnosed. If I thought about death at all, it was in terms of the loss of my parents, or my fear of losing you, or one of our children. I will never take my life for granted again." Could she have begun this exploration without a cancer diagnosis? "You never know," she said. "There are some lessons that have to be learned in their own time." Yet having been with Sharland on this journey, neither our children or I will ever take our lives for granted.

Sharland mused about a core theme of this book, the paradox of solitude and connection. She quoted one of her favorite writers on human psychology, Donald Winnicott. "Winnicott said that the capacity to be securely alone is born in the child's solitary play in the presence of the mother. The parent is an emblem of safety and security, but doesn't interrupt the child's inner fantasy world. The capacity to sooth one's self, to comfort one's self, to be comfortable alone, is, paradoxically, what enables you to engage deeply with other people. Death, ultimately, is the most alone experience there is. Yet, along the way, if you're brave enough to invite people in, relationships deepen. I feel that all the relationships I care about have deepened over the past years. It's strange to say, but at this moment, I feel happy— enriched, blessed, and deeply sad all at once, but alive and connected. I haven't withdrawn from my life. I haven't withdrawn from other people."

Some people have a hard time with terminal candor. Many experience it with relief and appreciation. A recent friend of Sharland felt empowered to write her a note, in the last weeks of her life: "I am a latecomer to your circle, and in some ways that makes me feel even more bereft to not have more time to know you better. You are not the first person important in my life who has faced death, but you are the only one who has shared some of the experience with me. Thank you. I want you to know I love you and I wish you eternal peace." Reflecting on the healing circle and the whole three-year process, another dear friend of Sharland's observed it helped her realize, amid great sadness, that Sharland was living for three years, not dying for three years.

As the weather turned cold, Sharland's health worsened. Finally, in mid-November, when she was confined to her bed and in and out of consciousness, we had one session of the healing circle where Sharland was in the house but not in the room. She had had many talks with Dr. Schnipper about just how she hoped to spend her last days. She would of course be at home, surrounded by family and friends. She had planned her memorial, down to the music that would be played, the poems that would be read, those who would speak, and the party that would immediately follow.

She had inquired of Dr. Schnipper what the end would be like. As cancer deaths go, he explained, it would be fairly gentle. Her liver would gradually cease functioning. She would become more and more fatigued, fade into unconsciousness, and within a few days or weeks, she would die. In the meantime, however, as the cancer grew, she would be in escalating pain. This could be controlled with morphine. At the point where the dosage adequate to the control the pain began slowing her metabolic functions, the painkillers might hasten her death.

Sharland had tentatively decided that when she reached a point where her life had little quality left, she would say final good-byes and then raise the dosage of her painkillers to a near-lethal level. Dignity was very important. She did not want to spend her last days bedridden, incoherent and incontinent. We had one last conference with Dr. Schnipper at the hospital, and Sharland came home to have one last round of visits and to die. She limited the bedside callers to her closest friends, her brother, our children, and me. But as she got weaker and weaker, she was clear enough to decide that she did not want to end her life with painkillers, and for nearly two weeks she lingered in and out of consciousness.

At that final session of the healing circle while Sharland was alive, I read this poem that I had just written.

Providence

This storybook ending wasn't to be.
After the elegant bravery
after the goodbyes, comes the waiting.
The cosmos has one more trick
the spirit isn't ready to leave;
the body fools us,
and resolves to live on.
How did we dare think
we could script death?

It is almost awkward,
like a guest overstaying a welcome
or lingering after a rich dinner
when the waiters want to go home
a play persisting into a sixth act
imposing our drama on a restless audience.

Groping for metaphor and meaning,
Paula thinks of endless landing delays
on a wintry northeast corridor
with Logan Airport fogged in. She says:
"It's like circling over Providence."

Divine Providence has her own schedule
pilots and runways we can't imagine
as we circle and circle,
seeking some beacon,
straining out our tiny windows
looking for solid ground.

Along with the vivid connection and heroism we all felt was
just plain sadness. Acknowledging that sorrow was part of the
process of grieving that began in Sharland's presence.

It goes without saying that the healing circle was an unimagined source of support for Gabriel, Jessica, and me, as well as for

Sharland. But it was Sharland who had modeled how to engage death with vivid life. When Sharland did die, in late November, we felt an irreplaceable loss, yet we had shared a lot of the mourning while she was alive. Sharland was not a saint, I wrote in one poem, only a prophet.

It is important to acknowledge that our children's experience was not the same as ours. Sharland and I had experienced other deaths. We came to this process, of one of us dying, with some fierce determination. Gabe and Jess did not bring this prior history. For them, the overwhelming reality was that they were losing a mother. The way Sharland went about dying was secondary to that devastating reality. Yet engaging her own death and including her family in the process made it less awful and made each of us less alone.

Inviting others into the intimate business of dying is a gift we can give ourselves and others. It is particularly poignant when the others are our children, because all of our parental impulses are to protect them. Two dear friends of ours, Paul and Sandra Starr, went through a similar odyssey with cancer shortly after ours began. Just forty-four at the time she faced death, Sandra wanted to pass treasured family memories on to her young children. With the children sitting in bed beside her, she went through family albums, tape recording a description of the moment of each picture, beginning with each child's birth. The family planned to put the album onto a compact disk, with the recording accompanying each photo. This would be a lifelong gift to the children, a living family album narrated in their mother's voice. Perhaps more important, the act of making the tape with the children engaged Sandra in a narrative of her life and engaged her children in the emotional reality of her dying.

In Chapter 3, we quoted part of Dr. Rachel Remen's story of her fifteen-year-old leukemia patient, Gloria, who hoped to spare her parents knowledge of her impending death. Dr. Remen went on to explain that, once mortality was acknowledged, she subsequently had long conversations with the girl about dying. "We wondered together: Could life go on some other way. We spoke of heaven and other ideas about the possibility of life after death. She was surprised to learn that most of the people in the world believe there is life after death. I told her that philosophers and other people have always wondered about the mystery of death and written about it, and asked her if she would like me to bring her any of these writings. She accepted the offer."

Their talks continued. Eventually, Gloria was able to discuss her incipient death with her parents.

"She felt the depth of their love. She had always known how much her mother had loved her, but her father was undemonstrative; she had not known how deeply he cared. 'Dr. Remen,' she said. 'He even cried.'"

"At her request, her father brought her a picture of the spot where she would be buried. He reminded her that someday he and her mother would be buried there, too. It was terribly, terribly sad, but it was not lonely."

Finally, Gloria slipped into a coma and died. Their private doctor, an older man, went in to console the parents. "He assured them that everything possible, everything scientifically known, had been done, but it just hadn't been enough. He told them sincerely how very sorry he was. He spoke of her courage and what good parents they had been to her. Both of them had been with her at the end, he said. She had not died alone. And she had not known she was dying, so she had not been afraid."

"When he finished we all sat together for a while. Then her father looked at me for the first time."

"'Thank you,' he said."

"She had not died alone, but it had been such a near thing."

Lorraine David, whose essay "The Use of Terminal Candor" we quoted in our first chapter, described how her children, then in their early twenties, responded to her impending death. Like Sharland, she was determined not to try to shelter them. She felt fortunate, she wrote, because "Needless energies have not been dissipated in 'keeping secrets' or in playing the draining charade of 'protecting each other.' Her own candor, she added, emboldened her younger son, then twenty-two.

Some months after my illness [began], he asked if he might

do an interview with me as part of a communications course assignment. He had always had assumed the role of family comedian and up to this point I had found it very difficult to talk to him about our feelings, because he would always turn me off with a flip comment. But when he called, I suspected he was choosing this way, on his own terms, where he might be in control, to discuss my impending death. I guessed right, and our encounter turned out to be one of the most moving and meaningful exchanges I have ever had with someone near and dear to me. He wanted to know how it felt to be in my position, and in turn, shared his own feelings. More importantly, he wanted to know how I felt about the way he had turned out and expressed his feelings about how I stacked up as a mother. Spurred on by a new sense of confidence and freeing of self, he next interviewed my husband about his plans after I die. Did he plan to sell the house? Would he remarry? He did a magnificent job of dealing with anticipatory grief—my husband's as well as my own.

Dan Lowenstein, in one of the Commonweal poems, wrote:

> Help me
> To weave
> The Threads of my life
> Into a tapestry that will
> Keep my children warm
> When I die.

What has been called a "good death" is the final chance that one has to repair and intensify emotional bonds between parents and children. Our tragedy is that Gabe and Jess will not have their mother to participate in benchmark events—career achievements, the birth of children, family crises, chances just to compare notes on living. Nobody will know them the way Sharland did. That she was such an accessible mother and such an alive person makes the loss that much more irreplaceable. But Sharland's gift to our children was a wholeness in our family that lives beyond her death—a continuing reunion. Long life, though universally sought, is no guarantee of such connection. Sharland left our children an emotional vocabulary and intelligence, rare for their years, that will serve them throughout their lives. It is hard to imagine a richer legacy.

Acknowledgments

A wide variety of people helped us with this book and supported us as we were living a very different family reunion than we intended. The late Martin Kessler believed in this project and was the first of several editors to work with us. The book's current editor, Philip Rappaport, was willing to keep it alive even after one of the authors was no longer living. Our agent, John Brockman, steadfastly believed in it.

We received wise counsel from Faye Snider, Barry Dym, Ralph Engel, Henry Gruenbaum, Gerald Adler, Robert Butler, and Sylvia Staub. We thank Jon Kabat-Zinn, Michael Lerner and colleagues at Commonweal, Lowell Schnipper and Paddy Connally and the team at Boston's Beth Israel Hospital, and Bob Mayer of the Dana Farber Cancer Institute.

All or part of the manuscript was read by Bea Chorover, Constance Bloomfield, Bill MacFarlane, Paula Rayman, Robert Read, Sydney Reed, Larry Aber, Orli Avi-Yonah, Judy Salzman, John Brockman, Katinka Matson, Gabriel Kuttner, Jessica Kuttner, Polly Levy, and Joan Fitzgerald.

We are grateful to the Radcliffe Public Policy Institute, its director Paula Rayman and its staff, especially Chris Locke, Sue Shefte, and Abby Elmore for giving Sharland a fellowship to work on this book, and making Bob a fellow to continue the work after Sharland's death. We had research help from Jill Denny, Runa Islam, Karen Hallman, and Joellen Valentine.

We owe a particular debt to Sharland's healing circle: James

Carroll and Lexa Marshall, Peter and Ann Anderson, Orli and Reuven Avi-Yonah, Constance Bloomfield and Bill McFarlane, Bea and Steve Chorover, Ross and Anne Gelbspan, Barney Geller and Jeff Packard, Christopher Jencks and Jane Mansbridge, Gabriel Kuttner and Kate Milne, Jessica Kuttner, Polly Levy, Susan Linn and Clifford Crane, Pat Peterson, Paula Rayman and Rob Read, Robert Reich and Clare Dalton, Carl and Judy Salzman, John and Ellie Trotter, Susan Wadsworth, Shannon Woolley and Tom Gutheil.

Special thanks are due to Gabriel and Jessica Kuttner, who are part of a continuing reunion as strong, autonomously attached, loving adults; to Polly Levy, who has demonstrated an ongoing capacity for growth and compassion as she approaches ninety; and to Joan Fitzgerald, who married into this unusual project and who has supported it with uncommon grace.

Notes

Chapter 1

1 **Metropolitan Diary:** Lawrence Feinman, "Metropolitan Diary,"*New York Times*, November 7, 1993, C2.

2 **Dickens:** Charles Dickens, *David Copperfield* (New York: Dodd, Mead & Co., 1943), 1 ("Whether I shall turn out to be the hero of my own life, or whether that station will be held by anybody else, these pages must show").

9 **Framo quote:** James Framo, *Explorations in Marital and Family Therapy* (New York: Springer Publishing Co., 1982), 178.

9 **David quote:** Lorraine David (pseudonym), "The Use of Terminal Candor," in Peter Titelman, ed., *The Therapist's Own Family* (Northvale, NJ: Jason Aronson, 1987), 279–300.

9 **Edelman reference** Hope Edelman, *Motherless Daughters* (Reading, MA: Addison-Wesley, 1994).

10 **Edelman quote:** Ibid., 82.

Chapter 2

17 **Wolf:** Anthony E. Wolf, *Get Out of My Life (But First Could You Drive Me and Cheryl to the Mall?)* (New York, Noonday Press, 1991), 165.

18 **Linn:** Susan Linn, "Take Another Look: Learning to Rethink Anger" (videotape). Brookline, MA: Institute for Mental Health Initiatives, 1990.

19 **Williamson:** Donald S. Williamson, "Personal Authority via Termination of the Intergenerational Hierarchical Boundary: A 'New' Stage in the Family Life Cycle," *Journal of Marital and Family Therapy* (October 1981) 444–45.

21 **Jonas and Nissenson:** Susan Jonas and Marilyn Nissenson, *Friends for Life: Enriching the Bond Between Mothers and Their Adult Daughters* (New York: William Morrow, 1997), xiv.

22   **Jonas and Nissenson:** Ibid., 80.

23   **"prize pig":** The Boston Women's Health Collective, *Ourselves and Our Children* (New York: Random House, 1978), 116.

25   **Kabat-Zinn:** Jon Kabat-Zinn, *Full Catastrophe Living* (New York: Delta/Dell, 1991).

27   **Callahan:** Sidney Callahan, *Parents Forever* (New York: Crossroad Publishing Co 1992), 58–59.

28   **Klingelhofer:** Edwin L. Klingelhofer, *Coping with Your Grown Children* (Clifton, NJ: Humana Press, 1989), 219.

28   *Fantasticks:* Tom Jones and Harvey Schmidt, *The Fantasticks* (New York: The Fantasticks Company, 1960).

34   **Zax and Poulter:** Barbara Zax and Stephan Poulter, *Mending the Broken Bough: Restoring the Promise of the Mother-Daughter Relationship* (New York: Berkley Books, 1998), 68.

Chapter 3

36   **Joyce:** James Joyce, *Portrait of the Artist as a Young Man* (New York: Viking Press, 1962/1916), 14.

37   **Roth**/Portnoy: Philip Roth, *Portnoy's Complaint* (New York: Vintage Books, 1967), 111.

37   **Turgenev:** Ivan Turgenev, *Fathers and Sons*, trans. Rosemary Edmonds (New York: Penguin Books, 1965), 87.

39   **Nagy:** See Ivan Boszormenyi-Nagy and Geraldine M. Spark, *Invisible Loyalties* (Levittown, PA: Bruner/Mazel, 1984), esp. chaps. 2–5.

40   **Remen:** Rachel Naomi Remen, *Kitchen Table Wisdom* (New York: Riverhead Books, 1997), 121.

46   **Bloomfield:** Harold H. Bloomfield, *Making Peace with Your Parents* (New York: Ballantine Books, 1983), 8, 9, 16.

46   **Framo ("smothering bitch"):** James L. Framo, *Family-of-Origin Therapy: An Intergenerational Approach* (New York: Brunner/Mazel, 1992), 9–10.

47   **Framo ("therapeutic resource"):** Ibid., 8.

47   **McGoldrick:** Monica McGoldrick, *You Can Go Home Again* (New York: W. W. Norton, 1995), 111.

47   **Minuchin:** Salvador Minuchin, *Families and Family Therapy* (Cambridge, MA: Harvard University Press, 1974), 4–5.

48   **System rather than individual dysfunctional:** Roberta Gilbert, *Extraordinary Relationships* (New York: John Wiley, 1992), 66.

48   **McGoldrick:** McGoldrick, *You Can Go Home Again*, 114.

49   **Lerner: ("I stopped feeling angry")** Harriet Goldhor Lerner, *The Dance of Anger* (New York, Harper & Row, 1985), 155.

49   **Lerner: ("correspondence between the generations"):** Ibid.

50   **Lerner: ("real emotional issue"):** Ibid., 156.

50   **Compliance with and rebellion against family system:** Michael E. Care,
        M.D. "Darwin to Freud to Bowen," *Georgetown* (Spring 1988), 17–19;
        44–45; quote at 19.

50   **Well-differentiated people:** See Gilbert, *Extraordinary Relationships,* 22.

52   **Gilbert:** Ibid., 7.

53   **Karen:** Robert Karen, *The Forgiving Self* (New York: Doubleday, 2001),
        249.

53   **Bowen:** Gilbert, *Extraordinary Relationships,* 119.

54   **Parents divested of magical power:** Framo, *Family-of-Origin Therapy,* 162.

54   **Framo:** Ibid., 27. See also 159–62.

55   **Framo:** Framo, *Explorations in Marital and Family Therapy,* 186.

55   **Osherson ("Big Al"):** Samuel Osherson, *Finding our Fathers* (New York:
        Free Press, 1986), 25.

55   **Susan Forward:** Susan Forward, *Toxic Parents* (New York: Bantam
        Books, 1989), 269.

56   **Framo: ("weeping father"):** Framo, *Family of Origin Therapy,* 64.

56   **Framo: (internalized father):** Ibid., 81.

        Chapter 4

62   **Nagy:** Boszormenyi-Nagy and Spark, *Invisible Loyalties,* 4.

62   **Haley:** Jay Haley, *Leaving Home* (New York: McGraw-Hill, 1980), 29.

62   **Haley: ("parents become unable to function"):** Ibid., 30.

62   **Wallerstein:** Judith S. Wallerstein, "Psychological Tasks of Marriage,"
        American Journal of Orthopsychiatry 64 (4), October 1994.

63   **Bowlby:** See John Bowlby, *Attachment and Loss.* Vol. 1: *Attachment*
        (New York: Basic Books, 1969).

67   **"Schizophrenogic mothers":** See Richard Pollak, *The Creation of Dr. B: A
        Biography of Bruno Bettelheim* (New York: Simon & Schuster, 1997).

69   **How attachment to spouse affects parenting:** Jane L. Pearson, Deborah
        A. Cohn, Philip A. Cowan, and Carolyn Paper Cowan, "Earned and
        Continuous Security in Adult Relations," *Development and Psychol-
        ogy,* 6 (1994), 369, 370.

70   **Mark Twain's father:** This famous remark, long attributed to Mark
        Twain, appears nowhere in his published writings. He is said to have
        expressed it orally. According to *Bartlett's,* the first printed reference
        is in *Reader's Digest* (September 1937).

71   **Bly's Iron John:** Robert Bly, *Iron John* (Reading, MA: Addison-Wesley,
        1990).

71   **Osherson and Homer's Odyssey:** Osherson, *Finding Our Fathers,* 42.

72   **Miller's Death of a Salesman:** See Arthur Miller, *Death of a Salesman*
        (New York: Quality Paperback Club, 1995).

73   **Greenberg: ("opening the floodgates"):** Vivian Greenberg, *Children of
        a Certain Age* (Lanham, MD: Lexington Books, 1994), 24.

74   **Chodorow:** Nancy Chodorow, "Family Structure and Feminine Person-
        ality," in Laurel Richardson, Verta Taylor and Nancy Whittier, eds.,
        Feminist Frontiers IV (New York: McGraw-Hill, 1996), 145.

74   **Klein:** Melanie Klein and Joan Riviere, *Love, Hate, and Reparation*
        (New York: W. W. Norton, 1937).

74   **Miller:** Jean Baker Miller, *Toward a New Psychology of Women*
        (Boston: Beacon Press, 1976).

74   **Gilligan:** Carol Gilligan, *In a Different Voice* (Cambridge, MA: Har-
        vard University Press, 1982).

76   **Instrumental fathers, expressive mothers:** See Olga Silverstein and
        Beth Rashbaum, *The Courage to Raise Good Men* (New York: Penguin
        Books, 1995), 30.

77   **Parker on maternal ambivalence:** Rozsika Parker, *Mother Hate,
        Mother Love* (New York: Basic Books, 1995), 21.

78   **Gornick's *Fierce Attachments:*** Vivian Gornick, *Fierce Attachments: A
        Memoir* (New York: Simon & Schuster, 1987), 6.

78   **Lively's *Moon Tiger* ("She was a disappointment . . .")**: Penelope
        Lively, *Moon Tiger* (London: Penguin Books, 1988), 51–52.

79   ***Moon Tiger* (daughter's thoughts):** Ibid., 56.

79   **Rubin:** Lillian B. Rubin, *Families on the Fault Line* (New York:
        HarperCollins, 1997), 151. See also: Lillian B. Rubin. *Tangled Lives:
        Daughters, Mothers, and the Crucible of Aging* (Boston: Beacon Press,
        2000).

80   **Secunda:** Victoria Secunda, *When You and Your Mother Can't Be
        Friends,* (New York: Dell/Delta, 1990), 103.

80   **Zax and Poulter:** Zax and Poulter, *Mending the Broken Bough,* 284.

82   **Carroll: *An American Requiem:*** James Carroll, *An American
        Requiem* (Boston: Houghton Mifflin, 1996), 248.

82   ***Requiem:* ("child-changed father")** Ibid., 249.

83   ***Requiem:* (father sobbing):** Ibid., 215.

83   ***Requiem:* (fathers and sons breaking hearts):** Ibid., 279.

83   **Osherson: Study:** Terrence Real, *I Don't Want to Talk About it.* (New
        York: Fireside, 1997). See also George E. Vaillant, *Adaptation to Life*
        (Boston: Little, Brown and Co., 1977).

84   **Osherson: ("forbidding creature"):** Osherson, *Finding Our Fathers,* 6.

84   **Osherson: ("judgmental quality"):** Ibid., 17.

84   **Osherson: ("devalue what is feminine"):** Ibid., 7.

85   **Hochschild:** See Arlie Hochschild, *The Second Shift* (New York: Viking
        Press, 1989), and *The Time Bind* (New York: Metropolitan/Holt, 1997).

85   ***Price of Motherhood:*** Ann Crittenden, *The Price of Motherhood* (New
        York: Metropolitan Books, 2000).

86   **Weissbourd anecdote:** Richard Weissbourd, "How Society Keeps Fathers
        Away from Children, *The American Prospect,* December 6, 1999, 28.

87   **Chodorow on child-rearing patterns:** Nancy Chodorow, "A Coda on Culture," in *The Power of Feelings* (New Haven: Yale University Press, 1999), 219–38.

87   **Chodorow on gender and relationality:** Nancy Chodorow, "Theoretical Gender and Clinical Gender: Epistemological Reflections of the Psychology of Women," *Journal of the American Psychoanalytic Association*, 44 suppl., 218–19.

Chapter 5

89   **Mutually affirming connections:** Robert Kegan, *The Evolving Self* (Cambridge, MA: Harvard University Press, 1982).

90   **Grown children living with parents:** Bureau of the Census, Census of Population and Housing (Washington DC, 2000).

90   **Housing costs:** Katherine Newman, *Declining Fortunes* (New York: Basic Books, 1993), 30.

90   **Downward mobility in the 1970s and 1980s:** See Frank Levy, *Dollars and Dreams* (New York: Basic Books, 1987).

91   **Okimoto and Stegall on Tom and Ann:** Jean Davies Okimoto and Phyllis Jackson Stegall, *Boomerang Kids* (Boston: Little, Brown, 1987), 17.

92   **"I want my wife back.":** Ibid., 18.

93   **Okimoto and Stegall:** Ibid., 30.

94   **"I keep asking myself what I did wrong.":** Greenberg, *Children of a Certain Age*, 140.

95   *Old Money:* Nelson Aldrich, *Old Money: The Mythology of America's Upper Class* (New York: Alfred A. Knopf, 1988), 137.

95   **Newman interview:** Newman, *Declining Fortunes*, 3.

96   **Newman on parental rescue missions:** Ibid., 21.

101   **Hausner's story of Phyllis:** Lee Hausner, *Children of Paradise*, (Los Angeles: Jeremy P. Tarcher, Inc, 1990) 234–36.

101   **Stockman and Graves' story of Tom:** Larry V. Stockman and Cynthia S. Graves, *Adult Children Who Won't Grow Up* (Chicago: Contemporary Books, 1989), 177.

106   **FDR's mother, wife, and mistress:** See McGoldrick, *You Can Go Home Again*, esp. pp. 225–29; also Joseph P. Lash, *Eleanor and Franklin* and Doris Kearns Goodwin, *No Ordinary Time*. (New York: W. W. Norton, 1991).

106   **Newman: (parents from the Old Country):** Katherine Newman, *Falling from Grace: The Experience of Downward Mobility in the American Middle Class* (New York: Free Press, 1987), 111.

107   **Newman: ("he could dominate her completely"):** Ibid., 139.

107   **Hidden injuries of class:** Richard Sennett, *The Hidden Injuries of Class* (New York: Vintage Books, 1973). See also Salvador Minuchin, et al., *Families of the Slums* (New York: Basic Books, 1967).

108   **Rubin:** Lillian B. Rubin, *Worlds of Pain* (New York: Basic Books, 1976), 130.

108   **Greenberg:** Greenberg, *Children of a Certain Age*, 164.

Chapter 6

109   **Yasmina Reza, *Art*** (London: Faber & Faber 1996), 30.

114   **Edelman ("hard even to have lunch with him"):** Edelman, *Motherless Daughters*, 127.

115   **Edelman: ("abandon his daughters") :** Ibid., 128–29.

115   **Karen:** Karen, *The Forgiving Self*, 13, 16.

116   **Carter on Roger and Cassie:** Betty Carter with Joan K. Peters, *Love, Honor and Negotiate* (New York: Pocket Books, 1996), 283–84.

120   **Emily and John Visher's clients:** Emily B. Visher and John S. Visher, *Stepfamilies: A Guide to Working with Stepparents and Stepchildren* (New York: Brunner/Mazel, 1979), 124–25.

124   **Lerner:** Harriet Lerner, *The Mother Dance* (New York: HarperCollins, 1999), 256.

124   **Stepfamilies stabilizing and integrating:** See Lerner, *The Dance of Anger*, 261.

124   **Bray:** James H. Bray and John Kelly, *Step Families* (New York: Broadway Books, 1999), 29.

125   **Family styles at holidays:** Clifford J. Sager et al., Treating the Remarried Family (New York: Brunner/Mazel, 1983), 277.

Chapter 7

128   **Herman on dissociation:** Judith Lewis Herman, *Trauma and Recovery* (New York: Basic Books, 1992), 111–12.

129   **Herman on terrible secrets:** Ibid., 96.

129   **Herman: ("So I had to go and be crazy"):** Ibid., 101.

130   **Herman ("guilt . . . where it belongs"):** Ibid., 200.

131   **Herman on family's limitations:** Ibid., 201.

132   **Forward:** Forward, *Toxic Parents*, 94–95.

134   **Callahan:** Callahan, *Parents Forever*, 104.

135   **The Cowans quoting John Pearce:** Paul Cowan with Rachel Cowan, *Mixed Blessings* (New York: Doubleday, 1987), 20.

135   **Cowans ("She punishes me with silences."):** Ibid., 20.

136   **McGoldrick:** Monica McGoldrick, in Monica McGoldrick, John K. Pearce, and Joseph Giordano, eds., *Ethnicity and Family Therapy* (New York: Guilford Press, 1982), 21.

137   **"White standard of beauty":** Paul C. Rosenblatt, Terri A. Karis, and Richard D. Powell, *Multiracial Couples: Black and White Voices* (Thousand Oaks, CA: Sage Publications, 1995), 108.

137   **Intermarriage and divorce:** Maria P. P. Root, *Love's Revolution: Interracial Marriage* (Philadelphia: Temple University Press, 2001), 107.

137   **"cultural baggage" in intermarriages:** Cowan and Cowan, *Mixed Blessings*, 51.

137   **Lerner ("he has to be Jewish"):** Ibid. 105.

138   **Fourth-generation Jewish-American client:** Quoted in Fredda M. Herz and Elliott J. Rosen, "Jewish Families," in McGoldrick, et al., eds., *Ethnicity and Family Therapy*, 366.

139   **Immigrants keep ties to homeland:** Alejandro Portes and Rubén G. Rumbaut. *Legacies: The Story of the Immigrant Second Generation* (Berkeley, CA: University of California Press, 1999).

139   ***Garcia Girls:*** Julia Alvarez, *How the Garcia Girls Lost Their Accents* (New York: Plume/Penguin 1992), 109.

139   **Maria Root on racial sameness and happiness:** Root, *Love's Revolution*, 21.

140   **"So I just left."** Rosenblatt, et al., *Multiracial Couples: Black and White Voices* (Thousand Oaks, CA: Sage Publications, 1995), 77.

140   **Root ("Recipe for marital failure"):** Root, *Love's Revolution*, 21.

140   **"Puts an edge on the marriage":** Ibid., 130.

140   **White disapproval of intermarriage in the 1950s:** Paul R. Spikard, *Mixed Blood* (Madison: University of Wisconsin Press, 1989), 292.

140   **Higher approval among younger adults:** Root, *Love's Revolution*, 38.

141   **Loving case and the Supreme Court:** Spikard, *Mixed Blood*, 295.

141   **"We just won't come to your house.":** Lise Funderburg, *Black, White, Other: Biracial Americans Talk About Race and Identity* (New York: William Morrow, 1994), 210.

141   **"the shame you've brought on me.":** Rosenblatt et al., *Multiracial Couples*, 66.

141   **"because I had to be poor.":** Ibid., 75.

142   **"I need to forgive him.":** Ibid., 91.

142   **"It would make him not white or something.":** Root, *Love's Revolution*, 43.

142   **"[My father took] ten years to apologize. . . .":** Rosenblatt et al., *Multiracial Couples*, 93.

143   **Julie's story:** Root, *Love's Revolution*, 108.

143   **Root's story of a white Seattle woman:** Ibid., 107.

143   **Study speculating about "charm of the child":** Rosenblatt et al., *Multiracial Couples*, 96.

143   **Incomplete healing, leftover racism:** Ibid., 99.

144   **Callahan's southern military family:** Callahan, *Parents Forever*, 67.

144   **Callahan quote on getting along with her adult children:** Ibid.

144   **Mixed marriage "between a man and a woman":** Rosenblatt et al., *Multiracial Couples*, 295.

144   **Quote on gender difference versus cultural difference:** Ibid.

144   **Sullivan's *Virtually Normal*:** Andrew Sullivan, *Virtually Normal* (New York: Vintage Books, 1996).

145   *Now That You Know:* Betty Fairchild and Nancy Hayward, *Now That You Know: A Parents' Guide to Understanding Their Gay and Lesbian Children* (New York: Harvest Press, Harcourt, Brace, 1979, 1998).

146   **"My heart ached for my son and other gays":** Ibid., 25.

147   **"I'm through pretending.":** Ibid., 31–32.

149   **Darrell, Chris, and Dad:** John Preston, ed., *A Member of the Family: Gay Men Write About Their Families* (New York: E. P. Dutton, 1992), 91.

Chapter 8

154   **Nagy and Spark:** Boszormenyi-Nagy and Spark, *Invisible Loyalties,* 4

154   **Nagy on unconscious rules for family systems:** Ibid., 2.

154   **Nagy rebelling against his father:** Ibid., 3.

155   **Roth: ". . . . in my liberation would be his.":** Roth, *Portnoy's Complaint,* 8–9.

155   **Roth on requited devotion:** Philip Roth, *Patrimony* (New York: Vintage Books, 1991), 80.

156   **Hochschild on his father:** Adam Hochschild, *Half the Way Home* (New York: Penguin Books, 1986), 68.

156   **Hochschild: "exiting the stage":** Ibid., 123.

156   **Hochschild: "Or have I broken the chain at last?":** Ibid., 181.

157   **Sissela Bok on coming to understand her mother gradually:** Sissela Bok, *Alva Myrdal* (Reading, MA: Addison-Wesley, 1991), 9.

157   **Bok on regrets about her mother:** Ibid., 179.

158   **Robert Karen:** Karen, *The Forgiving Self,* 246.

160   **Sophie Freud Loewenstein:** Sophie Freud Loewenstein, "Mother and Daughter—An Epitaph," *Family Process,* 20 (1981), 1.

162   **Donald Williamson:** Williamson, "Personal Authority via Termination of the Intergenerational Hierarchy Boundary: A 'New' Stage in the Family Life Cycle," *Journal of Marital and Family Therapy* (October 1981), 445.

162   **Williamson: "compassion for the people who used to be [one's] parents.":** Ibid., 448.

163   **Williamson: "essence of the change process.":** Ibid., 446.

163   **Nagy on psychological equality:** See Boszormenyi-Nagy and Spark, *Invisible Loyalties.*

163   **Consensual authority:** Williamson, "Personal Authority," 442–42, citing Ibid.

163   **Nagy on unbalanced emotional ledger:** See Boszormenyi-Nagy and Spark, *Invisible Loyalties,* and H. Stierlin, *Psychoanalysis and Family Therapy* (New York: Jason Aronson, 1977).

163   **Lynn Hoffman:** Lynn Hoffman, *Foundations of Family Therapy* (New York: Basic Books, 1981), 252.

164   **McGoldrick:** McGoldrick, *You Can Go Home Again,* 21.

165   **Titelman:** Peter Titelman, "The Therapist's Own Family," in Titel-
         man, ed., *The Therapist's Own Family*, 8.

168   **McGoldrick:** McGoldrick, *You Can Go Home Again*, 277.

168   **Dym and Glenn:** Barry Dym and Michael Glenn, *Couples* (New York:
         HarperCollins), 237.

169   **LaForte:** Jack T. LaForte, "Efforts to Modify One's Position in Interlock-
         ing Triangles," in Titelman, ed., *The Therapist's Own Family*, 126–27.

169   **LaForte on food conflicts:** Ibid., 131.

171   **Benswanger on her family history:** Ellen G. Benswanger, "Strategies to Ex-
         plore Cutoffs," in Titelman, ed., *The Therapist's Own Family*, 203.

170   **Benswanger on expressing anger:** Ibid., 204.

172   **McBride on his history:** James McBride, *The Color of Water* (New
         York: Riverhead Books, 1996), 207.

172   **McBride: "His own wife was scared of him.":** Ibid., 209.

173   **McBride: "devastating realization":** Ibid., 269.

Chapter 9

176   **Pipher:** Mary Pipher, *Another Country* (New York: Riverhead Books,
         1999), 276.

176   **"grandparents have the best of it":** Arthur Kornhaber with Sandra
         Forsyth, *Grandparent Power* (New York: Crown, 1994), 26.

177   **"practically a holiday":** Ibid.

177   **Pipher: "This time around I am present.":** Pipher, *Another Country*,
         279.

177   **Kornhaber: landmark survey:** Arthur Kornhaber, *Contemporary
         Grandparenting* (Thousand Oaks, CA: Sage Publications, 1996), 36.

179   **Lerner: "I just can't . . . [pretend] I don't hear her screaming."** Lerner,
         The Dance of Anger, 76.

180   **Lerner: "It does not mean emotional distance":** Ibid., 80, italics in the
         original.

181   **McFarland and Watson-Rouslin:** Barbara McFarland and Virginia Wat-
         son-Rouslin, *My Mother Was Right* (San Francisco: Jossey-Bass, 1997),
         92.

182   **Secunda:** Victoria Secunda, *When You and Your Mother Can't Be Friends*,
         341.

183   **Secunda: Julie's story:** Ibid., 342.

186   **Remen:** Rachel Naomi Remen, *My Grandfather's Blessings* (New
         York: Riverhead Books, 2000), 2.

187   **Kornhaber and Woodward on grandparents feeling pained distance:**
         Arthur Kornhaber and Kenneth Woodward, *Grandparents, Grandchil-
         dren: The Vital Connection* (New Brunswick, NJ: Transaction Books,
         1985).

187   **"Is this what I want?":** Ibid., 79.

191   **Cherlin and Furstenberg quote of "the Sergeant":** Andrew J. Cherlin and Frank F. Furstenberg, *The New American Grandparent* (Cambridge, MA: Harvard University Press, 1992), 128.

191   **"back seat to authority.":** Ibid., 130.

191   **"have love to spare.":** Ibid.

193   **Lerner:** Lerner, *The Dance of Anger*, 85.

193   **Okimoto and Stegall:** Okimoto and Stegall, *Boomerang Kids*, 110.

Chapter 10

200   **Data on Americans in nursing homes:** Betty Friedan, *The Fountain of Age* (New York: Touchstone Books, 1994), 57

202   **Friedan quote:** Ibid., 299.

202   **Erikson quote:** Erik H. Erikson, Joan M. Erikson, and Helen Q. Kivnick, *Vital Involvement in Old Age* (New York: W. W. Norton, 1994), 189.

202   **Pipher quote:** Mary Pipher, *Another Country*, 10.

203   **Butler on the life review:** See "The Life Review, An Interpretation of Reminiscence on the Aged," *Psychiatry*, 26 (1963), 65–76. 1. See also "Life Review," paper prepared for the *Encyclopedia of Gerontology*, (James Birren, ed., San Francisco: Academic Press, 1995), 2.

203   **Butler on lingering regrets:** Robert Butler and Henry L. Schwartz, "Looking Back, Looking Forward: The Life Review Revisited." Keynote paper, National Reminiscence and Life Review Conference, University of Wisconsin, Superior, WI, August 24–25, 1995, 14.

203   **Butler on older person as "garrulous:"** R. N. Butler, "The Life Review: An Interpretation of Reminiscence in the Aged," 65–73.

203   **Butler's life review as a "naturally occurring process:"** Ibid., See also R. N. Butler and Schwartz, "Looking Back, Looking Forward: The Life Review Revisited."

204   **Butler on proximity of death:** Robert N. Butler, et al., *Aging and Mental Health* (New York: Allyn & Bacon, 1998), 356.

206   ***Successful Aging:* and health of people "with social support:"** John W. Rowe and Robert L. Kahn, *Successful Aging* (New York: Pantheon Books, 1998), 163.

206   **Butler on autobiography:** Butler and Schwartz, "Looking Back, Looking Forward," 20.

208   ***Stone Diaries* dialogue:** Carol Shields, *The Stone Diaries* (New York: Penguin Books, 1993), 235–36.

209   **Shauna Smith on estrangement from grown children:** Shauna Smith, *Making Peace with Your Adult Children* (New York: Harper Perennial, 1991), 196.

209   **Robert Karen on his patient, "Norman":** Robert Karen, *The Forgiving Self*, (New York: Doubleday, 2001), 99.

210   **"Can you allow me my flaws?":** Ibid., 103.

210   **Framo on love and acceptance:** James L. Framo, *Explorations in Marital and Family Therapy*, 188.

210   **Butler's "most tragic situation":** Robert N. Butler, "The Life Review: An Interpretation of Reminiscence in the Aged," 68

212   **Stewart Alsop quote:** Stewart Alsop, *Stay of Execution* (New York: J. B. Lippincott, 1973), 11.

213   **Cicely Saunders' "real work of dying":** Quoted in Ira Byock, *Dying Well: The Prospect for Growth at the End of Life* (New York: Riverhead Books), 233.

214   **Byock on "dying well":** Ibid., 32.

Epilogue: Terminal Candor

218   **Kabat-Zinn, *Full Catastrophe Living*.** See also Kabat-Zinn's interview in Bill Moyers, *Healing and the Mind* (New York: Doubleday, 1993), 115–43, quote at 129.

220   **Rachel Naomi Remen,** "Mother knows Best . . ." in Remen, ed., *Wounded Healers*, (Bolinas, CA: Wounded Healer Press, 1994), 35

220   **Carole Munson.** "Untitled," in Remen, *op. cit.*, 47.

221   **Suzanne Lipsett,** "Beach Flowers," in Remen, *op. cit.*, 40–41.

231   **Jenny Mansbridge quote:** Ellen Goodman and Patricia O'Brien, *I Know Just What You Mean* (New York: Fireside/Simon & Schuster), 235.

232   **Alexandra Marshall,** *Gus in Bronze* (New York: Houghton Mifflin/Mariner, 1999), 174–76.

232   **Sherwin Nuland,** *How We Die* (New York: Vintage Books, 1995), 243.

242   Mary Oliver, "When Death Comes," in Mary Oliver, *New and Selected Poems* (Boston: Beacon Press, 1992). 10.

252   **Rachel Naomi Remen,** *Kitchen Table Wisdom*, 124

252   **Lorraine David quote:** In Titelman, ed., *The Therapist's Own Family*, 289.

253   **Dan Lowenstein,** "Help Me," in Remen, op. cit., 59.

Resources

Working on this book has taken us into diverse literatures. For nonspecialist readers who wish to delve further, here are our favorites. Some these books are written for mental health professionals, others as self-help books or memoirs. But all have in common accessibility, wisdom, and humanity

.

Readable Classics from the Psychology Literature:

Ivan Boszormenyi-Nagy and Geraldine M. Spark, *Invisible Loyalties: Reciprocity in Intergenerational Family Therapy* (New York: Brunner/Routledge, 1993).

James L. Framo, *Explorations in Marital and Family Therapy* (New York: Springer Publishing Co., 1982).

James L. Framo, *Family-of-Origin Therapy: An Intergenerational Approach* (New York: Brunner/Mazel, 1992).

Roberta M. Gilbert, *Extraordinary Relationships: A New Way of Thinking About Human Interactions* (New York: John Wiley, 1992). A readable summary of Murray Bowen's approach.

Jay Haley, *Leaving Home: The Therapy of Disturbed Young People* (New York: McGraw-Hill, 1980).

Lee A. Headley, *Adults and their Parents in Family Therapy: A New Direction in Treatment* (New York: Plenum Press, 1977).

Jon Kabat-Zinn, *Full Catastrophe Living: Using the Wisdom of Your Body and Mind to Face Stress, Pain and Illness* (New York: Delta/Dell, 1991).

Robert Karen, *Becoming Attached: Unfolding the Mystery of the Infant-Mother Bond and Its Impact on Later Life* (New York: Oxford University Press, 1998).

Robert Karen, *The Forgiving Self: The Road from Resentment to Connection* (New York: Doubleday, 2001).

Robert Kegan, *The Evolving Self: Problem and Process in Human Development* (Cambridge, MA: Harvard University Press, 1982).

Harriet Goldhor Lerner, *The Dance of Anger: A Woman's Guide to Changing the Patterns of Intimate Relationships* (New York: Harper and Row, 1985).

Monica McGoldrick, *You Can Go Home Again: Reconnecting with Your Family* (New York: W. W. Norton, 1995).

Salvador Minuchin, *Families and Family Therapy* (Cambridge, MA: Harvard University Press, 1974.)

Virginia M. Satir, The New Peoplemaking (Mountain View, CA.: Science and Behavior Books, 1988).

Peter Titelman, ed., *The Therapist's Own Family: Toward the Differentiation of Self* (Northvale, N.J.: Jason Aronson, 1987.)

For Parents of Grown Children:

Sidney Cornelia Callahan, *Parents Forever: You and Your Adult Children* (New York: Crossroads Publishing Co. 1992).

Edwin L. Klingelhofer, *Coping with Your Grown Children* (Clifton, N.J.: Humana Press, 1989).

Jean Davies Okimoto and Phyllis Jackson Stegall, *Boomerang Kids: How to Live with Adult Children Who Return Home* (Boston: Little, Brown and Company, 1987).

Shauna L. Smith, *Making Peace with Your Adult Children: A Guide to Family Healing* (New York: Harper Perennial, 1993).

For Grown Children Dealing with Parents:

Harold H. Bloomfield with Leonard Felder, *Making Peace with Your Parents* (New York: Ballantine Books, 1983).

Vivian E. Greenberg, *Children of a Certain Age: Adults and Their Aging Parents* (New York: Lexington Books, 1994).

On Mothers and Grown Children:

Nancy Chodorow, *The Reproduction of Mothering: Psychoanalysis and the Sociology of Gender* (Berkeley, CA: University of California Press, 1978, 1999).

Vivian Gornick, *Fierce Attachments: A Memoir* (Boston: Beacon Press, 1997).

Susan Jonas and Marilyn Nissenson, *Friends for Life: Enriching the Bond between Mothers and Their Adult Daughters* (San Diego: Harcourt Brace, 1998.)

Jean Baker Miller, *Toward a New Psychology of Women* (Boston: Beacon Press, 1986).

Olga Silverstein and Beth Rashbaum, *The Courage to Raise Good Men* (New York: Penguin Books, 1995).

Barbara Zax and Stephan Poulter, *Mending the Broken Bough: Restoring the Promise of the Mother-Daughter Relationship* (New York: Berkley Books, 1998).

On Fathers and Grown Children:

R. William Betcher and William S. Pollack, *In a Time of Fallen Heroes: The Re-creation of Masculinity* (New York: The Guilford Press, 1994).

Samuel Osherson, *Finding Our Fathers: How a Man's Life Is Shaped by His Relationship with His Father* (Chicago: Contemporary Books, 2001).

William S. Pollack, Real Boys: *Rescuing Our Sons from the Myths of Boyhood* (New York: Henry Holt, 1999).

Terrence Real, *I Don't Want to Talk About It: Overcoming the Secret Legacy of Male Depression* (New York: Fireside/Simon & Schuster, 1998).

On Families and Economic and Marital Stresses:

Ann Crittenden, *The Price of Motherhood: Why the Most Important Job in the World Is Still the Least Valued* (New York: Metropolitan Books, 2001).

Sylvia Ann Hewlett and Cornel West, *The War Against Parents: What We Can Do for America's Beleagured Moms and Dads* (Boston: Houghton Mifflin, 1998).

Arlie Russell Hochschild, *The Second Shift: Working Parents and the Revolution at Home* (New York: Viking Press, 1989).

Katherine S. Newman, *Declining Fortunes: The Withering of the American Dream* (New York: Basic Books, 1993).

Lillian B. Rubin, *Families on the Fault Line: America's Working Class Speaks About the Family, the Economy, Race, and Ethnicity* (New York: Harper Collins, 1994).

Lillian B. Rubin, *Worlds of Pain: Life in the Working-Class Family* (New York: Basic Books, 1976).

On Grandparenting and Healthy Aging:

Robert N. Butler et al., *Aging and Mental Health: Positive Psychosocial and Biomedical Approaches* (New York: Allyn & Bacon, 1998.)

Andrew J. Cherlin and Frank F. Furstenberg Jr., *The New American Grandparent: A Place in the Family, A Life Apart* (Cambridge, MA.: Harvard University Press, 1992).

Erik H. Erikson, Joan M. Erikson, and Helen Q. Kivnick, *Vital Involvement in Old Age* (New York: W. W. Norton, 1994.)

Betty Friedan, *The Fountain of Age* (New York: Touchstone Books, 1994).

David Gutmann, *Reclaimed Powers: Men and Women in Later Life* (Evanston, IL: Northwestern University Press, 1994.)

Arthur Kornhaber with Sondra Forsyth, *Grandparent Power!* (New York: Crown Books, 1994.)

Mary Pipher, *Another Country: Navigating the Emotional Terrain of Our Elders* (New York: Riverhead Books, 1999).

Lillian B. Rubin, *Tangled Lives: Daughters, Mothers, and the Crucible of Aging* (Boston: Beacon Press, 2000).

On Intermarriage and Stepfamilies:

James H. Bray and John Kelly, *Step Families: Love, Marriage, and Parenting in the First Decade* (New York: Broadway Books, 1999).

Paul Cowan with Rachel Cowan, *Mixed Blessings: Overcoming the Stumbling Blocks in an Interfaith Marriage* (New York: Penguin USA, 1988).

Maria P. P. Root, *Love's Revolution: Interracial Marriage* (Philadelphia: Temple University Press, 2001).

Paul C. Rosenblatt et al., *Multiracial Couples: Black and White Voices* (Thousand Oaks, CA.: Sage Publications, 1995).

Clifford J. Sager et al., *Treating the Remarried Family* (New York: Brunner/Mazel, 1983).

Emily B. Visher and John S. Visher, *Stepfamilies: A Guide to Working with Stepparents and Stepchildren* (New York: Brunner/Mazel, 1979).

On Abuse and Alcoholism:

Claudia A. Black: *"It Will Never Happen to Me!" Children of Alcholics* (New York: Ballantine Books, 1991).

Susan Forward with Craig Buck, *Toxic Parents: Overcoming Their Hurtful Legacy and Reclaiming Your Life* (New York: Bantam Books, 1989).

Judith Lewis Herman, *Trauma and Recovery* (New York: Basic Books, rev. ed., 1997).

On Gays and Lesbians and their Parents:

Robert A. Bernstein, *Straight Parents, Gay Children: Inspiring Families to Live Honestly and with Greater Understanding* (New York: Thunder's Mouth Press, 1999).

Betty Fairchild and Nancy Hayward, *Now That You Know: A Parents' Guide to Understanding Their Gay and Lesbian Children* (San Diego: Harcourt Brace, 1979, 1998).

Robb Forman Dew, *The Family Heart: A Memoir of When Our Son Came Out* (New York: Ballantine Books, 1995.)

Carolyn Welch Griffin, Marian J. Wirth, and Arthur G. Wirth, *Beyond Acceptance: Parents of Lesbians and Gays Talk About Their Experiences* (New York: St. Martin's Press, 1996.)

John Preston, ed., *A Member of the Family: Gay Men Write About Their Families* (New York, E.P. Dutton, 1992.)

On Parents and Adopted Children:

David M. Brodzinsky, Marshall D. Schechter, and Robin Marantz Henig, *Being Adopted: The Lifelong Search for Self* (New York: Anchor Books, 1993).

Betsy Keefer and Jayne E. Schooler, *Telling the Truth to Your Adopted or Foster Child: Making Sense of the Past* (Greenwood Publishing Group, 2000.)

Betty Jean Lifton, *Journey of the Adopted Self: A Quest for Wholeness* (New York: Perseus Books, 1995.)

Joyce Maguire Pavao, *The Family of Adoption* (Boston: Beacon Press, 1999).

On Death and Dying:

Ira Byock, *Dying Well: The Prospect for Growth at the End of Life* (New York: Riverhead Books, 1997).

Hope Edelman, *Motherless Daughters: The Legacy of Loss* (Reading, MA: Addison-Wesley, 1994.)

Michael Lerner, *Choices in Healing: Integrating the Best of Conventional and Complementary Approaches to Cancer* (Boston: MIT Press, 1994.)

Sherwin B. Nuland, *How We Die: Reflections on Life's Final Chapter* (New York: Vintage Books, 1995)

Index